ENGLISH - ITALIAN
ITALIAN - ENGLISH

BARNES & NOBLE BOOKS

A DIVISION OF HARPER & ROW, PUBLISHERS

New York, Hagerstown, San Francisco, London

Distributed in
the U.S. by
Harper & Row, Publishers, Inc.
10 East 53rd Street
New York, N.Y. 10022

ENGLISH-ITALIAN
DICTIONARY

PRONUNCIATION

a sounds as a in father

e „   „ e „ net

e „   „ e „ where

i „   „ i „ pin

y „   „ y „ yes

o „   „ o „ cot

$ò$ „   „ o „ mole

u „   „ u „ bull

a, e, i, e, u are always pronounced

h is never sounded.

gli.,., has a liquid sound as in *seraglie*, or the

Spanish *ll*.

Days of the Week.	Giorni Della Settimana
Sunday .. La Domenica	Thursday Il Giovedi
Monday .. Il Lunedi	Friday .. Il Venerdi
Tuesday .. Il Martedi	Saturday Il Sabato
Wednesday Il Mercoledi	Week .. La settimana

Months of the Year.	Mesi Dell'anno
January .. Gennaio	May .. .. Maggio
February .. Febbraio	June .. .. Giugno
March .. .. Marzo	July .. .. Luglio
April .. prile	August .. Agosto

Ordinal Numbers

First	primo
Second	secondo
Third	terzo
Fourth	quarto
Fifth	quinto
Sixth	sesto
Seventh	settimo
Eighth	ottavo
Ninth	nono
Tenth	decimo
Eleventh	undicesimo
Twelfth	dodicesimo
Thirteenth	decimo terzo
Fourteenth	quattordicesimo
Fifteenth	quindicesimo
Sixteenth	sedicesimo
Seventeenth	diciassettesimo
Eighteenth	diciottesimo
Nineteenth	diciannovesimo
Twentieth	ventesimo
Thirtieth	trentesimo
Fourtieth	quarantesimo
Fiftieth	cinquantesimo
Sixtieth	sessantesimo
Seventieth	settantesimo
Eightieth	ottantesimo
Ninetieth	novantesimo
Hundredth	centesimo
Thousandth	millesimo
Millionth	millionesimo

Dialogues.

Useful Phrases & Idioms.	Frasi Utili e Idiomi
I am very much obliged to you	Le sono molto obbligato
I beg your pardon	Mi scusi, Le domando scusa
I congratulate you	Congratulazioni, mi congratulo con Lei
I pity you	La compiagno
If you please	Per favore
Allow me	Mi permetta
Pray, do not mention it	Prega, non ne parli
Thank you; many thanks	Grazie, tante grazie
No, thank you	No, grazie
With your permission	Con permesso
Good morning, afternoon, day	Buon giorno
Good evening; good night	Buona sera; buona notte
Good-bye	Addio, arrivederci
A pleasant. journey	Buon viaggio
How do you do?	Come sta?
I am (not) very well	Molto bene. non molto bene
I am better	Sto meglio
I hope you are better	Spero che stia meglio
And how are you?	E come sta Lei?
Agreed	E'inteso
Are you ready?	E'pronto?
Ask him (her)	Lo domandi a lui (lei). Glielo domandi.
Ask him to come	Gli domandi di venire. Le domandi di venire
I want the bill of fare, please.	Mi favorisca la lista delle vivande.
Put a bottle of wine in ice for me.	Metta una bottiglia di vino in ghiaccio per me.
Bring glasses and some more bread.	Porti dei bicchieri e dell'altro pane.
This wine is corked.	Il vino sa di sughero.
This meat is not fresh.	Questa carne non è fresca.

9

To carry coals to New-castle	Portar l'acqua al mare
To commit a blunder	Pigliare un granchio
To deceive	Gettar della polvere negli occhi
To dismiss	Congedare
To drink like a fish	Bere come un pesce
To drive	Andare in vettura
To drive very fast	Andare a rompicollo
To fall backwards	Cadere all'indietro
To find it worth one's while	Trovare l'affar suo
To find out a good berth	Far casa
To fly into a passion	Lasciarsi trasportare dall ['ira
To get acquainted	Far la conoscenza di
To give a person permission to speak	Dare la parola a qualcuno
To give it up	Rinunciare
To give largely	Dare a piene mani
To go at full speed	Andare a spron battuto
To go for a sail for a row	Andare in barca
To go from one thing to another	Divagare
To go one's own way	Fare a modo proprio
To grieve	Affliggere, affliggersi
To have a narrow escape	Scamparla bella
To have at one's disposal	Avere sotto mano
To have bad luck	Esser sfortunato
To kick up a row	Fare del baccano
To kill by inches	Far morire a oncia
To laugh in one's sleeve	Ridere sotto i baffi
To lay a bet	Scommettere
To let one go his own way	Lasciargli la briglia su collo

Date. Age.	**Data. Età.**
What day of the week is it?	Che giorno è oggi?
What year is this?	In che anno siamo?
What month is it?	In che mese siamo?
What day of the month is it?	Quanti ne abbiamo oggi?

It is the first of January.	E'il primo di Gennaio.
Do you often come here?	Vien spesso qui?
Once a week.	Una volta la settimana.
Weekly.	Settimanalmente.
I arrived several days ago.	Arrivai alcuni giorni orsono.
I leave to-morrow week (fortnight).	Partirò in una settimana (in quindici giorni) da domani.
He is often late (5 minutes).	Egli è spesso in ritardo (cinque minuti).
To-day is Thursday.	Oggi è Giovedì.
To-morrow is Friday.	Domani è Venerdì.
How old are you?	Che età ha Lei?
I am twenty years old.	Ho venti anni.
How old do you think I am?	Che età crede Lei che io abbia?
I am ten years older (younger) than my brother.	Ho dieci anni di più (di meno) di mio fratello.
Younger brother—Elder brother.	Fratello minore—Fratello maggiore.
She is going on fifty years old.	Si avvicina ai cinquant' anni.
He is over forty.	Ha passato i quarant' anni.

Asking the Time. — Per domandare l'ora

What time is it?	Che ore sono?
Can you tell me what the time is?	Può dirmi che ore sono?
It is nearly six o'clock.	Sono quasi le sei.
It is past four o'clock.	Sono passate le quattro.
Exactly five o'clock	Le cinque precise.
It is exactly half past six.	Sono le sei e mezzo precise
Midday, Midnight.	Mezzogiorno, Mezzanotte.
A quarter past two.	Le due e un quarto.
Half past three.	Le tre e mezzo.
A quarter to eight.	Un quarto alle otto.
Twenty minutes to nine.	Venti minuti alle nove.
Ten minutes past one.	La una e dieci.
It is about to strike four.	Sono quasi le quattro.
It has just struck five.	Sono le cinque precise.

My watch is stopped.	Il mio orologio è fermato.
My watch is 15 minutes slow (fast).	Il mio orologio ritarda (avanza) di quindici minuti.
My watch is broken.	Il mio orologio è rotto.
I shall take it to the watchmaker.	Lo porterò dall'orologiaio.
It is a keyless watch.	E'un orologio senza chiavetta.
It has been repaired.	E'stato riparato.
I have forgotten to wind it.	Ho dimenticato di caricarlo.
I have lost my watchkey.	Ho perduto la chiavetta del mio orologio.

Health.   Saluti.

How do you do? How are you?	Come sta?
I am very well, and you?	Sto molto bene, e Lei?
Fairly well, thanks.	Abbastanza bene, grazie.
Is your father well?	Sta bene suo padre?
Father and mother are both well.	Papà e Mamma stanno bene.
I am not very well myself.	Io non sto troppo bene.
I have caught a cold.	Ho preso un raffreddore.
I have a cold in my head and toothache.	Ho un raffreddore di testa e mal di denti.
I hope you will soon be better.	Spero che presto stia meglio.
I have sprained my wrist.	Mi sono slogato il polso.
You should see a doctor.	Dovrebbe farsi visitare dal medico.
Where does he live?	Dove abita?
What are his consulting hours?	Quali sono le sue ore di consultazione?
Six to eight o'clock every evening.	Dalle sei alle otto ogni sera.
I shall go to see him this evening.	Andrò da lui questa sera.
I feel very ill.	Mi sento molto male.
I shall get a prescription from the doctor.	Mi farò dare una ricetta dal medico.

Visiting.

Is Mr. X., Mrs. X., at home?
What name please?
Please take my card.

Mr. X. is not at home.
Can you tell me when he will be at home?
He will be back to-morrow morning.
My friend, Mr. Z., asked me to call on you.

Please sit down.
I have called on business
What can I do for you?

I called yesterday, but you had just gone out.
I was very sorry to miss seeing you.
I am delighted to make your acquaintance.
It is very kind of you to have called.

La Visita.

Riceve il Signor X., la Signora X.?
Chi posso annunciare?
Questa è la mia carta da visita.

Il Signor X. non è in casa.
Può dirmi quando sarà in casa?
Ritornerà domani mattina.
Il mio amico, Signor Z., mi chiese di venirla a visitare.

Favorisca sedersi.
Sono venuto per affari.
Che cosa posso fare per Lei?

Venni ieri ma Ella era appena uscito.
Mi spiacque molto non aver La incontrata.
Ho molto piacere di conoscer La.
Ella è molto genti di essere venuto

At the Hotel.

Drive me to the Grand Hotel.
Bring in my luggage, porter.
Have you any rooms?
Yes sir, several.
On which floor do you want?
Can I have a single (double) bedded room?
Certainly, either on the first or second floor.

Do you want a front or a back room?

All'Albergo.

Mi conduca al Grand Hotel.
Portiere, porti dentro il mio bagaglio.
Ha una stanza?
Sì Signore, varie stanze.
A che piano la desidera?
Posso avere una camera con un letto (doppia)?
Certamente, tanto al primo che al secondo piano.
Desidera una camera sulla parte anteriore o sulla parte posteriore dell'Albergo?

abandon abbandonare

abandoned abbandonato

abandonment abbandono
m; cessione f

abate abbattere; diminuire

abatement diminuzione f

abbey badia f

abbot abbate m

abbreviate abbreviare

abbreviation n abbrevia-
zione f

abdicate abdicare

abdication abdicazione f

abdomen addome; basso
ventre m   [m & f

abdominal addominale

abduct rimuovere; rapire

abduction abduzione f

abductor n abduttore m

aberration aberrazione f

abet incoraggiare

abettor fautore m; isti-
gatore m

abeyance vacanza f;
in - vacante

abhor abborrire; detestare

abhorrence orrore m

abhorrent colpito d'orrore

abide dimorare

abiding soggiorno m,
stabilità f   [f

abigail serva f; cameriera

ability abilità; capacità f

abject abbietto; vile;
- ly bassamente

abjection abbiezione f

able capace; abile; to
be - to esser in istato
di; - ness n capacità
f; forza f

abode dimora f; sog-
giorno m   [lare

abolish abolire; annul-

abolition abolizione f;
annientamento m

abominable abbomina-
bile; detestabile m & f

abominate abbominare

abomination abbomina-
zione f; orrore m

aboriginal primitivo

abortion aborto m

abortive abortivo; abor-

abound abbondare [tito

abounding abbondanza;
soverchio m

about intorno; circa;
verso; sopra; da; in;
in quanto a; - noon
verso il mezzogiorno;
to be - to essere sul
punto di

above al di sopra; di
sopra; - mentioned,
said suddetto

abrade logorare

abrasion abrasione f

abreast di fronte; - of
dirimpetto   [tringere

abridge abbreviare; ris-

abridgment sommario m;
diminuzione f

abrupt precipitato; brusco; - ly av bruscamente;
- ness n asprezza f;
precipitazione f

absence assenza f; lontananza f; - of mind
distrazione f; leave of -
congedo m

absent assente; to be -
essere distratto m

absentee assente dal suo
paese m

absolute assoluto; perfetto; - ly assoluta-

mente; affatto

absolution assoluzione *f*

absolve assolvere; slegare

absorb assorbire; inghiottire [*m & f*

absorbent assorbente

abstention astinenza *f*

abstinence astinenza *f*; **day of –** giorno di digiuno *m*

abstract astratto; compendio *m*; **– ly** astrattamente

abstract estrarre; involare

abstraction astrazione *f*; sottrazione *f*

absurd assurdo; insensato *m*

absurdity assurdità *f*

abundance abbondanza *f*

abundant abbondante; **– ly** copiosamente

abuse abuzare; maltrattare [*f p*; errore *m*

abuse abuso *m*; ingiure

abusive abusivo; ingiurioso; **– ness** *n* abuso

academic, academical accademico *m* [*m*

academy accademia *f*

accede aderi e; consentire

accelerate accelerare

acceleration acceleramento *m* : prestezza *f*

accent accento *m*; pronuncia *f* [colare

accent accentuare; articolare

accentuate accentuare

accentuation accentuazione *f* [dire

accept accettare; aggradire

acceptable accettabile

acceptance accettazione *f*

accessibility accessibilità *f*

accessible accessibile *m & f*

accessory accessorio

accident accidente *m*;

accidental accidentale; fortuito; **– ly** accidentalmente; per caso

accommodate accomodare; aggiustare; regolare

accommodation adattazione *f*; aggiustamento *m*; convenienza *f*

accompaniment accompagnamento *m*

accompanist accompagnatore *m*, trice *f*

accompany accompagnare

accomplice complice *m & f*

accomplish effettuare; eseguire [terminato

accomplished compito;

accomplishment *n* compimento *m*; talento *m*

accord accordo *m*; consenso *m*; **of one's own –** di sua propria volontà *f*; accordare

according, – as secondo che; **– to** secondo; **– ly** in conseguenze

account conto *m*; contare; rendere conto di; **by all – s** secondo il detto generale; **on that –** per questo motivo; **on no –** con nessun pretesto;

to keep – s tener libri; **– book** libro *m* de' conti

accountability risponsabilità *f* [*m & f*

accountable risponsabile

accountant calcolatore *m*; che tiene i libri

accumulation accumulazione *f* [mula

accumulative chi accu-

15

accumulator accumulatore *m*, trice *f*

accuracy esattezza

accurate esatto; corretto; – ly esattamente

accurse maledire

accursed maledeto

accusation accusa *f*

accuse accusare

accustom accostumare; to – one's self avvezzarsi

accustomed abituato

acetate acetato *m*

ache far male; soffrire; my head – s io ho mal alla testa; male *m*; dolore *m*

achieve compiere; finire

achievement compimento *m*; fatto *m*

aching dolore *m*

acid acido *m*

acidity aciddezza *f*

acknowledge riconoscere; confessare

acknowledgment *n* recognizione *f*; confessione

acme apogeo *m*; colmo *m*

acoustic acustico

acquaint avvertire; apprendere

acquaintance conoscenza *f*

acquiesce acconsentire

acquiescence consenso *m*

acquire acquistare; ottenere

acquit pagare; assolvere; –tance *n* pagamento *m*

acre misura di terreno (4046 m. quad)

acrimonious acrimonico; acre; – ly con acrimonia

across per mezzo; a traverso; per sopra

act fare; operare; atto *m*; in the very – in

flagrante delitto

action azione *f*; fatto *m*; battaglia *f*; processo *m*

active attivo; lesto

activity attività

actor attore *m*; commediante *m*

actress attrice *f*; commediante *f*

actual attuale; reale; – ly attualmente

acute acuto; sottile; – ly sottilmente; – ness perspicacia *f*

adage proverbio *m*

adamant diamante *m*

adapt adattare; aggiustare

adaptable adattabile

adapted adattato; proprio

add aggiungere; to – up sommare

adder vipera *f*; serpente *m*

addict, to – one's self addarsi; applicarsi

addition *n* somma; addizione *f*

additional addizionale

addle stantio; guastato; – headed, – pated scervellato

address indirizzo *m*

address indirizzare; parlare a

addresser mittente *m*

adduce addurre; allegare

adept adetto; dotto

adequacy sufficienza *f*

adequate uguale; – ness sufficienza *f*

adhere aderire

adherence aderenza *f*

adherent aderente *m*

adjust aggiustare

adjustment aggiustamento *m*

adjutant aiutante *m*

administer amministrare;

fornire [tivo
administerial ammistra-
administrate amministrare [trazione *f*
administration amminis-
administrator amminis-
tratore *m*; direttore *m*
admirable ammirabile
admirably ammirabil-
mente
admiral ammiraglio *m*
admiration ammirazione *f*
admire ammirare
admirer ammiratore *m*
admissible ammissibile
admission ammissione *f*;
entrata *f*; – **ticket** biglietto *m* d'entrata *f*
admit accordare; am
mettere
admittance entrata *f*,
concessione *f*; **no – here**
non si entra qui
admonish avvertire; riprendere
admonition ammoni-
zione *f*; avviso *m*
adolescence adolescenza *f*
adolescent adolescente
m
adopt adottare
adorable adorabile
adoration adorazione *f*
adore adorare
adorn ornare
adrift alla deriva *f*;
abbandono *m*
adroit destro; abile;
– **ness** destrezza *f*
adult adulto; adoles-
cente *m*
adulterate adulterare
adulteration adultera-
zione *f*; falsificazione *f*
adulterer adultero *m*

adulteress adultera *f*
adultery adulterio *m*
advance avvicinamento
m; progresso *m*; **in** -
anticipatamente
advancement promozione
f; progresso *m*
advantage vantaggio *m*;
superiorità *f*; **to take** –
profittare
advantageous vantag-
gioso; – **ly** vantaggio-
samente
adventure avventura *f* ;
accidente *m*; avven-
turare
adventurer avventuriere
m
adventuresome arrischi-
ante; ardito
adverb avverbio *m*
adversary avversario *m*
adverse avverso; con-
trario
adversity avversità *f*
advertise annunziare

advertisement avverti-
mento *m*; avviso *m*;
annunzio *m* [siglio *m*
advice avviso *m*; con-
advisable prudente; av-
visato *m* [visare
advise consigliare; av
advisedly prudentemente
advocate avvocato *m*;
difensore *m*; difendere;
aeronaut aeronauta *m*
aerostat aerostato *m*;
pallone *m* [lontano
afar lungi; – **off** da
affability affabilità *f*
affable affabile
affair affare *m*
affect affettare
affectation affettazione *f*
affection affezione *f*;

17

tenerezza *f*
affectionate affettuoso
affiliate adottare
affiliation filiazione *f*
affinity affinità *f*
affirm affermare
affirmation affermazione *f*
affirmative affermativo;
in the – affermativo-
mente
affix aggiugnere
afflict affliggere
affliction afflizione *f*
affluence affluenza *f*
affluent abbondante
afford fornire; dare
afloat a galla
afore innanzi; prima;
avanti; piuttosto; –
mentioned suddetto; –
named sullodato; – said
suddetto; – time già
suddetto;
afraid spaventato
afresh di nuovo
afront di fronte
after dopo; conforme
aftermost ultimo
afternoon vespro *m*;
dopo mezzodì *m*
afterwards dopo; più
tardi
again ancora; di nuovo;
di più
against contro; sopra;
verso; – the grain con-
trapelo

age età *f*; generazione;
of – maggiore *m & f*;
under – minore *m & f*
aged vecchio
agency azione *f*; agenzia *f*
agenda giornale *m*; tac-
agent agente *m* [cuino *m*
agression agressione *f*
aggressive ostile
aggressor aggressore *m*
aggrieve affliggere

aghast spaventato
agile agile
agility agilità *f*
agitate agitare; discutere
agitation agitazione *f*
agitator agitatore *m*
ago passato; long – gran
tempo fa; two days –
due giorni fa; how
long – ? da quanto
tempo?
agonise agonizzare
agonising straziante;
atroce
agony agonia *f*
agree accordarsi; convenire; consentire; ac-
cordare
agreeable conforme; gradevole   [accordo
agreed convenuto; d'
agreement accordo *m*;
contratto; to come to
an – venir d'accordo
agricultural d'agricoltura
agriculture agricoltura *f*
ahead avanti; innanzi
aid aiuto *m*; assistenza;
aiutare; soccorrere; in
– of a beneficio di
ail soffrire; what – s you?
ove soffrite, ch'avete?
ailing malaticcio
ailment male *m*; pena *f*
aim mira *f*; punto *m*;
prender di mira *f*;
dirigere; mirare
air aria *f*; vento *m*;
canto *m*; ciera *f*;
aspetto *m*; – balloon
serostato *m*; –blad-
der vescica natatoria;
– gun fucile *m* a vento
m; – hole spiraglio
m; – pump macchina

f; pneumatica; **– shaft**
ozzo *m*; da far
entrare l'aria *f*; **– tight**
a impermeabile all'aria
f; far prender aria *f*;
espore all'aria *f*; ventilare
airiness leggerezza *f*
airing passeggiata *f*
airless senz'aria *f*
airy aereo; leggiero
aisle parte *f*; laterale
d'una chiesa *f*
alarm allarme *m*; risveglio *m*; **– clock** orologio-sveglia *f*; allarmare
alcohol alcool *m*
alcoholic alcoolico
alcove alcova *m*
alder alno *m* (albero)
alderman consigliere municipale
ale birra *f*; **– brewer**
birraio *m*; **– house**
taverna *f*; **– housekeeper** tavernaio *m*
alert alerte; vigilante; on
the **–** stante allerta
algebra algebra *f*
alien straniero; strano;
straniero *m*, ra *f*
alienable alienabile *m & f*
alienate alienare
alienation alienazione *f*;
– of mind pazzia *f*
alight discendere; cadere
alight accesso
alike somigliante *m & f*
aliment alimento *m*
alimony pensione *f*
all tutto; tutti; **all the
better** tanto meglio;
with – speed prestissimo;
by – means a qualunque
prezzo; **not at – punto
punto**; **nothing at –**

niente affatto; **– of us**
tutti noi; **– along** lungo
11; **that is all** ecco tutto;
– at once di subito;
– powerful onnipotente;
allegation allegazione *f*
allege allegare; ad durre;
dichiarare
allegiance fedeltà *f*
allegory allegoria
alleviate alleggiare
alleviation allievamento *m*
alley andito *m*; vicolo *m*;
**blind – angiporto *f*
alliance allenza
alliteration alliterazione *f*
allot ripartire; assegnare
allotment ripartizione *f*
nezzo *m* di terra *f*
allow assegnare; permettere
allowance allocazione *f*;
pensione *f*; **to make –
for** tenir conto di
alloy lega *f*; miscuglio *m*;
allegare; alterare
allspice pimento *m*
allude alludere
allure attrarre; sedurre
allurement vezzo *m*;
seduzione *f*
allusion allusione *f*
ally unire; alleato *m*
almighty onnipotente *m
& f*
almond mandoria; **burnt
– mandoria tostata
almost quasi; presso a
poco

aloft in alto; in aria
alone solo; solamente
along per lungo; di
lungo; alla lunga;
come – venite dunque;
andiamo
alongside accanto; bordo

19

a bordo
aloof lungi; **at largo**
aloud alto; *ad* alta voce
alpaca alpaca *m* (stoffa)
alphabet alfabeto *m*
alphabetic alphabetical
alfabetico
alpine alpino; alpestre
already già   [ancora
also anche ugualmente;
altar altare *m*; – piece
cornice *f*; quadro *m*
d'altare
alternate alternare; alternativo; alterno
alternation alternativa *f*
alternative alternativo
although sebbene; quantunque
altogether interamente
alum allume *m*
always sempre
a.m. iniziali di: **anno
mundi** l'anno del mondo;
artium magister maestro
m d'arti; **ante meri-
diem** antimeridiano
amadou esca *f*
amain vigorosamente
amalgam amalgama *f*
amalgamate amalgamare
amanuensis, amanuenses
secretario *m*; scrivano *m*
amass ammassare
amateur dilettante; virtuoso *m*   [prendere
amaze sbigottire; sor-
amazement stupore *m*
amazon amazzone *f*
ambassador ambasciatore
m   [trice *f*
ambassadress ambascia-
ambition ambizione *f*
ambitious ambizioso
amble ambio *m*; andar
all' ambio
ambrosia ambrosia *f*

ambulance ambulanza *f*
amenable risponsabile
amend emendare; cor-
reggere   [f
amendment emendazione
amends riparazione *f*
amenity amenità *f*
amethyst amatista *m*
amiability amabilità
amiable amabile *m & f*
amicable benevolente
amid, amidst nel mezzo
ammonia ammoniaca *f*
ammunition munizione *f*
amnesty amnistia *f*
among, amongst tra;
fra; appresso
amount montante *m*;
totale *m*; montare
amplifier amplificatore *m*
amplify amplificare
amply ampiamente
amputate amputare   [f
amputation amputazione
amuck furiosamente; **to
run** – attaccare con furia
amuse divertire
amusement divertimento
m; ricreazione *f*
an uno *m*; una *f*
anachronism anacronis-
mo *m*
analogous analogo
analogy analogia *f*
analysis analisi *f*
analyst analista *m*
analytic, analytical ana-
analyze analizzare [litico
anarchist anarchista *m*
anarchy anarchia *f*
anatomist anatomista *m*
anatomy anatomia *f*
ancestor antenato *m*
ancestral ereditario
ancestry antenati *m pl*
anchor ancora *f*; to ride

at – esser a l'àncora;
to weigh – levar l'àncora

anchorage ancoraggio *m*

ancient àntico; vecchio

and e

angel angelo *m*

angelic angelico

angelus avemaria *m*

anger collera *f*

angle angolo *m*; canto *m*;
pescare colla lenza *f*;
accalappiare

angler pescatore *m*
colla lenza

anglican anglicano; inglese *m & f*

angling pesca *f* colla
lenza; – **ling** lenza da
pesca *f*; – **rod** canna
da pesca

angry in collera

anguish angoscia *f*

angular angolare *m & f*

animadvert riprendere

animal animale *m*

animate animare; vivificare; animato

animation animazione

animosity animosità *f*

annihilate annichilare

annihilation annichila-
mento *m*   [*m*

anniversary anniversario

annotate annotare

annotation annotazione *f*

announce annunziare;
– **ment** annunzio *m*

announcer chi annun-
zia *m*   [estare

annoy incomodare; mol-

annoyance incomodità *f*

annual annuale

annuitant censuario *m*

annuity somma *f* an-
nuale d'una rendita

anoint ungere; fregare

anointed unto

anomalous anomalo

anomaly anomalia *f*

anon subito; or ora

anonymous anonimo

another un altro; ancor
un altro

answer rispondere; risposta *f*; soluzione *f*

answerable risponsabile
m & f

ant formica *f*   [*m*

antagonism antagonismo

antagonist antagonista *m*

antarctic antartico

antecedent antecedente
m & f   [*f*

antelope antilopo *f*

anterior anteriore *m & f*

anthem antifona *f*

anthology antologia *f*

anthropology *n* antropo-
logia *f*

antic antico *m*

anticipate anticipare

anticipation anticipazione

antidote antidoto *m*   [*f*

antipathy antipatia *f*

antiquated antico   [*f*

antique antico; antichità

antiquity antichità *f*

antiseptic antisettico

antithesis antitesi *f*

anus ano *m*

anvil incudine *f*

anxiety ansietà; in-
quietudine

anxious ansioso; in-
quieto *m*

any qualche; del; della;
degli; alcuno; – **body**
qualsia; – **where** dap-
pertutto; (preceduto
d'un negativo) in nes-
suna parte; – **more** di
più   [to

apart a parte

apartment appartamento
apathetic apatico
apathy apatia *f*
ape scimia *f*; imitare
apex sommità *f*; cima *f*
apiece il pezzo; per testa
apologetic, apologetical apologetico
apologize far l'apologia
apology apologia *f*
apostrophize apostrofare
apothecary farmacista *m*;
 – 's shop farmacia *f*
appal spaventare
appanage appannaggio *m*
apparatus apparecchio *m*
apparel abito *m*; vestimento *m*; vestire
apparent apparente *m & f*
apparition apparizione *f*
appeal appello *m*; appellare [parire
appear apparire; comappearance apparizione *f*; aspetto *m*
appease placare; calmare
appellant appellante *m & f*
appellation appellazione *f*
append appendere
appendage pertinenza *f*; accessorio *m*
applaud applaudire
applause applauso *m*
apple mela *f*; pupilla *f* (dell' occhio) – tree melo *m*
appliance applicazione *f*
applicable applicabile *m & f* [*m & f*
applicant postulante
application applicazione *f*; make – indirizzarsi
apply applicare [nare
appoint nominare; designappointment nomina *f*;
apportion ripartire [& f

apposite convenevole *n.*
appraise apprezzare
appreciable apprezzabile
appreciate apprezzare
appreciation estimazione *f*; valutazione *f*
apprehend pigliare; arrestare [*f*; arresto *m*
apprehension apprensione *f*
apprentice apprendista *f*
apprise apprendere; informare
approach avvicinare; avvicinamento *m* [zione *f*
approbation approvaappropriation appropriazione *f*
approval approvazione *f*
approve approvare
approximate ravvicinare: -ly per approssimazione *f* [*f*
apricot albicocca *f*; -tree albicocco *m*
apron grembiale *m*
apropos a proposito [& *f*
apt atto; intelligente *m*
aptitude attitudine *f*
aqueduct acquedotto *m*
arbiter arbitro *m*
arbitrary arbitrario
arbitrate arbitrare
arbitration arbitraggio *m*
arbitrator arbitro *m*
arbor albero *m*
arcade vaito *f*; arcata *f*
arch arca *f*; volta *f*; arco *m*; --way volta *f*
archaeological archeologico
archaeology archeologia *f*
archbishop arcivescovo *m*
archer arciere *m*
archery tiro dell' arco *m*
architect architetto
architecture architettura *f*
archives archivio *m*

22

arctic artico
ardent ardente *m & f* – **ly** ardentemente
irdor ardore *m*
arduous arduo *m & f*
area area *f*; superficie
arena arena *f*
argue argomentare
argument argomento *m*
argumentative argomenaria *f* [tativo
arise alzarsi; levarsi
aristocracy aristocrazia *f*
aristocrat aristocratico *m*
arithmetic aritmetica *f*
ark arca *f*; cassa *f*
arm braccio *m*; ramo *m*; arma *f*; – **in** – a braccetto; –**chair** sedia *f*; a bracciuoli; – **hole** ascella *f*; armarsi
armistice armistizio *m*
armless senza bracchi
armourer armaiuolo *m*
armorial d'armedi stemma *f*
armoury arsenale *m*; sala d'armi; armatura *f*
armour armatura *f*
arms armi *pl*; men at – gente d'armi *m pl*
army esercito *m*; armata *f*
aroma aroma *m* [*f*
aromatic aromatico *m*
around intorno; in giro
arquebus archibugio *m*
arraign accusare
arrange assettare
arrangement acconciamento *m*
arrear prodotto d'una rendita *f*; arretrato *m*
arrest arresto *m*; arrestare
arrival venuta *f*; arrivo *m*
arrive arrivare
arrogance arroganza *f*

arrogant arrogante *m & f*
arrow saetta *f*; strale *m*
arse culo *m*
arsenal arsenale *m*
arsenic arsenico *m*
arson incendio *m*
art arte *f*; abilità *f*
arterial arteriale *m & f*
artery arteria *f*
artful artistico; astuto
artichoke carciofo *m*
article articolo *m*; stipulazione *f*; materia *f*
articulate articolare; articolato [*f*
articulation articolazione
artifice artifizio *m*
artificial artifiziale *m & f*
artillery artiglieria *f*
artisan artigiano *m*; operaio *m*
artist artista *m* [to
artless senz'arte *f*; schiet**as** come; anche; siccome; conforme; – **for** in quanto a; – **well** così bene che; – **soon** – tosto chè
ascribe attribuire
ash frassino *m*; legno *m*; –**tree** frassino *m*
ash cenere *f*; – **coloured** cenerino; – **Wednesday** mercoledì delle ceneri
ashamed vergognoso [*f pl*
ashes cenceri *pl*
aside da canto; a parte; lay – metter da parte
asinine asinino
ask domandare

asleep in riposo
asparagus asparago *m*
aspect aspetto *m*
asphalt asfalto *m*
aspirant aspirante *m & f*
aspirate aspirare

23

aspire aspirare
assailant assalitore
assassin assassino *m*
assassinate assassinare
assassination assassinio *m*
assault assalto *m* [giare
assay saggio *m*; assag-
assayer saggiatore *m*
assemblage complesso *m*
assemble raccogliere
assembly assemblea *f*
assent consentire; assen-
tire; approvazione *f*
assert affermare
assertion asserzione *f*
assess tassare [posta *f*
assessment tassa; im-
assessor assessore *m*
assign assegnare
assignment assegnazione
assimilate assimilare
assimilation assimila-
assist assistere [zione
assistance assistenza *f*
assistant aiutante; assis-
tente *m & f*
assize corte *f*
associate associare; –
with frequentare; as-
sociato *m*; socio *m*
association società; as-
sociazione *f*
assort assortire [*m*
assortment assortimento
assuage placare; calmare
assuagement mitigazione
assume prendere [*f*
assuming presuntuoso
assumption presunzione
f; assunzione *f*
assurance assicurazione *f*;
fiducia *f*
assure assicurare
asterisk asterisco *m*
asthma asma *m*
astonish sorprendere
astonishing stupendo

astonishment stupore *m*
astray fuori del cam-
mino; go – aviarsi
at a; in; dentro; sopra;
dopo; contro; da; –
home in casa; – first
prima; – length final-
mente
atmosphere atmosfera *f*
atmospheric atmospher-
atom atomo *m* [ico *m*
atone espiare; redimere
atonement espia
atop in alto; alla sommità
atrocious atroce *m & f*
atrocity atrocità *f*
atrophy atrofia *f*
attach attaccare; pigliare
attachment affezione *f*;
attaccamento *m*
attack assalire
attacker assalitore *m*
attain pervenire a; otte-
nere [talento *m*
attainment acquisizione *f*
attaint dichiarare
attempt tentare; assalire;
tentativo *m*; attentato *m*
attend seguire; accom-
pagnare; attendere
attendance servizio *m*;
cura *f* [dipendente *m*
attendant domestico *m*;
attention attenzione *f*;
pay – far attenzione;
give – prestar attenzione
attentive attento
attic attico; mansarda *f*
attire veste *f*; ornamento
m [posa *f*
attitude attitudine *f*;
attorney procuratore *m*;
regio; power of – pro-
cura *f*
attract attrarre; attirare
attraction attrazione *f*
attractive attrattivo *m*
attribute attribuire; im-

putare

attribute attributo
attune accordare
auction incanto m; subasta f; - sale vendita all'incanto m
auctioneer commissario m stimatore
audacious audace m & f
audacity audacia f
audible udibile m & f
audience udienza f; uditorio m
audit revisione f (di conti); udizione
auditor uditore m
augment aumentare
augmentation aumento m
aunt zia f
auspicious propizio
austere austero; severo
austerity austerità f
authenticity autenticità f
authenticate autenticare
authentication conferma-
author autore m [zione f
authoress autrice f [m
authoritative autorizzato
authority autorità f
authorization autorizza-
zione f
authorize autorizzare
autocracy autocrazia f
autocrat autocrata m
autograph autografo m
automaton automato m
autopsy autopsia f
auxiliary ausiliario
avail vantaggio m; utilità f; servire; profittare

available disponibile
avalanche valanga f
avenge vendicare; punire
avenger vendicatore m
avenue viale m
aver affermare

average mezzo termine m
averse contrario a
avert distrarre
aviary uccelliera f
avidity avidità f
avocation occupazione f
avoid evitare
await aspettare; attendere
awake vigilante
awaken svegliare
award aggiudicare; sentenza f; decisione
aware vigilante; attento
away, go - andarsène; take - togliere; send - rimandare
awe timore m; rispetto m
awful imponente; solenne, terrible
awhile per qualche tempo
awkward disadatto; sconcio; - ness goffaggine f; incommodità f
axe scure f
axiom assioma m
axis asse f
axle asse f; -pin acciarino m; -tree asse f
ay, aye si; sicuramente; certamente

aye sempre; per sempre
azote azoto m
azure azzurro m

B

b. - flat bemolle m
babble ciarlare; ciarla f
babbler chiaccherone m
babe bimbo m; bambino m
baby bambino; bimbo; — linea corredo m de

25

bimbi

back dorso m; posteriore m; dossiere m; fondo m; rovescio m; indietro; di ritorno; ritornare; appoggiare; far – indietreggiare; rinculare

background fondo m; in the – all'ombra f

backward indietro; a ritroreo

bacon lardo m; **rasher of** – fetta f di lardo

bad cattivo; male; infermo; **-ly** male

badge marchio m

baffle sventare; frustrare

bag sacco m; valigia f; insaccare

baggage bagaglio m; meretrice f

bail cauzione f; sicurtà; scarecrarc sotto cauzione

bailiff bailo m; usciere m

bait esca f; adescare

bake far pane; coucere

baker panattiere m

bakery bottega f di fornaio m

balance bilancia f; equilibrio m; bilanciere m; saldo m; bilanciare; aggiustare; dubitare

balcony balcone m

bald calvo; **-ness** n calvizie f

bale balla f; imbalare

balk trave f; contrariare

ball palla f; globo m; ballo m

ballad ballata f

balloon pallone m; aerostrato m

ballot scrutinio m; ballottaggio m; per votare; **–box** urna f

bamboo bambu

bank banca f; **-note** biglietto m di banca

banker banchiere m

bankrupt fallimento f

bankruptcy fallimento m

banner bandiera f

banquet banchetto m

banter scherzo m

baptism battesimo m

bar barra f; stanga f

barbarian barbaro

barber barbiere m

bard bardo m

bare nudo

barefaced a viso m

barefooted coi piedi

bareheaded col capo m

bargain mercato m

barge battello m

barley orzo m

barn granaio m

barnacle morsa f

barometer barometro m

baron barone m

barque barca f

barrack baracca f

barrel barile m

barren sterile

barricade barricata f

barrier barriera f

basin bacino m

basket cesta f

bass stuola f

bassoon fagotto m

bastard bastardo m

bastinade bastonata f

bastion bastione m

bat nottola f

batch fornata f

bate sbattere

bath bagno m

bathe bagnare

bather bagnaiuolo m

battalion battaglione m

batten impinguare

batter pasta f

26

battery batteria *f*
battle battaglia *f*
battledore racchetta *f*
battlement merlo *m*
bawl gracchiare
bay alloro *m*; báia *f*;
– **window** finestra *f*
bayonet baionetta *f*
bazaar bazar *m*
be essere
beach ripa *f*
beacon fanale *m*
bead grano; di rosario *n*
beak becco *m*
beam trave *f*; raggio *m*
bean fava *f*
bear orso *m*: she – orsa *f*
bear portare
beard barba *f*
bearer portatore *m*
beast bestia *f*
beat vincere; battere
beau elegante *m*
beautiful bello *m*; bella *f*
beautify abbellire
beauty beltà *f*
beaver castore *m*
because ché; perciochè
become divenire; con-
venire
bed letto *m*; talamo *m*;
-room, **-chamber** camera *f* da letto; –
clothes lenzuola *f pl*;
– **stead** lettiera *f*
bedlam ospedale *m* dei
pazzi *m pl*
bedridden a in letto
bee ape *f*; – **hive** alveare
m   [faggiuola *f*
beech faggio *m*; – **nut**
beef bue *m*; **boiled** –
lesso *m*; **roast** – rosbif
– **steak** bifteck
beer birra *f*
beet bietola *f*; – **root**

barbabietola *f*
beetle scarafaggio *m*;
scarabeo *m*
befall accadere
before prima;
beg domandare; sollecit-
tare; mendicare
beggar mendicante *m*;
impoverire
begin cominciare
beginner principiante *m*;
novizio *m*   [origine *f*
beginning principio *m*;
begone vattene!
begrime annerare
beguile ingannare [dursi
behave regolarsi; con-
behaviour condotta *f*
behead decapitare
behest comando *m*
behind dietro; dopo
behold guardare
beholder spettatore *m*
belabour battere
belatedness ritardo *m*
belch rutto *m*; eruttare
believe credere
believer credente *m & f*
bell campana *f*; sonaglio
m; **-clapper** batocchio
m; **-rope** cordone di
campanella *f*; **-ringer**
campanaio *m*
belligerent belligerante
bellow muggire [*m & f*
bellows soffietto *m*
belly ventre *m*
belong appartenere
beloved diletto; caro
below al di sotto di;
agiù; laggiù
belt cinturino *m*
bench banco *m*; panca *f*;
corte *f* [incurvatura *f*
bend bendare; curvare

27

beneath sotto giù
benediction benedizione *f*
benefactor benefattore *m*
benefice beneficio *m*
beneficial vantaggioso
beneficence beneficenza *f*
beneficiary beneficiario *m*
benefit profitto *m*; vantaggio *m*; profittare
benevolent benefico
benign benigno
bent tendenza *f*; curvato
benumb stupefare
benzine belzuino *m*
bequeath legare
bestow dare; concedere
bet scommessa *f*; ._commettere
betray tradire
betrayal tradimento *m*
betroth fidanzare
better migliore; get the - of prevalere
between fra
betwixt fra   [a sbieco
bevel squadra *f*; tagliare
beverage beveraggio *m*
bevy brigata *f*
beware guardarsi
bewitch ammaliare
beyond al di là di; oltre; da lungi; lungi
bias sbieco; linea; tendenza *f*; inclinare
Bible Bibbia *f*

bibliography bibliografia *f*
bibulous spugnoso   [*m*
bicarbonate bicarbonato
bicker arrissarsi
bid pregare; offerire; offerta *f*   [*m & f*
bidder maggior offerente
big grosso; grande *m & f*
bigamy bigamia *f*
bigot bacchettone *m*

bile bile *f*
bilge fondo *m*; minore;
bilious bilioso [pancia *f*
bilk frustrare
bill serpe *f*; becco *m*; scritto *m*; annunzio *m*; fattura *f*; nota *f*; - of exchange cambiale *f*; - of fare carta *f* di trattoria; - of lading lettera di carico; **stick no - s!** proibita l'affissione *f*; -**sticker** attaccatore *m* di cartelli
billet biglietto *m*
billiards bigliardo *m*
bind legare; bendare: obbligare
binder legatore di libri
binding legatura *f*
biographer biografo
biography biografia *f*
bird uccello *m*; - **cage** uccelliera *f*; - **catcher** uccelatore *m*; - **lime** vischio *m*; - **'s-eye view** a vista d'uccello
birth nascità *f*; - **day** giorno *m* di nascità; - **place** luogo *m* nativo; - **right** primogenitura *f*
biscuit biscotto *m*
bishop vescovo *m*
bishopric vescovado *m*
bit boccone *m*; punta *f*
bitch cagna *f*
bite mordere; morsura *f*
bitter amaro *m & f*
black nero; oscuro; annerare; - **amoor** negro *m*; - **art** magia *f* nera; - **berry** mora *f* di ronco; - **bird** merlo
blacken annerare
blacking incerato *m*
blackish nericcio
bladder vescica *f*

blade fusto *m*; lama *f*
blameable biasimevole
blame biasimo; torto *m*
blameless irreprensibile
blameworthy degno di biasimo *m*
blanch imbiancare
bland dolce
blank bianco
blanket coperta da letto *m*
blarney adulazione *f*
blaspheme bestemmiare
blast colpo *m* di vento; suono *m*; distruggere; bruciare; **- furnace** fucina *f*
blaze fiamma *f*; lustro *m*; avvampare; brilliare
bleach imbiancare
bleak pallido; freddo
bleat be are; belamento
bleed salassare [*m*
bleeding salasso *m*
blemish difetto *m*; macchiare
blend mescolare
bless benedire
blessed benedetto
blessing benedizione *f*
blight nebbia *f*; peste *f*
blind cieco; oscuro; stuoia *f*; persiana *f*; accecare; mascherare; **- ness** cecità *f*
blindfold bendar gli occhi
blink batter gli occhi
bliss felicità *f*
bloated enfiato
block ammasso *m*
blockade blocco *m*; bloccare
blond bionda *f*
blood sangue *m*; **-horse** cavallo *m* di puro sangue
bloodshed effusione di sangue
bloodshot iniettato di sangue
bloodthirsty sanguinario
bloody sanguinario
bloom fiore *m*; fiorire
blossom fiore *m*
blot scarabocchio *m*
blotch pustola *f*
blotting scarabocchio; **- case** cartario *m*; **- paper** carta *f* asciugante
blow colpo *m*; puntura *f*; soffiare; **- up** saltare; **- one's nose** soffiare il naso
blowpipe zampogna *f*
blue turchino; azzurro
bluff grosso
blunt grossolano; brusco; rintuzzare *f*
blur macchia *f*
blush rossore *m*; arrossire
boar cinghiale *m*
board tavola *f*; cartone *m*; scrittoio *m*; consiglio *m*; esser in pensione *f*
boarder pensionario *m*
boarding pensione *f*; **-house** casa di pensione; **- school** pensionato *m* [tars
boast vanteria *m*; van**boat** battello *m*; barca *f*; **steam -** battello *m* a vapore;
body corpo *m*; **--guard** guardia *f* del corpo
bog palude *f*; infangare
boggy paludoso
boil bollire [*m*
boiler caldaia; calderone
boiling bollimento *m*
boisterous impetuoso

29

bold ardito; coraggioso;
  –ness arditezza *f*
bole tronco *m*
bolster capezzale *m*
bolt saetta *f*; strale *m*;
  scapparsi; schivarsi
bomb bomba *f*
bond legame *m*; obbli-
  gazione *f*; buono *m*;
  –man schiavo *m*
bondage servitù *f*
bone osso *m* disossare
bonfire fuoco *m* di gioia
bonnet cappello; ber-
  rettino *m*
bonus benefizio *m*
bony osseo; ossuto
booby goffo *m*
book libro *m*; memoriale
  m; registrare; **– binder**
  legatore *m*; **– case**
  biblioteca *f*; **– keeper**
  computista *m*; **– keeping** tenuta *f* dei registri
  m pl; **–seller** libraio
  m; **– store** magazzino
  m di libri
boot stivale *m*; profitto
  m; stivalare; profit-
  tare; **–hook**, **–jack**
  cavastivali *m*; **–maker**
  stivalaio *m*; **–tree**
  forma *f*
booted stivalato
booth tenda *f* baracca *f*
boots garzone *m*

border bordo *m*; bordare
bore buco *m*; calibro *m*;
  scandaglio *m*; persona
  f tedio *m*; forare;
  bucare; scandagliare
born nato; be **– nascere**
borough borgo *m*
borrow prestare
bosom seno *m*; cuore *m*
botanist botanico *m*
botany botanica *f*

both ambo; l'uno e
  l'altro; alla volta
bother imbarazzare; im-
  barazzo *m*
bottle bottiglia
bottom fondo *m*; fondarsi
bottomless senza fondo
bough ramo *m*   [*m*
bounce saltare; strepito
bound limitare; saltare;
  limite; balzo *m*
boundary limite *m*

bounty bontà *f*

bow inchinarsi; saluto *m*
bow arco *m*; archetto *m*;
  –window finestra *f*
  sagliente
bowel intestino *m*; **– s**
  viscere *f pl*
bowl bollo *m*; baso *m*;
  lanciar una palla
box bosso *m*; scatola *f*;
  cassa *f*; palco (di teatro)
  schiaffo *m*; sedia (di
  cocchiere); camerino;
  –office uffizio *m* di
  locazione *f*
boxing lotta *f* a pugni
boy ragazzo *m*
boyhood fanciullezza *f*
brace paio *m*
bracelet braciletto *m*
brad punta *f*; **– awl** pun-
brag vantarsi [teruolo *m*
braggart millantatore *m*
braid treccia *f*; intrecciare
brain cervella *m*; intelletto *m*; **– less** scervellato
brake freno *m*
bramble ronco *m*
bran crusca *f*
branch ramo *m*; suc-
  cursale *f*
brand torcia *f*; macchia *f*;
  marcare

brandish vibrare
brandy acquavite *f*
brazier calderaio *m*
bravery bravura *f*
brawl gridare; zuffa *f*
brawn carne *f* di porco; forza *f*; muscolare
bread pane *m*; **brown – pane** *m* bigio
breadth altezza *f*
break spezzare; **rompere**; **– open** rompere; **– off** staccare; **– away** staccarsi; **– down** abbattersi; **– in** entrare per forza; **–out** scappare; **– up** rompersi; rottura *f*; interruzione *f*; lacuna *f*; freno *m*
breakage frattura *f*
breaker spezzatore *m*
breakfast far colazione *f*
breast petto *m*; seno *m*; cuore *m*; **–bone** sterno *m*; **– plate** corazza *f* pettorale *m*; **– work** parapetto *m*
breath respiro *m*; fiato *m*; **be out of –** aver perduto il fiato in
breed generare; procreare; razza *f*; covata *f*; specie
breeder allevatore *m*
breeding educazione *f*
breeze brezza *f*; vento
brethren fratelli *m* pl
breviary breviario *m*
brevity brevità *f*
brew mescolare; far la birra *f*; mescolarsi; **– er** birraio fabbricante
bribe regalo *m*; corrompere
bribery corruzione *f*

brick mattone *m*; **–layer** muratore *m*
bride sposa *f*; **-groom** sposo *m*; **– 's-maid** damigella d'onore
bridge ponte *m*
bridle briglia *f*
brief breve; breve *m*
bright brillante
brighten brillare
brilliancy lustro *m*
brilliant brillante
brim orlo *m*
brine salamora *f*
bring portare; menare; **– about** compiere; **– forth** far uscire
broad largo; ampio; **–cloth** panno *m* fino; **–side** fianco *m* bordata *f*
broaden allargare
brocade broccato *m*
broil disputa *f*
broker sensale *m*
brokerage sensaria *f*
bronchitis bronchite *f*
bronze bronzo *m*
brook ruscello *m*
broom ginestra *f*
broth brodo *m*
brothel postribolo *m*
brother fratello *m*; **–in-law** cognato *m*
brow ciera *f*; fronte *f*
brown bruno
bruise ammaccare; ammaccatura *f*
brunette brunetta *f*
brush spazzola *f*; pennello *m*; attacco *m*; spazzolare; **–maker** *n* spazzolaio *m*
brutalise imbestiare
brute bruto *m*; bestia *m*
bubble bolla *f*

buck daino m; – skin pelle f di daino

bucket secchia f

buckle fibbia f; fibbiare

buffoon buffone m

bug climice f

bugbear spauracchio m

buggy carretta f

bugle lustrino m

build edificare; fabbricare

builder capomastro m; costruttore m

building edificio m;

bulb bulbo m [fabbrica f

bulge gonfio m; curvarsi

bulk grossezza f; volume; –head tramezzo m

bulkiness grossezza f

bulky grosso

bull toro m

bullet palla f

bulletin bollettino m

bullion oro m; argento m

bullock bue m

bully bravaccio m

bulrush giunco m

bulwark bastione m

bump bozza f

bumper pieno bicchiere m

bumpkin villano m

burden carica m; sopraccaricare

burdensome pesante

burgess borghese m & f

burg borgo m

burglar ladro m

burglary furto m

burgomaster borgomastro m

burial sepultura f; – ground cimeterio m

burlesque burlesco

burn bruciare; incendiare; scottatura f

burner brucciatore m

burnish abbrunire; pulire; – er brunitore m

burrow tana f

bursar economo m

burst crepare; rompersi; strepito m; esplosione f

bury sotterrare

bush cespuglio m

bushel staio m

bushy cespuglioso

business affare m; occupazione f

bust busto m [m

bustle affrettarsi; tumulto

busy occupato; attivo

but ma; che; che non; senza che; solamente; eccetto

butcher beccaio m

butler bottigliere m

butt groppa f; scopo m

butter butirro m burro m; bread and – pane m unto col butirro; –cup botton m d'oro; –fly farfalla f; – milk siero m

buttock natica f

button bottone m; abbottonare; –hole occhiello m;

buy comprare

buyer compratore m

buzz ronzo m; ronzare

buzzard babaccione m

by da; di; a; in; sopra; presso di; avanti; fra; tra; sotto; –all means ad ogni costo

bye dimora f; good – addio

C

cab biroccio; fiacre m; – man cocchiere m

cabbage cavolo m

cabin capanna f; cam-

32

erino *m*; **-boy** mozzo *m*
cabinet gabinetto *m*
  - maker ebanista *m*
cable gomena *f*; cavo *m*
caboose cucina
cackle chiocciare
cactus catto *m*
cake pasta; tavoletta *f*;
  indurire
calamitous calamitoso
calamity calamità *f*
calculable calcolabile
calculate calcolare
calculation calcolo *m*
calendar calendario *m*
call appello *m*; visita;
  vocazione *f*; chiamare;
  appellare; visitare
callosity callosità *f*
callous calloso [calma
calm calmo; **- ly** con
calm calma *f*; placare
calumniate calunniare
calumniator calunniatore
calumny calunnia *f* [*m*
camp campo *m*;
  campare
campaign campagna *f*
camphor canfora *f*
can boraccia *f*; potere;
canal canale *m* [sapere
canary-bird canarino *m*
cancel cancellare; annul-
cancer cancro *m* [lare
candid candido
candidate candidato *m*
candle candela *f*
candle-stick candeliere *m*
canoe canoa; piroga *f*
canon canone; canonico
canonical canonico [*m*
canopy baldacchino *m*;
  duomo *m* [teca *f*
canvas canavaccio *m*
canvass brigare
cap berretto *m*

capability capacità *f*
capable capace; abile
capacious vasto; spazioso
capacity capacità *f*
cape bavero; capo *m*
caper capriola *f*; far
  capriole
capital capitale; eccellente; capitale; lettera-
  maiuscola *f*
capitalist capitalista *m*
capitulate capitolare
capitulation capitolato *m*
capricious capriccioso
captain capitano *m*
captivate cattivare
captive prigioniere *m*
captivity cattività *f*
captor prenditore *m*
capture cattura *f*; cat-
  turare
car carro *m*; carretta *f*
caravan carovana *f*
carbon carbonio *m*
carbonize carbonizzare
card biglietto *m*; carta *f*;
  cardare
cardinal cardinale *m*
care cura; sollecitudine
  f; curare; stimare
career carriera *f* [dente
careful attentivo; pru-
carefulness accuratezza
careless negligente
carelessness trascuratezza
  [zare
caress carezza *f*; accarez-
cargo carico *m*
caricature caricatura *f*
carnation carnagione *f*
carnival carnevale *m*
carol carola *f*; cantare
carousal orgia *f*
carpenter carpentiere *m*
carpet tappeto *m*; **- bag**
  sacco *m*

carriage trasporto *m*; carrozza; vettura *f*;
carrier portatore *m*
carrot carota *f*
carry portare [*m*
cart carretta *f*; camione

cartoon cartone *m*

carve indicere; tagliare
carver incisore *m*
carving scultura; trinciatura *f*
cascade cascata *f*
case cassa; scatola *f*
casement finestra *f*
cash denaro; contante *m*; cambiare; scontare
cash-box cassetta *f*
cashier cassiere *m*
cashmere cascimirra *f*
cask botte *f*; barile *m*
casket cassetta *f*
cast getto; tiro *m*; figura; forma *f*; – **iron** ghisa *f*
cast gettare; shalzare; tirare; cambiare; fonçastigate castigare [dere
castigation castigo *m*
casting fusione *f*
castle castello *m*
castor oil olio di ricino *m*
casual casuale
casualty casualità *f*
cat gatto *m* [logare
catalogue catalogo; catacatastrophe catastrofe *f*
catch presa *f*; acchiappare; sorprendere
caterpillar bruco *m*
catgut minugia *f*
cathedral cattedrale *f*
catholic cattolico *m*
cattle bestiame *m*
cauliflower cavolfiore *m*
cause causa *f*; motivo *m*; causare
causeless senza causa

cautious cauto
cavalier cavaliere *m*
cavalry cavalleria *f*
cave cavern1;

ceaseless incessante
cedar cedro *m*
cede cedere
ceiling soffito *m*
celebrate celebrare
celebrated celebre
celebration celebrazione *f*
celebrity celebrità *f*
celerity celerità *f*
celery sedano *m*
celestial celeste
celibacy celibato *m*
cell cella; casella *f*
cellar cantina *f*
cellular cellulare
cement cemento *m*; cementare
cemetery cimitero *m*
censor censore *m*
censure censura *f*; cencensus censo *m* [surare
central centrale
centrifugal centrifugo
century secolo *m*
ceremonial ceremoniale *m*
ceremony ceremonia *f*
certain certo; sicuro
certainty certezza *f*; cosa certa *f*
certificate certificato *m*
certify certificare
cessation cessazione *f*
cession cessione *f*
chafe scaldare
chagrin stizza *f*
chain catena; trama *f*; incatenare
chair sedia *f*; seggio *m*; – **man** presidente *m*
chalk creta *f* [vocare
challenge sfida *f*; prochamber camera *f*; gab-

inetto *m*;

champagne sciampagna *f*

champion campione *m*

chance azzardo *m*

chancellor cancelliere *m*

change cambiamento *m*; variazione *f*; resto *m*; cambiare; alterare

changeable cambiabile; incostante

channel canale *m*

chaos caos *m*

chaotic caotico

chapel cappella *f*

chaplain cappellano *m*

chapter capitolo *m*

character carattere *m*; parte *f* [tico

characteristic caratteris-

characterize caratteriz-

charade sciarada *f* [zare

charcoal carbone di legno *m*

charge peso; carico *m*; carica *f*; prezzo; incarico *m*; caricare; affidare; incaricare; accusare; far pagare

charitable caritatevole

charity carità; elemosina *f*

charm incanto; fascino *m*; incantare; invaghire

charter carta *f*; statuto *m*

chase caccia *f*; cacciare

chasm burone *m* fessura *f*

chaste casto

chastise castigare

chastisement castigo *m*

chastity castità *f*

cheap buon mercato

cheat baro; inganno *m*; imbrogliare

check freno; scacco *m*; frenare; controllare

checkmate scaccomatto

m; dare scaccomatto

cheek guancia; coscia *f*

cheer festino; applauso *m*

cheer incoraggiare; applaudire; rallegrarsi

cheerful allegro

cheerfulness allegrezza *f*

cheerless tristo

cheese formaggio *m*; – monger formaggiaio *m*

chemical chimico

chemist chimico *m*

chemistry chimica *f*

cherry ciliegia *f*

chess scacchi *m pl*

chess-board scacchiere *m*

chess-man pedina *f*

chest cassa *f*; petto *m*; – of drawers armadio *m*

chestnut castagna *f*; marrone *m*

chew ciccare; masticare

chicken pollastra *f*

child ragazzo; bimbo *m*; – hood infanzia; fanciullezza *f*; – ish fanciullesco; puerile; –less senza figlioli; – like da ragazzo; – ren ragazzi *m pl*

chill freddo; ghiacciare

chilly freddoloso

chime carriglione *m*; scampanare

chimney camino *m*; – sweeper spazzacamino

chin mento [*m*

china porcellana *f*

chirp cinguettio *m*

chisel cesello; scalpello *m*; cesellare

chivalry cavalleria *f*

chloride clorite *m*

chloroform cloroformio *m*

chocolate cioccolata *f*

choice scelta; elezione *f*

choir coro *m*

choose scegliere; eleggere
chop costoletta /; spaccare
chord corda /
chorus coro m
Christ Cristo m
Christian cristiano m
Christianity cristianità /
Christmas Natale m
chronic cronico
chronicle cronaca /
chronology cronologia /
chrysanthemum crisantemo
chubby paffuto [temo m
chuckle sogghignare
church chiesa /
churchyard cimitero m
churn zangola /; follare
cider sidro m
cigar sigaro m; —holder fumasigari m
cinder cenere /
cipher cifra /; zero m
circle cerchio; circolo m
circuit circuito; giro m
circular circulare
circulate circolare
circulation circolazione /
circumcision circoncisione / [enza /
circumference circonferenza
circumstance circostanza /
circus circo m
citation citazione /
cite citare
citizen cittadino;
city città /

civic civico
civil civile; cortese
civilian borghese m
civility civiltà; cortesia /
civilization civilizzazione/
civilize civilizzare

clack battolare
claim reclamo m; rivendicazione /; reclamare; pretendere
clang clangore m
clank tintinnire
clap scoppio m; battere le mani
class classe /; classate
classic(al) classico
classify classificare
clatter chiasso m; far rimbombare
clause clausola /
claw artiglio m
clay argilla /
clean netto; pulito; nettare; pulire
cleanliness pulitezza
cleanly pulitamente
cleanse purificare; pulire
clear chiaro; limpido; manifesto; chiarire; nettare; dissodare
clearance disimpegno m; quitanza /
clearing dissodamento m
cleave fendere
cleaver fenditoio m
cleft fessura /
clemency clemenza /
clement clemente
clergy clero m
clergyman ecclesiastico m
clerical clericale
clerk commesso m
clever abile; capace
cleverness abilità /
client cliente m
cliff balza /
climate clima /
climax cima /
climb arrampicare
clime clima /
clinch ribadire
cling attaccarsi

clip tosare; tondere
cloak mantello *m*
clock pendola *f*; orologio *m*; –maker oriuolaio *m*
close chiuso; serrato; pesante; chiudere
closet camerino; gabinetto *m*
clot grumo *m*; coagulare
cloth panno; tessuto *m*;
clothe vestire [drappo *m*
clothes abiti *m pl*
clothing abbigliamento *m*; vestiti *m pl*
cloud nube *f*; nuvolo *m*
cloudy nuvoloso
clove garofano *m*
clover trifoglio *m*
clown mascalzone *m*
club circolo; casino *m*; mazza *f*; fiore (carte) *m*; contribuire
clump blocco; gruppo *m*
clumsy rozzo; malaccorto
cluster grappolo; capannello *m*
clutch afferrare; artiglio *f*

coach carrozza *f*; ripetitore *m*;
coagulate coagulare [*f*
coagulation coagulazione *f*
coal carbone *m*; –cellar buca del carbone *f*
coalition coalizione *f*
coarse grossolano
coarseness ruvidezza *f*
coast costa *f*; costeggiare
coat veste *f*; abito *m*; intonacare
coax accarezzare
cobweb ragnatelo *m*
cock gallo *m*; chiave *f*; – fight combattimento di galli; – sure certissimo
cocoa cacao *m*

cocoa-nut cocco *m*
cod merluzzo *m*
code codice *m*
coffin bara *f*; feretro *m*
cog dente *m*
cogitate meditare
cogitation escogitazione *f*
cognizance conoscenza *f*
cogwheel ruota dentata *f*
cohabit coabitare
coherent coerente
coil rotolo (corda) *m*; spira *f*; ravvolgere
coin moneta *f*; denaro *m*; coniare
coinage monetaggio *m*
coincide coincidere
coke coke *m*
cold freddo
collar collare; colletto *m*
collar-bone clavicola *f*
collate collazionare
collateral collaterale
colleague collega; socio *m*
collect raccogliere; riunire; colletta *f* [colta *f*
collection collezione; raccollective collettivo
collector collezionista *m* [*f*
college collegio *m*; facoltà
colloquial di conversazione
colon due punti *m pl*
colonist colono *m*
colonize colonizzare
colony colonia *f*
colossal colossale
colour colore; colorito *m*; colorare; pingere
colt puledro *m*
column colonna *f*
comb pettine; favo *m*; pettinare; cardare
combat combattimento *m*; combattere *m*
combatant combattente

combination combina-
zione; coalizione *f*
combine unire
combustible combustibile
combustion combustione
f   [provenire
come venire; avvenire;
comedian comico *m*
comedy commedia *f*
comet cometa *f*
comfort conforto; benessere *m*; comodità *f*;
confortare; racconsolare
comfortable confortevole
comforter consolatore *m*
comma virgola *f*
command comando *m*;
comandare   [*m*
commander comandante
commandment coman-
damento *m*   [orare
commemorate commem-
commemoration com-
memorazione *f*
commence comiciare
commencement comin-
ciamento *m*
commend commendare;
raccomandare
commendable commen-
dabile
commendation commen-
dazione: lode *f*
commensurate commen-
surato   [commentare
comment commento *m*;
commentary commen-
tario *m*
commerce commercio *m*
commercial commerciale
commission commissione
f; dar commissione;
incaricare   [sionario *m*
commissioner commis-
commit commettere
committee comitato *m*
commodity comodità *f*

common comune; or-
dinario; terre comunali
f pl; **-ly** comunemente;
          law
giustizia *m*; comune;
- place luogo *m* comune;
- sense buon senso;
- wealth repubblica *f*

commotion commozione *f*
commune comune *m*;
conferire
communicable comuni-
cabile
communicate comunicare
communication comuni-
cazione *f*   [cativo
communicative comuni-
communion comunione *f*
commuity comunità *f*
commutable commutabile
commute commutare
compact patto *m*
compact compatto; **- ly**
compattamente
companion compagno;
camerata *m*
company compagnia;
società *f*
comparable comparabile
comparative comparativo
compare comparare
comparison compara-
zione *f*   [mento *m*
compartment comparti-
compass bussola *f*
compasses compasso *m*
compassion compassione *f*
compassionate compas-
sionare
compel costringere
complainant querelante
m & f   [male *m*
complaint lagnanza *f*;
complaisant compiacente
complement complemen-
to *m*

38

complete completo; completare; finire [m

completion compimento

complex complesso

complexion colorito m; complessione f

compliance compiacenza f

complicate complicare

complication complicazione f

compliment complimento m; complimentare

complimentary complimentoso

compose comporre; calcomposed calmo [mare

composer compositore m

composition composizione f [m

composure calma; posatezza f

compound composto m; comporre; combinare

comprehend comprendere

comprehension comprensione f [sivo

comprehensive comprencompress compressa f; comprimere

comprise comprendere

compromise compromesso m; compromettere

compulsion compulsione f

compulsory compulsivo

computation computo m

compute computare

comrade camerata m

conceal nascondere

concede concedere

conceit vanità f; concetto m

conceive concepire

concentrate concentrare

conception concezione f; concetto m

concern affare; interesse m; inquietudine; casa f; concernere; riguardare; importare a

concerned interessato; inquieto

concert concerto m; concertare

concession concessione f

concise conciso

conclude conchiudere; terminarsi

conclusion conclusione f

conclusive conclusivo

concrete concreto m

concur concorrere

concussion concussione

condemn condannare

condemnation condanna f

condensation condensazione f

condense condensare

condescend condiscendere

conduce condurre; contribuire

conducive conducevole

conduct condotta f; condurre; dirigere

conductor conduttore m

confectionery confettureria f [zione f

confederacy confederaconfederate confederato

confer conferire; donare

conference conferenza f

confess confessare

confession confessione

confessional confessionale

confessor confessore m [m

confide confidare

confidence confidenza f

confident certo; sicuro

confidential confidenziale

confine confine m; confinare; imprigionare

confinement confinamento m; detenzione f
confirm confermare
confirmation confermazione f
confiscate confiscare
conflagration incendio m; conflagrazione f
conflict conflitto m; lottare
conform conformare
conformable conforme
conformity conformità f
confound confondere
confront confrontare
confuse confondere
confusion confusione f
confute confutare
congeal congelare; gelare
congenial congeniale
congratulation congratulazione f
congregate congregare
congregation congregazione f
congress congresso m
conjecture congettura f; congetturare
conjugate congiugare
conjunction congiunzione f
connect connettere; riunire [clientela f
connection connessione ;
conquer conquistare; vincere [vincitore m
conqueror conquistatore;
conquest conquista f
conscience coscienza f
consecration consacrazione f
consecutive consecutivo
consent consenso; consentimento m; consentire [f

consequence conseguenza
consequential d'importanza
conservative conservativo
conservatory serra f
conserve conservare
consider considerare
considerable considerevole
considerate considerato
consideration considerazione f; motivo m
consign consegnare; affidare [m
consignee consegnatario
consignment consegna f
consist consistere
consistency consistenza f
consistent consistente
consolable consolabile
consolation consolazione f
console consolare
consolidate consolidare
consonant conforme; consonante f
conspicuous cospicuo
conspiracy cospirazione f,
conspirator cospiratore
conspire cospirare [m
constancy costanza f
constant costante
constellation costellazione f [zione f
consternation costernaconstipation stitichezza f
constituent costituente; elettore m
constitute costituire
constitution costituzione f
constrain costringere
constraint costringimento
construct costruire [m
construction costrutto m struttura f
consumption consumo m; consunzione f [tisico
consumptive consuntivo;
contact contatto m

contagion contagio *m*
contagious contagioso; morboso
contain contenere
contaminate contaminare
contamination contaminazione *f*
contemn sprezzare
contemplate contemplare
contemplation contemplazione *f* [poraneo *m*
contemporary contem-
contempt sprezzo *m*
contemptible sprezzabile
contemptuous sprezzante
contiguous contiguo
continence continenza *f*
continent continente *m*
continental continentale
contingency contingenza *f*
contingent contingente *m*
continual continuo
continuance continuanza *f*
continuation continuazione *f*
continue continuare; prolungare; dimorare
continuity continuità *f*
contortion contorsione *f*
contour contorno *m*
contraband di contrabando; contrabbando *m*
contract contratto *m*; contrarre
contraction contrazione *f*
contractor contraente *m*
contradict contraddire
contradiction contraddizione *f*
contrary contrario; opposto [contrastare
contrast contrasto *m*;
contribute contribuire
contribution contribuzione *f*
contrite contrito

contrivance invenzione *f*
contrive inventare
control controllo *m*; autorità *f*; controllare; dirigere [arbitro *m*
controller controllore;
controversial di controversia
controversy controversia *f*
convalescence convalescenza *f* [cente *m & f*
convalescent convalescene** convocare [f
convenience convenienza *f*
convenient conveniente; comodo
convent convento *m*,
convention convenienza *f*
conventional convenzionale** convergere [ale
conversation conversazione *f*
converse intrattenersi
conversion conversione *f*; convertimento *m*
convert convertito *m*; convertire
converter convertitore *m*
convey trasportare
convict condannato *m*; condannare
conviction convinzione *f*
cook cuoco *m*; cucinare
cookery cucina *f*
cook-shop rosticceria *f*
cool fresco; freddo rinfrescare
cope contendere
copious copioso
copper rame; cupro *m*; caldaia *f* [*m*
coppice, copse bosco ceduo
copy copia *f*; esemplare *m*; copiare; imitare;
—**book** quaderno *m*

copying-press copialettere *m*

copyist copiatore *m*

copyright proprietà letteraria *f*

coquet civettare

coquette civetta *f*

coquettish da civetta

coral corallo *m*

cord corda *f*; incordare

cordial cordiale; cordiale *m*

cordiality cordialità *f*

core torso *m*

cork sughero; turacciolo *m*; turare; **– screw** cavaturacciolo *m*

corn grano; callo *m*; **– flower** fioraliso *m*

cornelian cornalina *f*

corner cantone; angolo *m*

coronation incoronazione

coroner procuratore del re *m*   [orale *m*

corporal corporale; caporale *m*

corps corpo *m*

corpse cadavere *m*

corpulence corpulenza *f*

corpulent corpulento

correct corretto; giusto; correggere

correction correzione *f*

correspond corrispondere; **– ence** corrispondenza *f*; **– ent** corrispondente *m* & *f*

corridor corridoio *m*

corroborate corroborare

corrode corrodere

corrosion corrosione *f*

corrupt corrotto; corrompere

corruption corruzione *f*

corset busto *m*; fascetta *f*

cosmetic cosmetico *m*

cosmopolitan cosmopolita *m* & *f*   [costare

cost costo; prezzo *m*;

cosy ad agio [villico *m*

cottage casetta *f*; **– r**

cotton di cotone; cotone *m*; bambagia *f*

couch letto; canapè

cough tosse *f*; tossire

council consiglio *m*

councillor counsellor consigliere *m*

counsel consiglio; avvocato *m*; consigliare

count, – ess conte *m*; contessa *f*

count contare; calcolare

countenance cera; faccia *f*; approvare

counter contra; banco *m*; **– act** contraporre; **– feit** contrafatto; contrafazione *f*; contraffare; **– mand** contrordine *m*; contromandare; **– part** controparte *f*; **– sign** controfirmare

countless innumerevole

country paese *m*;

– man contadino; villico *m*   [accoppiare

couple coppia *f*; paio *m*;

courage coraggio *m*

courageous coraggioso

course corsa *f*; corso *m*; correre; **ol – ben** inteso

court corte *f*; tribunale *m*; **–martial** corte marziale *f*;

courteous cortese [enza *f*

courtesy cortesia *f*; river-

cousin cugino *m*; cugina *f*

cove baia *f*   [contrattare

covenant contratto *m*;

cover coperta *f*; coperto *m*; coprire

covey covata *f*

cow vacca *f*; intimidire

coward(ly) codardo *m*
cowardice codardia *f*
cower tremare
cowl cappuccio *m*
cowslip tasso barbasso *m*
coy schifiltoso
crab granchio di mare *m*
crack crepatura; spac-
catura *f*; crepare;
spaccare; fendere
crackle scoppiettare
cradle culla *f*; cullare
craft mestiere *m*; astuzia
crafty astuto
crag rupe; balza *f*
cram impinzare
cramp granchio *m*
cranberry mortella palus-
crane grù; grua *f* [tre *f*
crank manovella; leva *f*
cranny screpolatura *f*
crape crespo *m*
crash scroscio *m*; catastrofe *f*; scrosciare
crate gabbia *f*
crazy matto
creak scricchiolare
cream crema *f*
crease piega *f*; spiegazzare
create creare
creation creazione *f*
creator creatore *m*
creature creatura *f*
credence credenza *f* [*pl*
credentials credenziali *m*
credible credibile
credit credenza *f*; credito *m*; credere
creditable onorevole;
degno di fede
creditor creditore *m*
credulous credulo
creed credenza *f*; credo *m*
creek seno *m*; cala *f*
creep tracinarsi; – **er**

piantra rampante *m*
crescent crescente; luna
nuova *f*
crime delitto; reato *m*
criminal criminale; reo
m; delinquente *m & f*
cringe abbassarsi
cripple storpio; zoppo
m; storpiare
crisis crisi *f* [increspare
crisp croccante; friabile;
critic critico *m*
critical critico
criticise criticare
criticism criticismo *m*
croak gracchiare
crocodile coccodrillo *m*
crook pastorale; uncino *m*.
crooked tortuoso
crop messe; raccolta *f*;
seminare; tosare
cross obliquo; contrario;
croce *f*; incrociare;
attraversare; – **bow**
balestra *f*; – **examination**
interpellazione *f*
crossing traversata *f*
crotchet ghiribizzo *m*
crow corvo *m*; cantare;
vantarsi
crowd folla; ressa *f*
crown corona *f*; cima *f*;
(in)coronare
crucial severo; rigoroso
crucible crogiuolo *m*
crucifix crocifisso *m*
crucifixion crocifissione *f*
crucify crocifiggere
crude crudo
cruel crudele
cruelty crudeltà *f*
cruise crociera *f*; incrociare
crumb mollica *f*
crumble sbriciolarsi
crumple spiegazzare

43

crusade crociata *f*

crush folla *f*; urtare

crust crosta *f*; incrostare

crutch gruccia *f*

cry grido; pianto *m*; gridare; piangere

cue stecca *f*; motivo *m*

cuff paramano; polsino *m*; schiaffeggiare

cuirass corazza *f*

cuirassier corazziere *m*

culinary culinario

cull cogliere

culminate culminare

culpable colpevole

culprit prevenuto *m*

cultivate coltivare

cultivation, culture coltivazione; cultura *f*

cumbersome pesante

cunning astuzia *f*; astuto

cup coppa; tazza *f*

cupboard credenza *f*; armadio *m*

cupidity cupidità *f*

cupping-glass ventosa *f*

cur mastino *m*

curable curabile

curacy cura *f*

curate curato; vicario *m*

curator curatore *m*

curb freno *m*; frenare

curd giuncata *f*

curdle quagliare

cure cura *f*; rimedio *m*; curare; guarire

curiosity curiosità *f*

currency corso *m*; circolazione *f*

current corrente *f*

cursory superficiale; – ily rapidamente

curt corto

curtail restringere

curtain cortina *f*

curtsey riverenza *f*

curve curva *f*; curvare

cushion cuscino *m*

custard crema *f* [lione *f*

custody custodia; priz-

custom costume; uso *m*; – ary abituale; ordinario; -er cliente *m* & *f*; - -house dogana *f*

cut taglio *m*; ferita; stampa *f*; tagliare; fendere

cutlass scimitara *f*

cycle ciclo; biciclo *m*

cymbal cembalo *m*

cylinder cilindro *m*

cynic cinico *m*

czar(ina) czar(ina) *m* & *f*

D

dab colpetto *m*; percuoter leggiermente

dabble imbrattare

daffodil affodillo *m*

dagger pugnale *m*

daily quotidiano; giornaliero; ogni giorno

daintiness delicatezza *f*

dainty delicato

dairy latteria *f*; – maid venditrice di latte *f*

daisy margherita *f*

dam diga *f*; arginare

damage danno; male *m* danneggiare |

dame dama; signora *f*

damn dannare; condannare

damnation dannazione *f*

damp umido; umidità *f*

dance danza *f*; ballo *m*; danzare [ballerina *f*

dancer ballerino *m*;

dandelion smirnio *m*

dandy elegante *m*

danger pericolo *m*
dangerous pericoloso
dangle dondolare
dare osare
daring audace
dark oscuro; tenebroso
darken oscurrare
darkness oscurità *f*
darling caro; diletto *m*
darn rammendare
dart dardo *m*; dardeggiare
data dati; questio
date data *f*; dattero *m*;
daughter figlia; figliola *f*;
  − −in-law nuora *f*
dawn alba; aurora *f*;
  spuntare
day giorno; di *m*
dazzle abbagliare
deacon diacono *m*
dead morto; inanimato;
  − letter office officio
  lettere rifiutate
deaden indurire
deadly mortale; funesto
deaf sordo
deafen assordare
deafness sordità *f*
deal abete *m*; quantità;
  a great − molto
dealer negoziante *m*
dean decano *m*
dear caro; costoso
dearness carezza *f*; caro
  m
dearth scarsezza *f*
death morte *f*; −−bed
  letto di morte; − like
  di morte

debit debito *m*; addebi
debtor debitore *m*
decamp levar il campo
decant decantare
decanter caraffa *f*

decapitate decapitare
decay decadenza ; decadere [*f*; morire
decease decesso *m*; morte
deceased defunto *m*
deceit inganno *m*
deceitful perfido
deceitfulness falsità
deceive ingannare
deceiver ingannatore *m*
decency decenza *f*
decent decente; modesto
deception inganno *m*;
  illusione *f*
decide decidere
decision decisione *f*
decisive decisivo
deck ponte *m*; ornare
declaration dichiarazione
declare dichiarare [*f*
decline declino *m*; decadenza *f*; declinare
decompose decomporre
decorate decorare; ornare
decoration decorazione *f*;
  ornamento *m*
decoy allettamento *m*;
  allettare [*m*; diminuire
decrease decrescimento
decree decreto *m*; decretare
decrepit decrepito

dedicate dedicare
dedication dedica; consacrazione *f*
deduce, deduct dedurre
deduction deduzione *f*
deed fatto; atto *m*;
  azione *f*; gesta *f pl*
deem stimare; pensare
deep profondo; alto;
deepen affondare [oscuro
deer daino *m*; daina *f*
default difetto *m*; defalcare; − er contumace *m*
defeat sconfitta; rotta *f*;

45

sconfiggere
defect difetto *m*

defence difesa; fortificazione *f*
defend difendere
defendant difendente
defensive difensivo
defer deferire
deference deferenza *f*
defiance sfida *f*; sprezzo
deficiency deficienza *f*
deficient deficiente
deficit deficit *m*
define definire
definite definito
definition definizione

deformed deforme
deformity deformità
defraud defraudare
defy sfidare
degenerate degenerato; degenerare
degradation degradazione
degrade degradare [*f*
degree grado; stato *m*
deity divinità; deità
deliberate deliberato; deliberare
delicacy delicatezza *f*
delicate delicato
delicious delizioso
delight delizia *f*; dilettare
delightful delizioso; piacevole
delineate delineare
delinquency delinquenza *f*
delinquent delinquente *m*
delirious delirante [& *f*
delirium delirio *m* [are
deliver consegnare; liberare
deliverance, delivery liberazione; consegna *f*;
dell valletta *f* [parto *m*
delude deludere [dare
deluge diluvio *m*; inon-

delusion delusione *f*
delusive illusorio
demand domanda *f*; reclamo *m*; domandare; chiedere
democracy democrazia *f*
democratic democratico
demolish demolire
demolition demolizione *f*
demon demone; demonio *m* [diabolico
demoniac(al) demoniaco;
demonstrate dimostrare
demonstration dimostrazione *f*
den tana *f*; antro *m*
denial diniego; negamento *m*
denominate denominare
denote denotare
denounce denunciare
dense denso; fitto
density densità *f*
dentist dentista *m*
denunciation denunzia *f*
deny negare; rifiutare
depart partire; ritirarsi
department dipartimento *m*
departure partenza *f*
depend dipendere
dependence, – cy dipendenza
dependent dipendente *m* & *f*
depict dipingere
depilatory depilatorio *m*
deplorable deplorevole
deplore deplorare
deportment contegno *m*
depose deporre [positare
deposit deposito *m*; deposition** deposizione *f*
depraved depravato
depravity depravazione *f*
deprecate deprecare [*f*
deprecation deprecazione

46

depreciate deprezzare [f
depredation depredazione
depredator depredatore
depress deprimere
depression depressione f
deprivation privazione f
deprive privare   [f
depth profondità; altezza
derange scompigliare
derangement sconcerto m
derelict abbandonato
derivation derivazione f
derive derivare
derogatory derogatorio
descend discendere
descendant discendente
m & f   [pendio m
descent ascesa; origine f;
describe descrivere; di-
pingere   [genere m
description descrizione f;
desecrate profanare
desert deserto; merito
m; disertare
deserter disertore m
deserve meritare
design disegno; scopo m;
disegnare
designate designato
designation designazione f
designing intrigante
desirable desiderabile
desire desiderio m; desi-
derare
desk leggio m; cattedra f
desolate desolato; devas-
tare
desolation desolazione f
despair disperazione f;
disperare
despatch dispaccio; invio
m; prontezza f; spedire
desperate disperato
desperation disperazione f
despicable sprezzabile

despise sdegnare
dessert frutta f
destination destinazione f
destine destinare
destiny destino; fato m
destitute destituto
destitution destituzione f
destroy distruggere
destruction distruzione f
desultory sconnesso
detach staccare; distac-
care
detached isolato
detachment staccamento
detail dettaglio m; detta-
gliare
detain ditenere; ritardare
detect scoprire
detection scoperta f [m
detective agente segreto
deteriorate deteriorare
determinate, determinato
determination determina-
zione f   [risolvere
determine determinare;
detest detestare
detestable detestabile
dethrone detronizzare
detract detrarre
detraction detrazione f
detractor calunniatore m
detriment detrimento m
detrimental pregiudizic-
vole
deuce due; diavolo!
devastate devastare
develop sviluppare
development sviluppo m
deviate deviare [divisa f
device spediente m;
devil diavolo; demone m
devilish diabolico
devious sviato
devise inventare
dexterity destrezza f
diabetes diabete f

47

diabolical diabolico
diagonal diagonale *f*
diagram diagramma *m*
dial meridiana *f*
dialect dialetto; idioma *m*
dialogue dialogo *m*
diameter diametro *m*
diamond diamante; quadro (carte) *m*   [cata *f*
diaper biancheria damas-
diarrhœa diarrea *f*
diary diario; giornale *m*
dice dadi *m pl*   [tare
dictate dettame *m*; det-
dictation dettatura *f*
dictatorial dittatorio
diction dizione *f*
dictionary dizionario *m*
die dado; punzone *m*;
diet dieta *f*   [morire
differ differire
difference differenza *f*
different differente
difficult difficile
difficulty difficoltà *f*
diffidence diffidenza; timidità *f*
diffusion diffusione *f*
dig scavare
digest digerire
digestion digestione *f*
dignify esaltare; onorare
dignity dignità *f*
digress digredire
dilate dilatare
dilemma dilemma *m*
diligence diligenza *f*
dim oscuro; vago; offuscare
dimension dimensione *f*
diminish diminuire
diminutive diminutivo
dimple fossetta *f*
din baccano *m*
dine pranzare
dining-room sala da pran-

zo *f*
dinner pranzo *m*
diocese diocesi *f*
direct diretto; dirigere
direction direzione *f*; consiglio; indirizzo *m*
dirt fango *m*
dirty sporco; sporcare
disability incapacità *f*
disable invalidare   [*m*
disadvantage svantaggio
disadvantageous svantaggioso
disaffected disaffezionato
disagree discordare
disagreeable sgradevole[*m*
disagreement disaccordo
disallow disapprovare
disappear scomparire   [*f*
disappearance scomparsa
disappoint far mancare
disappointment disappunto *m*   [zione *f*
disapproval disapprova-
disaster disastro *m*
disastrous disastroso
disavow sconfessare
disband disperdere
disbelief incredulità *f*
disbelieve non credere
disburse sborsare
disc disco *m*
discard rigettare; scartare
discernible discernibile
discernment discernimento *m*
discharge scarico *m*; suppurazione *f*; congedo *m*; scaricare; suppurare; pagare; congedare
disciple discepolo *m*
discipline disciplina *f*
disclaim sconfessare
disclose rivelare
disclosure scoperta *f*

discolour scolorire
discomfit sconfiggere
discomfort disagio *m*
discompose turbare
disconcert sconcertare
disconsolate desolato
discontent malcontento *m*
discontented scontento
discontinue discontinuare
discount sconto *m*; scontare
discourage scoraggiare
discourse discorso *m*; discutere
discover scoprire
discovery scoperta *f*
discredit scredito *m*; non
discreet discreto [credere
discrepancy discrepanza *f*
discretion discrezione *f*
discriminate distinguere
discuss discutere
discussion discussione *f*
disdain sdegno *m*; sdegnare
disease malattia *f*; male *m*
diseased ammalato
disembark sbarcare
disfigure sfigurare
disgrace disgrazia; onta *f*; svergognare
disgraceful disonorevole
disguise travestimento *m*; camuffare [gustare
disgust disgusto *m*; disdish piatto *m*; piatti *m pl*; servire
dishonest disonesto
dishonesty disonestà *f*
dishonourable disonorevole [*f*
disinherit diserdare
disinterested disinteres-
disjoin disunire [sato
dislike avversione *f*
dislocate dislogare

disloyal sleale; perfido
dismal lugubre
dismay spavento *m*; spaventare
dismiss licenziare
dismissal licenziamento; congedo *m*
disobedience disobbedienza *f*
disobedient disobbediente
disobey disobbedire
disoblige disobbligare
disorder disordine; male *m*
disorderly in disordine
disorganize disorganiz-
disown ripudiare [zare
disparage screditare
disparity disparità *f*
dispassionate spassionato
dispel dissipare
dispensary dispensario *m*
dispensation dispensa *f*
dispense dispensare
disperse disperdere
disposal disposizione *f*
dispose disporre; vendere
disposition disposizione *f*
dispossess spossessare
disproportionate sproporzionato
disputant disputante *m*
dispute disputa *f*; disputare [incapacità *f*
disqualification inabilità;
disqualify rendere incapace; disabilitare
disregard noncuranza *f*; sprezzare
disreputable screditabile
disrespectful irriverente
dissatisfaction scontento
dissect dissecare [*m*
dissection dissezione *f*
dissemble dissimulare

disseminate disseminare
dissension dissensione *f*
dissent dissenso *m*; dissentire [*f*
dissertation dissertazione
dissimilar dissimile
dissipate dissipare
dissipated dissipato
dissolute dissoluto
distort storcere
distortion storsione *f*
distract distrarre
distracted distratto
distrain sequestrare
distress stretta *f*; affliggere
distribute distribuire
district distretto *m*
distrust diffidenza *f*; sospetto *m*
disturb disturbare
disturbance disturbo *m*; agitazione *f*
dive immergersi
diver palombaro *m*
diverge divergere
diverse diverso
diversity diversificare
diversion diversione *f*; divertimento *m*
divert sviare; divertire
divide dividere; disunire
dividend dividendo *m*
divine divino; prete *m*; indovinare
divinity divinità *f*
division divisione; votazione *f*
divorce divorzio *m*; divorziare
divulge divolgare
dizziness vertigine *f*
dizzy vertiginoso
do fare ; effettuare
docile docile
dock bacino; banco *m*;

dauco *m*
doctor dottore; medico *m*
doctrine dottrina *f*
document documento *m*
dodge rigiro *m*; rigirare
dog cane *m*
dogged ostinato
dogma domma *m*
doll bambola; fantoccia *f*
dollar dollaro *m*
dome duomo *m*; cupola *f*
domestic domestico *m*; domestica *f* [care
domesticate addomesticdominant dominante
dominate dominare
dominion dominio *m*
donation donazione *f*
donkey asino; asinello *m*
donor donatore *m*
doom destino *m*
door porta *f*
dose pressa; dose *f*; dosare [giare
dot punto *m*; puntegdotage rimbambimento *m*
double doppio *m*; doppiare
doubt dubbio *m*; dubitare
doubtful dubbio; incerto
doubtless indubitabile
dough pasta *f*
dove colomba *f*
dowager vedova *f*
dower dote *f*
down giù; in basso; a terra; piumino *m*; duna *f*; – cast abbassato; – fall caduta *f*; – ward, – wards giù; in giù; a basso [nechiare
doze sonnetto *m*; sondozen dozzina *f*
drachm dramma *f*
draft tratta *f*; disegnare
drag tramaglio *m*; tirare
dragon, dragoon dragone

drain canale; fossa *f*;
prosciugare   [*m*
drainage prosciugamento
drake anitra *m*
draw tirare; trascinare;
disegnare;   infondere;
cavare; – **back** svantaggio *m*; – **ee** trattario *m*;
drawing-room salotto *m*
drawl strascicare (parole)
dread timore *m*; temere
dreadful terribile
dress abito; costume *m*;
veste *f*; vestire; abbigliare; guarnire;

drift tendenza *f*; mucchio
m; galleggiare
drill trivella *f*; esercizio
m; forare; esercitare
drink beveraggio *m*; bere
drip gocciolare
dripping sugo dell'arrosto
drive scarrozzata *f*;
spingere; cacciare
driver cocchiere; conduttore *m*
drizzle pioviggina *f*
droll comico
droop languire
drop goccia; scesa *f*;
lasciar cadere; cessare
drought siccità; sete *f*
drover mandriano *m*
drown annegare; innon-
dare
drowning annegamento *m*
drowsy sonnolente
drudgery lavoro faticoso
m
drug droga *f*
druggist droghiere *m*
drum tamburo *m*
drummer tamburino *m*
drunk(en) ubbriaco; ebbro
drunkenness ebbrezza *f*
dry secco; seccare; –

goods merceria *f*; –
nurse aia *f*
dubious dubioso
duchess duchessa *f*
duck anitra *f*; immergere
duel duello *m*
duet duetto *m*
duke duca *m*
dull tupido; pesante;
scuro; stupidire; offus-
care; stancare
dullness stupidità; oscurità *f*
duly debitamente
dumb muto; – **found**
rendere muto; – **ness**
mutezza *f*
dungeon prigione (sot-
terranea) *f*
duplicate duplicato; duplicare
duplicity duplicità *f*
durable durevole
duration durata *f*
during durante
dusk crepuscolo *m*
dust polvere *m*; spolue-
rare; –**er** strofinaccio
m; – **hole** mondezzaio
m; – **man** spazzino *m*;
– **y** polveroso
dutiful obbediente
duty dovere; servizio;
dwell dimorare; abitare;
– **ing** abitazione *f*
dwindle diminuire
dye tingere; tinta *f*
dyer tintore *m*
dying morente; spento
dynamite dinamite *f*

E

each ciascuno; ognuno;
– **other** l'un l'altro
eager ardente; vivo;

- **ly** ardentemente; -
ness ardore *m*
eagle aquila *f*; -**t**
aquilino *m*
ear orecchio *m*; spica *f*;
early primaticcio; precoce; matiniero; per
tempo; di buon ora
earn guadagnare; meritare
earnest serio; premuroso;
sincero; caparra *f*
earnestness serietà; pre-
mura; sincerità
earth terra; argilla *f*;
- **en** di terra cotta; - **en-
ware** terraglia *f*; - **ly**
terrestre; - **quake** terre-
moto *m*
earwig forfecchia *f*
ease facilità *f*; sollevare
easel cavalletto *m*
easiness facilità *f*
east d'est; orientale;
est; oriente *m*; - **erly**
all'est; dell'est
Easter Pasqua *f*
easy facile; agevole
easily facilmente
eat mangiare
eatable commestibile
eatables commestibili *m*
eccentric eccentrico; [*m*
ecclesiastic ecclesiastico
echo eco *m*; echeggiare
eclipse ecclisse *f*
economical economico
economist economista *m*
& *f*
economize economizzare
economy, economics eco-
ecstacy estasi *f* [nomia *f*
eddy vortice ; *m*
edge taglio; filo; orlo
m; affilare; orlare
edible mangiabile
edict editto *m*

edification edificazione *f*
edifice edificio *m*
edit compilare
edition edizione *f* [*m*
editor editore; redattore
educate educare
education educazione *f*
eel anguilla *f*
efface cancellare
effect effetto *m*; effet-
effective effettivo [tuare
effects effetti; beni *m pl*
effectual efficace
effeminate effeminato
efficient efficiente
effort sforzo; tentativo *m*
effrontery sfrontatezza *f*
egg ovo *m*; - **cup**
ovaiolo *m*; - **shell** guscio d'uovo
egoism, egotism egoismo;
egotismo *m*
egotist egoista *m & f*
eight otto *m*
eighteen diciotto *m*
eighteenth diciotesimo;
decimottavo *m*
eighth ottavo *m*
eighty ottanta *m*
either l'uno o l'altro;
qualunque; ciascuno
ejaculation giaculazione *f*
eject gettare (fuori);
spossessare; espellere

elastic elastico *m*
elasticity elasticità *f*
elate esaltare
elation esaltazione *f*
elbow gomito *m*
elder maggiore; seniore;
sambuco *m*
elderly attempato
eldest primogenito
elect eletto; eleggere
election elezione *f*
elector elettore *m*

electrical elettrico
electrician elettricista m.
electricity elettricità f
electrify elettrizzare
electrotype elettrotipia f
elegance eleganza f
elegant elegante
elegy elegia f
element elemento; — ary
  elementare
elephant elefante m
elevate elevare
elevation elevazione f
elevator elevatore m
eleven undici m
eleventh undecimo m
elicit elicere
eligible eleggibile
eliminate eliminare
elope fuggire con un'
  amante
eloquence eloquenza
eloquent eloquente
else altro; altrimenti
elsewhere altrove
elucidate dilucidare
emancipate emancipare
embalm imbalsamare
embankment arginamen-
  to m
embargo embargo m
embark imbarcare
embarrass imbarazzare
embarrassment imbaraz-
  zo m
embassy ambasciata
embellish abellire
embers ceneri f pl
embezzle appropriarsi
embroidery ricamo m
embroil imbrogliare; con-
  fondere
emerald smeraldo m
emerge emergere
emergency emergenza f
emetic emetico m

emigrant emigrante m & f
emigrate emigrare
emigration emigrazione f
eminence eminenza; cele-
  brità f   [bre
eminent eminente; cele-
emissary emissario m
emission emissone f
emit emettere
emollient emolliente
emotion emozione f [m
emperor imperatore m
emphasis enfasi f
emphatic enfatico
empire impero m
employ impiegare
employee impiegato m
employer padrone m
employment impiego m
empress imperatrice f
empty vuoto; vuotare
emulate emulare
enable metter in grado
enact decretare [tare
enamel smalto m; smal-
enclose inchiudere
enclosure chiusa; cinta f
encompass circondare
encore bis! bissare
encounter incontro m;
  incontrare
encourage incoraggiare
encouragement incorag-
  giamento m
encyclopaedia enciclope-
  dia f
end fine; estremita f;
  finire; terminare
endanger metter in peri-
  colo   [tentare
endeavour sforzo m;
endless senza fine; eterno
endorse girare
endorsement girata f
endow dotare; donare

53

endowment dote *f*; dono
endurable sopportabile [*m*
endurance tolleranza *f*
endure tollerare
enemy nemico *m*
energetic energico
energy energia *f*
engage ingaggiare; impegnare; prendere a servizio
engagement impegno ; invito; combattimento
engender generare [*m*
engine macchine; locomotiva *f*
engineer ingegnere *m*
engrave intagliare
engraver incisore *m*
engraving intaglio *m*
engross ingrossare
enhance far risaltare
enigma ennima *f*
enigmatical enimmatico
enjoin commandare
enjoy godere
enlarge allargare
enlargement ingrandimento *m*
enough abbastanza;
enrage esasperare [basta
enrich arricchire
ensign bandiera *f*; portabandiera *m*; - bearer porta bandiera *m*
enslave far schiavo
ensue seguire [sostituire
entail bene sostituto;
entangle intralciare
enter entrare; inscrivere
enterprize impresa *f*
enterprising intraprendente [tire
entertain trattenere; ver-
entertainment trattenimento; divertimento *m*
enthusiasm entusiasmo *m*
enthusiast entusiasta *m*

enthusiastic entusiatico
entice sedurre; indurre
entire intiero
entitle intitolare
entrance entrata *f*
entreat supplicare
entry entrata *f*; registratura *f*
enumerate enumerare
enunciate enunciare
envelope busta *f*
enviable invidiabile
envious invidioso
envoy inviato *m*
envy invidia *f*; invidiare
epicure epicureo *m*
epidemic epidemico; epidemia *f*
epilepsy epilessia *f*
episcopal episcopale
episode episodio *m*
epitaph epitaffo *m*
epoch epoca; era *f*
equal eguale; eguagliare
equality egualità *f*
equalize egualizzare
equanimity equanimità *f*
equator equatore *m*
equilibrium equilibrio *m*
equinox equinozio *m*
equip equipaggiare
equipment equipaggio *m*
equitable equo
equity equità *f*
equivalent equivalente *m*
equivocate equivocare
era era; epoca *f*
eradicate sradicare; estir-
erase raschiare [pare
erasure raschitura *f*
erect diritto; erigere
erection erezione *f*
ermine ermellino *m*
err errare; ingannarsi
errand messagio *m*
erratic errante; erratico

erroneous erroneo

error errore; sbaglio m

eruption eruzione f

escape fuga f; sfuggire

escort scorta f; scortare

essay saggio m; tentare

essence essenza f

essential essenziale

establish stabilire

establishment stabilimento f

estate stato m; terra; fortuna f

esteem stima f; stimare

estimate stima f; stimare

estrange alienare

estuary estuario m

eternal eterno

eternity eternità f

ether etere m

ethereal etereo

ethical etico

ethics etica f

evacuate evacuare

evade evitare; eludere

evaporate svaporare

evasion evasione f; sotterfuggio m

evasive evasivo

even eguale; pari; giusto; anche; persino

evening sera f

event evento; caso m

eventual eventuale

ever sempre

evergreen sempre verdi m

everlasting eterno

every ogni; ognuno; tutti i; tutte le

eviction evizione f

evidence evidenza; testimonianza f

evident evidente

evil cattivo; male

exalt elevare

examination esame; in

terrogatorio m; in spezione f [pesionare

examine esaminare; is

example esempio m

exasperate esasperare

excavate scavare

excavation escavazione f

exceed eccedere

exceedingly eccessiva-

excel eccellere [mente

excellence - cy eccellenza f

excellent eccellente

except eccetto; fuorchè; eccettuare [eccetto m

exception eccezione f;

exceptional eccezionale

excess eccesso m

excessive eccessivo

exchange cambio; aggio m; borsa f; cambiare; permutare

excite eccitare

excitement eccitamento m

exclaim esclamare [f

exclamation esclamazione

exclude escludere

exclusive esclusivo

excommunicate scommunicare

excruciating crucciante

excursion escursione f

excuse scusa f; scusare

execute eseguire

execution esecuzione f

executioner giustiziere m

executive potestà esecutiva f

executor esecutore m

exemplify esemplificare

exempt esentare

exercise esercizio; dovere m; esercitare

exert impiegare

exertion sforzo m

exhale esalare
exhaust esaurire [m.
exhaustion esaurimento
exhibit mostrare; — er mostratore
exhibition esposizione f
exhilarate esilarare
exhilaration esilaramento m
exhort esortare
exile esilio; esule m; esiliare
exist esistere; essere
existence esistenza f
exit esito m; uscita f
exonerate esonerare
exorbitant esorbitante
expand espandere
expanse estensione f
expansion espansione f
expect aspettare; attendere; — ancy aspettativa
expectation aspettazione; speranza; pretesa f
expectorate espettorare
expediency espediente m
expedient spediente m
expedite spedire
expedition spedizione f
expel espellere
expend spendere
expenditure spesa f
expense spesa f
expensive dispendioso; costoso [provare
experience esperienza f;
experiment prova f; sperimentare
expert esperto
expiration termine m
expire spirare; morire
explain esplicare
explanation explicazione f
explanatory spiegativo
explicit esplicito
explode esplodere
exploit gesta f
exploration esplorazione f

explore esplorare
explosion esplosione f
explosive esplosivo
export esportare
exportation esportazione f
export duty dazio d'uscita
expostulate rimostrare [f
expostulation rimostranza f
exposure esposizione f
expound esplicare
express espresso m; esprimere
expression espressione f
expressive espressivo
extension estensione f
extensive estensivo
extent estensione f
extenuate estenuare [f
extenuation estenuazione
exterior esteriore m
exterminate estirpare [m
extermination sterminio
external esterno
extinct estinto
extinction estinzione f
extinguish estinguere
extinguisher spegnitolo m
extraordinary straordinario
extravagance stravaganza f
extravagant stravagante
extreme estremo m
extremity estremità f
exultation esultazione f
eye occhio m; cruna (d'ago) f; guardare; osservare; --ball pupilla f; —brow ciglio m; - -lash ciglio m; - -lid palpebra f; - sight vista f; - -witness testimonio oculare m

F

fable tavola *f*; – d favoloso

fabric fabbrica *f*; edificio *m*; tessuto *m*

fabricate fabbricare

fabrication fabbricazione; costruzione *f*

fabulous favoloso

face faccia *f*; volto *m*; faccetta *f*; affrontare

facilitate facilitare

facility facilità *f*

fact fatto; atto *m*; in – infatti

faction fazione *f*

factor fattore; agente *m*

factory fabbrica; manifattura *f*

faculty facoltà *f*; talento *m*

fade languire

fail mancare

failure mancanza *f*; fallimento *m*

faint svenuto; svenire

fair bello; biondo;

fairly bene [fiera *f*

fairy fata *f*

faith fede; credenza *f*

faithful fedele

fall caduta *f*; cadere; diminuire; – asleep addormentarsi; – back indietreggiarsi; – in love innamorarsi;

falsehood menzogna *f*

falsification falsificazione *f*

falsify falsificare

falter esitare

fame fama *f*; –d famoso

familiar familiare; intimo

familiarity familiarità *f*

familiarize familiarizzare

family famiglia; spezie *f*

famine fame *f*

famish affamare

famous famoso [tilare

fan ventaglio *m*; ventilare

fanatic(al) fanatico *m*

fanciful capriccioso

fancy fantasia; idea *f*; immaginare

fang dente *m*

fantastical fantastico

far lontano; distante; – fetched ricercato

farce farsa *f*

farm masseria *f*; coltivare

farmer affittaiuolo *m*

farming coltivazione *f*

fashion moda; voga *f*

fashionable alla moda

fast fermo; rapido; dissoluto; subito; digiuno

fasten attaccare [*m*

fastidious fastidioso

fat grasso *m*

fatal fatale

fatality fatalità *f*

fate fato *m*

fated fatato

father padre *m*; – in-law suocero *m*; – land patria *f*; – less orfano; – ly paterno

fathom braccio *m*; penetrare; – less senza fondo

fatigue fatica *f*; affatigare

fatness grassezza *f* [care

fatten ingrassare

fault fallo; errore *m*; pecca *f*; – less senza colpa; – y imperfetto

favour favore *m*; – able favorevole [favorita *f*

favourite favorito *m*;

fear timore *m*; temere;

- ful timido; terribile;
- fully terribilmente;
- less senza paura
feasible fattibile
feast festa *f*; festeggiare
feat fatto; atto *m*
feather penna; piuma
feature lineamento *f*
federal federale
federation federazione *f*
fee emolumento
feeble debole
feed cibo *m*; cibare
feel tasto; - er antenna *f*
feeling sensazione; sensibilità *f*
feeling sensibile; vivo
feline felino
fell pelle *f*; abbattere
fellow socio; compagno; simile *m* [associazione
fellowship compagnia;
felon fellone *m*
felony fellonia *f*
felt feltro *m* [*f*
female femminile; donna
feminine femminile
fence palificata; cinta; *f*: palificare; cingere
fender parafuoco *m*
fern felce *f*
ferocious feroce
ferry batello *m*; - man tragittatore *m*
fertile fertile
fertility fertilità *f*
fertilize fertilizzare
fervent, fervid fervido
fester corrompere
festival festa *f*
festive festivo; gaio
festivity festività *f*
feud guerra intestina *f*
feudal feudale
fever febbre *f*
feverish febbroso

flow corrente *f*; colare
flower fiore *m*; fiorire;
- -girl fioraia *f*; - y fiorito
fluctuate fluttuare
fluctuation fluttuazione *f*
flue gola di camino *f*
fluent fluente
fluid fluido *n* [agitare
flurry trambusto *m*;
flush rossore *m*; arrossire [agitare
fluster agitazione *f*;
flute flauto *m*; - d scanalato [giare
flutter battito *m*; aleggiare
fly mosca *f*; volare; fuggire
foal puledro *m*; figliare
foam schiuma *f*; spumare
foaming spumante
fob borsellino *m*
focus foco *m*
fodder foraggio *m*
foe nemico *m*
fog nebbia *f*
foggy nebbioso
foil fioretto *m*; frustrare
fold piega *f*
foliage fogliame *f*
folk gente
follow seguire
follower seguace *m*
folly follia *f*
food cibo; vitto *m*
fool(ish) stupido *m*
fool gabbare
foot piede *m*; zampa *f*;
for perchè; perocchè; per; quanto a; come
forage foraggio *m*
forbearance pazienza *f*
forbid proibire; interdire
force forza *f*
forcible energico; forte
ford guado *m*; guadare
fore anteriore; antece-

dente; prima; – **arm**
cubito; – **bode** presagire; – **fathers** antenati
m pl; – **finger** indice *m*;

field campo *m*
fiend demonio *m*
fierce feroce; ardente
fiery di fuoco; ardente
fife piffero *m*
fifteen quindici *m*
fifteenth quindicesimo *m*
fifth quinto *m*
fiftieth quinquagesimo; cinquantesimo
fifty cinquanta *m*
fig fico   [combattere
fight combattimento *m*;
figurative figurativo
figure figura *f*; forma *f*; figurare
filbert nocciola; avellana
filch birbanteggiare
file fila; lima *f*; filare;
filial filiale   [limare
filigree filigrano *m*
film membrana *f*; velo *m*
filter filtro *m*; filtrare
filth fango *m*
find trovare
fine bello; fine
fine ammenda *f*; multare
finery ornamento *m*
finger dito *m*
finish finitezza *f*; finire
finite limitato
fire fuoco; incendio *m*; incendiare;   – **-arms**
armi da fuoco *m pl*;
– **brick** mattone ritroso;
– **-brigade** corpo dei pompieri; – **damp** fuoco di mina; – **-engine**
pompa per incendio *f*;
– **-escape** apparecchio di salvataggio *f*; **--grate**
grata del camino; – **man**

pompiere *m*; – **-proof**
a prova di fuoco; – **works** fuoco artificiale *m*
firm fermo; stabile
firmament firmamento *m*
first primo; principio;
– **born** primogenito; – **-rate** eccelente
fish pesce *f*; pescare
--bone resta *f*; – **erman** pescatore *m*;
fist pugno *m*
fit atto; idoneo; degno di; accesso; parossismo *m*; adattare; aggiustare; assettare
five cinque *m*
fix dilemma *m*; fissare;
– **ture** rattenuta
flabby floscio
flag bandiera *f*;
flake fiocco *m* [me giare
flame fuoco *m* **fiam-**
flank fianco *m*; fiancare
flannel flanella *f*
flap lembo *m*; falda *f*; battere leggermente
flare fiamma *f* brillare
flash sprazza di luce *m*; far splendere
flask fiasca; boccetta *f*
flat piatto; piano; stup-
flatten appianare [ido *m*
flatter adulare; – **er** adulatore *m*; – **y** adulazione *f*
flavour sapore; gusto *m*; far gustoso
flaw difetto *m*
flea pulce *m*
flee fuggire
fleece vello *m*
fleet rapido; flotta *f*
flesh carne *f*
flexible flessibile
flicker tremolare

59

flight volo *m*; – **y** leggiero
flinch tergiversare
fling lanciare
flirt civetta *f*; civettare
flock fiocco *m*; affollare
flood diluvio *m*; inondare
floor piano; palco *m*
florid florido
florist florista *m*
flounder impantanarsi;
flour farina *f* [dimenarsi
flourish fanfara *f*; fiorire;
prosperare
four quattro *m*
fourteen quattordici *m*
fourteenth quattordicesi-
mo; decimoquarto
fourth quarto *m*
fox volpe *f*; – -**glove**
digitale *f*; – **y** volpino;
astuto
fraction frazione *f*
fracture frattura *f*; rom-
fragile fragile [pere
fragment frammento *m*
fragrant fragrante
frail frale; debole
frailty fralezza *f*
frame forma; armatura;
struttura; inteleiatura
f; corpo *m*; formare;
disporre; corniciare
franchise franchigia *f*
frank franco; affrancare
fraternity fraternità *f*
free libero; franco;
gratuito; liberare
freedom libertà *f*
freemason frammassone
freeze gelare [*m*
freight nolo; carico *m*
frenzy frenesia *f*
frequent frequente; numeroso; frequentare
fresh fresco; recente;
– **en** rinfrescare; – **ness**

trescura; – **water** acqua
fret rodere [dolce
fretful afflitto
friar monaco *m*
friction frizione *f*
friend amico *m*; amica *f*
friendship amicizia *f*
fright paura *f*; – **en**
spaventare; – **ful** spav-
frigid frigido [entevole
fringe franzia *f*; bordo *m*
frisk saltellare
frivolity frivolezza *f*
frivolous frivolo
frock vestina; veste *f*
frog rana; granocchia *f*
frolic scherzo *m*; – **some**
scherzoso [sino da
from da; con; per;
foreign(er) straniero *m*
forest foresta *f*; bosco *m*
forfeit confisca *f*
forge ferriera *f*; fucinare
f
forgery contraffazione *f*
forget obliare; – **ful** immemore; – **fulness** di-
menticanza *f*; –**me-not**
miosotide *f*
forgive perdonare
forgiveness perdono *m*
fork forchetta *f*; biforcarsi; – **ed** forcuto
forlorn abbandonato
form forma; guisa *f*;
banco *m*; formare
formal formale
formality formalità *f*
former primo; prece-
dente; – **ly** altre volte
gia; prima
formidable formidabile
formula formola *f*
fornication fornicazione
fort forte *m*
forth avanti; and so –

e così di seguito; –
coming **a** presso ad apparire; – with subito
fortieth quarantesimo *m*
fortification fortificazione
fortify fortificare [*f*
fortnight quindicina *f*; – ly quindicinale
fortunate fortunato
fortune fortuna *f*
forty quaranta *m*
forward avanzato; presuntuoso; avanti; spe-
fossil fossile *m* [dire
foster nutrire; – -brother fratello di latte *m*; – -father balio *m*; – -mother balia *f*
foul sporco; impuro;
found fondare [sporcare
foundation base *f*; fondamento *m*
founder fondatore *m*
frost gelo *m*; – bitten a gelato; – y glaciale
froth spuma; schiuma *f*; spumare; – y spumante
froward perverso
frown cipiglio *m*
frozen gelato
frugal frugale
frugality frugalità *f*
fruit frutto *m*;
fruitless sterile
frustrate frustrare
fry frittura *f*; friggere
fudge sciocchezza!
fuel combustibile *m*
fugitive fuggitivo *m*
fugue fuga *f*
fulfil adempire
fulfilment realizzazione *f*
full pieno; intero
fuller follone *m*
fume fumo *m*; fumare
fumigate far suffumigi

fumigatlon suffumigio *m*
fun scherzo *m*
function funzione *f* [*m*
fund fondo *m*
fundamental fondamen-
funeral funerale *m* [tale
fungus fungo *m*
funnel imbuto *m*
funny comico *f*
fur pelliccia *f*
furious furioso
furl serrare
furnace fornace *f*
furnish fornire; mobiliare
furniture mobilia *f*
fury furia *f*
futile futile
futility futilità; inanità *f*
future futuro [*m*
futurity futuro; avvenire

G

gabardine gabbano *m*
gabble ciaramellare
gag sbarra *f*; imbavag-
gage pegno *m* [liare
gaff rampone *m*
gaiety gaiezza *f*
gaily gaiamente
gain guadagno *m*; guadagnare; lucrare; otten-
gainsay contraddire [ere
gait andatura *f*
gaiter ghetta *f*
gala gala *f*
galaxy costellazione *f*
gale tempesta *f*
gall noce di galla; bile *f*; irritare
gallant galante
gallantry eroismo *m*; galanteria *f*
gallery galleria *f*
galleon gallion *m*
galley galera *f*

61

gallic francise
gallon hallone m [litr. 1.54) · [pare
gallop galoppo m; galop-
gallows patibolo m
galosh galoscia f
galvanize galvanizzare
gamble giuocare
gambler giuocatore m
gang banda f
gangway passavanti m
gap breccia; apertura f
gape sbadigliare
garb vestito; abito m
garbage rifiuto m
garble troncare; alterare
garden giardino m; -er giardiniere m; - ing giardinaggio m
gargle gargarismo m; gargarizzare
garland ghirlanda f
garlic aglio m
garment abito; vestito m
garner ammassare
garnet granato m
garnish guarnire
garret soffitta f
garrison guarnigione f
gas gas m; - burner-lamp becco di gas; - light illuminazione a gas;
gash ferita larga f; sfregiare
gasp anelito m; anelare
gate porta f; portone m
gather raccogliere; accumularsi; - er raccoglitore m; - ing riunione f; ascesso m
gaudy ostentato
gaunt magro
gauze garza f
gay vivace [templare
gaze sguardo m; con-
gear ingranaggio; ap-

parecchio m
gelatine gelatina f
gem gemma ; gioia f
gender genere m
general generale m
generalize generalizzare
generate generare
generation generazione f
generic generico
generosity generosità f
generous generoso
genial geniale
genius genio m
gentle gentile; grazioso; - man gentiluomo m; - ness gentilezza f
genuine genuino
geography geografia f
geology geologia f
geometry geometria f
geranium geranio m
germ germe m
gesture gesto m
get ottenere; acquistare; - away andarsene; - off togliere; - over sormontare; - the better of vincere; - up levarsi
ghastly orrido
ghost spettro m
giant gigante m
gift dono m
gifted dotato
gigantic gigantesco
gills branchie f pl
gin gin m; trappola f
ginger zenzero m; - bread pan pepato m
girl ragazza; fanciulla f
girlish di ragazza
girth giro m
give dare; donare; - in, - up, - way cedere
glacial glaciale
glad felice; - den ralle-

grare; allietare; — **ness**
gaiezza *f*; — **some** gaio
glade radura *f*; viale *m*
glance piglio *m*
gland glandula *f*
glare luce smagliante *f*;
guardo feroce *m*
glass vetro; specchio *m*;
— **blower** soffiatore; —
house vetreria; — **shade**
globe di vetro; — **works**
vetrerie
glaze inverniciare
glazier vetraio *m*
gleam scintilla *f*; scintillare   [olatore *m*
glean spigolare; —**er** spig-
glee gioia *f*
glen gola; valle *f*
glide scorrere
glimpse occhiata *f*
glisten, glitter brillare;
lustro *m*
gloat guardar fisso
globe globo *m*
gloom oscurità
gloomy oscuro; tristo
glorify glorificare
glorious glorioso
glory gloria; fama *f*
gloss lustro *m*; lustrare
glossary glossario *m*
glove guanto *m*; — **r**
guantaio *m*
glow calore; ardere;
— **ing** ardente; — **-worm**
lucciola *f*
glue colla *f*; incollare
glutton ghiotto *m*; — **ous**
goloso; — **y** ghiottoria
f
go andare; partire;
— **abroad** andar all'estero; — **after** seguire; —
— **ahead** inoltrarsi; —
mediatore *m*; — **by** passar

davanti; — **forth** uscire;
— **forward** avanzare; —
in entrare; — **off** andar-
sena; esplodere; — **on**
continuare; — **out** andar
fuori; — **over** attraversare; verificare; — **up**
salire; — **with** accom-
pagnare; — **without** far
senza
goal termine *f*
goat capro *m*
God Dio; Iddio *m*;
— **child** figlioccio *m*;
— **dess** dea *f*; — **father**
padrino; — **like** divino;
— **liness** pietà *f*; — **ly**
pio; devoto; — **mother**
matrina *f*
gold d'oro; oro *m*;
gonorrhœa gonorrea *f*
good buono; bene; —
bye! addio *m*; — **Friday**
Venerdì santo *m*; — **ly**
bello; — **natured** di
buon cuore; — **ness**
bontà *f*; — **s merci** *f pl*;
beni *m pl*
goose oca *f*
gorgeous magnifico
gory insanguinato
gospel vangelo *m*
gossip comare *f*; ciarla
govern governare; — **a**
governabile; — **ness**
vernante *f*; — **ment**
ministrazione *f*; —
governatore *m*
gown veste; toga *f*
grace grazia *f*; favo
— **ful** grazioso
gracious grazios
mente; — **ly** g
mente
grade grado *m*

gradual graduale
graduate laureato *m*;

graduation graduazione *f*
graft innestare [venare
grain grano *m*; vena *f*;
grammar grammatica *f*
granary granaio *m*
grand grande; grandioso;
  – **child** nipotino *m*; –
  eur grandezza *f*; –
  father nonno; avo *m*;
  – **mother** nonna; ava; *f*
granite granito *m*
grant concessione *f*; dare
granulated granato
grape uva *f*
grass erba *f*
grasshopper grillo *m*
grassy erboso
grate grata; graticola *f*
  grattugiare
grateful riconoscente
grater grattugia *f*
gratify gratificare
gravity gravità *f*
gravy sugo (di carne) *m*
gray grigio
graze pascere pascolare
grease grasso *m* ungere
greasy grasso
great grande; –**coat** soprabito *m*; – **ness** grandezza *f*
greediness avidità *f*
greedy avido
green verde; fresco;
  verdume *m*; – **gage**
  regina claudia *f*; –
  grocer fruttivendolo *m*;
  – **horn** sbarbatello *m*;
  – **house** serra *f*; – **ish**
  verdognolo; – **s legumi**
  m pl; – **sward** erbuccia
greet salutare; – **ing**
  saluto *m*
gridiron graticola *f*

grief dolore *m*
grievance querela *f*
grieve affliggere
grievous gravoso
grill arrostire sulla grati-
grim torvo; feroce; [cola
grimace smorfia *f*
grin sogghigno
grind macinare; **stone**
  macina *f*
grip presa *f*; stringere
groan gemito *m*; gemere
grocer droghiere *m*
grocery drogherie *f pl*
groin inguine; angolo *m*
groom palafreniere *m*
groove scanalatura *f*;
  scanalare
grope brancolare
gross grosso; grossa *f*
grotesque grottesco
ground terreno; fondo
  m; stabilire; toccare;
grove boschetto *m*
grovel strisciar per terra
grow crescere; coltivare
growl grugnito *m*; grug-
  nire   [aumento *m*
growth crescimento
grudge rancore *m*
gruff rauco

grumble brontolare
grunt grugnito *m*
guarantee garanzia *f*;
  garantire
guard guardia *f*; conduttore *m*; guardare
guardian guardiano *m*
guess congettura *f*;
  indovinare
guest convitato *m*
guidance condotta *f*
guide guida *f*; conduttore *m*; guidare; – **book**
  guida *f*
guild corporazione *f*

guile astuzia *f*
guilt delitto *m*
guiltless innocente
guilty colpevole
guitar chitarra *f*

gull gabbiano *m*; gabbare
gulp sorso *m*; ingozzare
gum gomma *f*; ingom-
 mare
gun fucile; cannone *m*;
 - -boat cannoniera *f*;
 - cotton cotone ful-
 minante;

gurgle gorgoglio *m*
gush sgorgo *m*; sgorgare
gusset borsellino *m*
gust colpo di vento *m*
gusty burrascoso [trare
gut intestino *m*; sven-
guttapercha guttaperca *f*
gutter gronda *f*; scolare

H

haberdasher merciaio *m*
haberdashery merceria *f*
habit uso; abito *m*
habitable abitabile
habitation abitazione *f*
haggard macilente
haggle stiracchiare
hail grandine; gragnola *f*;
 grandinare; salutare
hair capello *m*; pelo *m*;
 - brained scervellato;
 - -brush spazzola per
 capelli *f*; - -dresser
 barbiere *m*; - -dye tintura per capelli *f*; - less
 senza capelli; - -pin
 forcella *f*; - -wash
 lavatura cosmetica *f*;
 - y peloso
halcyon di alcione; calmo

hale robusto; sano
half metà *f*; mezzo *m*
halfpenny soldo *m*

hall entrata; sala *f*
hallow consacrare
hallucination illusione *f*
halo aureola *f*
halt zoppo; sosta; alto
 m; fare alto
halter capestro *m*
ham garetto *m*
hamlet casale *m*
hammer martello *m*
hammock amaca *f* [pare
hamper corba *f*; incep-
hand mano *f*; ago;
 operaio *m*; - barrow
 barella *f*; - bill annun-
 cio *m*; - book manuale
 m; - cuffs manette *f* pl;
 - ful manata *f*; - icraft
 mestiere *m*; - kerchief
 fazzoletto *m*; - - le mani-
 ico *m*; maneggiare;
 - maid serva *f*
handsome bello
[ndwriting scrittura *f*
handy destro
hang sospendere
hank matassa *f*
happen avvenire
happiness felicità *f*
happy felice; beato
harass affaticare
harbour porto; rifugio
 m; albergare
hard duro; difficile; - en
 indurire; - -hearted in-
 umano; - iness ardi-
 tezza *f*; - ly duramente;
 - ness durezza *f*; - of
 hearing duro d'orrechi;
 - ship privazione *f*;
 - ware chincaglieria *f*;
 - y robusto

hare lepre *m & f*

harm male *m*; far male; – ful dannoso; – less innocuo

harmonize armonizzare

harmony armonia *f*

harness finimenti *m pl*;

harp arpa *f*

harrow erpicare; erpice *m* [cordante

harsh aspro; duro; dis-

harshness asprezza *f*

harvest messe *f*; raccolto

hassock cuscino *m*

haste fretta *f*

hasten accelerare

hasty frettoloso

hat cappello *m*; –box cappelliera *f*; –rack cappellinaio *m*;

hatch covare; nascere

hatchet accetta *f* [(uccelli)

hate odio *m*; detestare; – ful odioso

hatred odio *m*

haunt soggiorno *m*; bazzicare; visitare

have avere; tenere

haven porto *m*; rada *f*

havoc guasto *m*

hawk falco; sparviere *m*

hawker merciaiolo *m*

hawser ansiera *f*

hawthorn biancospino *m*

hay fieno *m*

haystack maragnuola *f*

hazard azzardo

hazardous azzardoso

haze nebbia *f*

hazel nocciola *f*; di

hazy nebbioso [nocciola

he egli; lui; quegli; colui

head testa *f*; capo *m*; – ache mal di testa *m*;

health salute; sanità *f*

healthy sano [amassare

heap mucchio *m*;

hear sentire; intendere; ascoltare; – er uditore *m*; – ing udito *m*; – ken ascoltare; –say inteso-dire

hearse carro funebre *m*

heart cuore; centro *m*

hearth focolare *m*

heartily cordialmente

heartless senza cuore;

hearty cordiale [vigliacco

heat calore *m*; scaldare

heater scaldatore *m*

heath erica; brughiera *f*

heathen pagano *m*

heather erica *f*

heave elevare [*m*

heaven cielo; firmamento

heavenly celeste

heavy grave; pesante

heckle diliscare

hectic etico; tisico

hedge siepe *f*; assiepare

hedgehog spinoso *m*

heed cura; guardia *f*;

heir, heiress erede *m & f*

heirloom mobile; inalien-

hell inferno *m* [abile *m*

helm timone *m*

helmet elmo; casco *m*

help aiuto *m*; assistere; – ful utile; – less senza soccorso; – lessness abbandono *m*;

hem orlo *m*; orlare

hemisphere emisfero *m*

hemorrhage emorragia *f*

hemp canapa *f*

hen gallina *f*

hence quindi; di quà

henceforth ormai

henpecked governato dalla moglie [suoi; sue

her la; lei; suo; sua;

herb erba *f*

herd gregge *m*; mandria *f*
here quà; qui; di quà; — about(s) di quà; quà vicino; — after d'ora innanzi; vita futura *f*; — by con questo mezzo; così; — in in ciò; in codesto; — of di codesto; — on su codesto; su ciò; — tofore finora; un
hereditary ereditario
heresy eresia *f*
heritage eredità *f*
hermit eremita *m*
hero eroe *m*; — ic eroico; — ically eroicamente; — ine eroina *f*; — ism eroismo *m*
herring aringa *f*
hers suo; sua; d'essa; il di lei; la di lei
herself essa; se stessa; si
hesitate esitare
hesitation esitazione *f*
heterogeneous eterogeneo
hew tagliare
hibernate invernare
hide cuoio *m*; pelle *f*; nascondere; celare
hideous orrendo
high alto; elevato; — land paese montagnoso; — lander montanaro; — ly grandemente; — ness
hind cerva *f*; villico *m*
hinder impedire
hinge cardine *m*
hint avviso *m*; insinuare
hip anca *f*
hire nolo *m*; pigione *f*
his suo; sua; tuoi; sue
hiss sibilo *m*; zittire
historian, historical stori-
history storia *f* [co *m*

hit colpo *m*; botta *f*; colpire; battere
hitch intoppo *m*; attaccare
hither quà; di quà
hive arnia *f*
hoar bianco; canuto
hoard gruzzolo *m*; cumu-
[lare
hold presa; stiva *f*; contenere; arrestare
holder possessore *m*
holdfast rampone *m*
hole buco *m*; apertura *f*
holiday festa; vacanza *f*
holiness santità *f*
hollow cavo; scavare
holly agrifoglio *m*
holster fonda da pistola *f*
holy santo; benedetto
homage omaggio *m*
home dimora; casa; patria *f*; — less sezza dimora; — liness semplicità *f*; — ly semplice; — sickness nostalgia *f*; — wards verso casa
homicide omicida *m* & *f*
honest onesto
honesty onestà; probità *f*
honey miele *m*; — moon luna di miele *f*; — suckle caprifoglio *m*
honorary onorario
honour onore *m*; onorare
honourable onorevole
hood cuffia *f*; cappuccio *m*
hoof unghia *f*
hook gancio *m*; uncinare
hop salterello; luppolo *m*; saltare
hope speranza *f*; sperare; — ful pieno di speranza; — less senza speranza
horizon orizzonte &
horizontal orizzontale

horn corno m

hornet calabrone m

horrible orribile; orrendo

horror orrore m

horse cavallo m; cavalleria f; on - back, a cavallo, --dealer marcante di cavalli m; --fly tafano m; - -hair crine (di cavallo) m; - -manship equitazione f; - -power forza d'un cavallo f;

horticulture orticoltura f

horticulturist orticoltore m

hose calza f; tubo m

hosiery calzatura f

hospitable ospitale [m

hospital ospedale; ospizio

hospitality ospitalità f

host ospite; oste m

hostage ostaggio m

hostess ostessa f

hotel albergo m; osteria f

hound bracco m

hour ora f; - glass oriuolo a sabbia

hourly di ora in ora

house casa; dimora f; alloggiare; - breaker ladro per frattura; - hold casalingo; casa f; m; - keeper. - wife massaia f; - less senza casa; - maid serva di casa f

how come; quanto; - ever pero; pure; - much quanto

howl grido; urlo m; gridare; urlare

hug abbracciare

huge enorme

hull baccello; scafo m

hum ronzio m; mor- human umano [morare

humane umano

humanity umanità f

humble umile; umiliare

humbug ciarlatano m

humidity umidità f

humiliate umiliare

humility umiltà f

humming-bird colibri m

humorous umoristico

humour umore

hundred cento; centina f; - fold centuplo; - th centesimo m; - weight mezzo quintale m

hunger fame f; aver fame

hungry affamato

hunt caccia f; cacciare

hunter, huntsman cacciatore m

hurdle canniccio m; - race corsa delli siea f pl

hurl lanciare

hurricane uragano m

hurry fretta; precipitazione f; affrettare

hurt male; danno m; - ful dannoso

husband marito; sposo m; risparmiare;

hutch madia f

hyacinth giacinto m

hydraulic idraulico

hydrogen idrogeno m

hydrophobia idrofobia f

hyena iena f

hygiene igiene f

hymen imene m

hymn inno m

hyperbole iperbole f

hyphen lineetta d'unione f

hypnotism ipnotismo m

hypocrisy ipocrisia f

hypocrite, hypocritical ipocritico m

hypothesis ipotesi f

I

I io
iambic iambico
ice ghiaccio *m*; ghiacciare; – **cream** sorbetto
icicle ghiacciuolo *m*
icy glaciale
idea idea *f*; – l ideale
identical identico
identify identificare
idiom idioma *m*
idle(r) ozioso *m*; – **ness** pigrizia *f*
idol idolo *m*;
if se
ignite accendere
ignorance ignoranza *f*
ignoramus ignorante *m*
ignorant ignorante
ignore ignorare
ill indisposto; cattivo;
illegal illegale   [male
illegible illeggibile
illegitimate illegittimo

illiterate illetterato
illness malattia *f*
illogical illogico
illuminate illuminare
illusion illusione *f*
illusive, illusory illusorio
illustrate illustrare
illustration illustrazione *f*
illustrious illustre
image immagine *f*
imaginable immaginabile
imaginary immaginario
imagination immaginazione *f*
imagine immaginare
imbecile imbecille *m*
imitate imitare

imitation imitazione *f*
immaculate immacolato
immaterial immateriale
immature immaturo
immediate immediato
immemorial immemorabile
immense immenso [bile
immerge, immerse immergere   [*m & f*
immigrant immigrante
immigrate immigrare
imminent imminente
immobility immobilità *f*
immoderate smoderato
immodest immodesto
immolate immolare
immoral immorale
immortal immortale
immortality immortalità *f*
immoveable immobile
immunity immunità *f*
immure murare
imp folletto *m*
impair deteriorare
impale impalare
impart impartire
impartial imparziale
impassable impassabile
impassioned appassionato
impassive impassibile
impatience impazienza *f*
impatient impaziente
impeach denunciare
impeachment imputazione *f*
impede impedire   [*m*
impediment impedimento
impel impellere
impend essere sospeso
impersonate rappresentare   [enza *f*
impertinence impertinenza
impervious impervio
impetuosity impetuosità *f*
impetuous impetuoso
implacable implacabile

implant implantare
implement arnese *m*
implicate implicare
implicit implicito
implore implorare
imply implicare
impolite inurbano
import importare
importance importanza *f*
important importante [*f*
imposition imposizione;
 impostura *f* [*f*]
impossibility impossibilità
impossible impossibile
impostor impostore *m*
impotent impotente
impoverish impoverire
impracticable impratica-
 bile [*f*]
impregnable imprendibile
impregnate impregnare
impress impronta *f* im-
  prontare
impression impressione *f*
impressive espressivo
imprint imprimere
improbable improbabile
improper sconvenevole
improve migliorare
improvement migliora-
 mento; progresso *m*
imprudence imprudenza *f*
imprudent imprudente
impudence impudenza *f*
impudent impudente
impulse impulso *m*
impunity impunità *f*
impure impuro
in in; tra, fra; per; su;
inability inabilità *f*
inaccessible inaccessibile
inaccuracy inesattezza *f*
inaccurate inesatto
inactive inattivo
inadequate inadequato
inadmissible inammissi-

bile
inadvertent inavvertente
inalienable inalienabile
inanimate inanimato
inanity inanità; vanità *f*
inapplicable inapplicabile
inappropriate disadatto
inattentive disattento
inaudible inaudibile
inaugurate inaugurare
inborn innato
incandescent incandes-
 cente [*m*]
incantation incantesimo
incapable incapace
inch pollice *m*
incident incidente *m*
incise incidere
incision incisione *f*
incite incitare
incivility inciviltà *f*
inclemency inclemenza *f*
inclination inclinazione
incline pendenza *f*; in-
 clinare [prendere]
include inchiudere; com-
inclusive inclusivo
incoherent incoerente
income rendita
incomparable incompar-
 abile [bile]
incompatible incompati-
incompetent incapace
incomplete incompleto
incomprehensible incom-
 prensibile [bile]
inconceivable inconcepi-
inconclusive inconclu-
 dente
incongruous ncongruo
inconsistent inconsistente
inconsolable inconsolabile
inconstant incostante
incontestable incontesta-
 bile
incontinent incontinente

inconvenience inconvenienza

inconvenient incomodo

incorporate incorporare

incorporation incorporazione

incorrect scorretto

incorrigible incorreggibile

increase aumento m; accrescere

incredible incredibile

incredulity incredulità

increment incremento m

incrust incrostare

inculcate inculcare

incumbent incombente; beneficiario m

incur contrarre

incurable incurabile

indebted indebitato; obbligato

indecisive inconcludente

indeed in verità

indefinite indefinito

indelible indelebile

indelicate indelicato

indemnify indennizzare

indemnity indenni ;f

indent intaccare; indentatura

independence indipendenza

independent indipendente

index indice m; lista f

indicate indicare

indication indicazione f

indict accusare

indifference indifferenza f

indigenous indigeno

indigent povero

indigestion indigestione f

indignant indignato [f

indignation indignazione

indignity indegnità f

indisposition indisposi-

zione f

individual individuale; individuo m

ndomitable indomabile

indubitable indubitabile

induce indurre

inducement ragione f; motivo m

indulge concedere

indulgence indulgenza f

industrial industriale

industrious industrioso

industry lavoro m; industria f

ineffectual inutile

ineligible ineleggibile

inequality inegualità f

inert inerte; pigro

inertia inerzia f

inevitable inevitabile

inexcusable inescusabile

inexhaustible inesauribile

inexorable inesorabile

inexperienced, inexpert inesperto

inexplicable inesplicabile

inexpressible inesprimibile

infancy infanzia f [m

infant bambino; infante

infantry fanteria f

infatuate infatuare

infect infettare

infectious contagioso

infer inferire

inferior inferiore m

inferiority inferiorità f

infernal infernale

infest infestare

infidel infedele m

infinite infinito

infirm infermo

infirmary infermeria f

inflame infiammare
inflammation infiamma-
zione *f*
inflate gonfiare; enfiare -
inflation gonfiamento *m*
inflexible inflessibile
inflict infliggere [influire
influence influenza *f*;
influential influente
inform informare
informal senza ceerimoni
informant informatore *m*
information avviso *m*
infringe infrangere
infuriate render furioso
infuse infondere
infusion infusione; in-
troduzione *f*
ingenious ingegnoso
ingenuity ingegnosità *f*
inhale inspirare
inherent inerente; innato
inherit ereditare
inheritance eredità *f*
inhuman inumano
inimical ostile
inimitable inimitabile
iniquitous iniquo
initial primo; iniziale *m*
initiate iniziare
initiation iniziazione *f*
inject iniettare
injection iniezione *f*
injunction ingiunzione *f*
injure ingiuriare
injury ingiuria *f*
injustice ingiustizia *f*
ink inchiostro *m*
inland interno; interiore
inlet entrata *f*
inmate convivente *m & f*
inn albergo *m*;
innate innato
inner interiore; interno
innocence innocenza *f*
innocent innocente
innovation innovazione *f*

innumerable innumere-
vole
inopportune inopportuno
inquest inchiesta *f*
inquire chiedere
inquisitive curioso
insane insano
insanity demenza *f*
inscribe nscrivere
insect insetto *m*
insecure non sicuro
insecurity mancanza di
sicurezza *f*; pericolo *m*
insert inserire
inside del didentro
insight conoscenza in
tima *f*   [cante
insignificant insignifi-
insincere poco sincero
insinuate insinuare
insist insistere; esigere
insolence insolenza *f*
insolent insolente
insoluble insolubile
insolvency fallimento *m*
insolvent insolvibile
fallito
inspect esaminare
inspection ispezione *f*
inspector ispettore *m*
inspire ispirare
install installare   [*m*
installation installamento
instalment pagamento a
termine [esempio *m*
instance istanza *f*
instant istante; urgente
instantaneous istantaneo
istantly all'istante ;
subito
instead invece; in luogo
instep collo del piede *m*
instigate instigare; inci-
instil istillare   [tare
instinct istinto *m*
instinctive istintivo
institute istituire

72

institution istituo *m*
instruct istruire
instruction istruzione *f*
instructive istruttivo
instrument instrumento
insufferable insopporta-
bile

insurance assicurazione *f*
insure assicurare
insurer assicuratore *m*
insurgent insorto *m*
insurmountable insuper-
abile

integrity probità *f*
intellect intelletto *m*
intelligence intelligenza
intelligent intelligente
intelligible intelligibile
intemperate intemperante
intend intendere
intense intenso
intensity intensità *f*
intent intento *m*; – ion
intenzione *f*; – ional
intenzionale
inter seppellire; inter-
rare
intercede intercedere
intercept intercettare
intercession intercessione
interchange cambiare *[f*
intercourse relazione *f*
interdict interdire
interest interesse *m*; interessare
interfere intervenire
interim interim *m*
interior interiore *m*
interlace intrecciare
interloper intruso *m*
interlude intermezzo *m*
interment sepoltura *f*
international internazion-
ale
interpret interpretare
interpreter interprete *m*

interrogate interrogare
interrupt interrompere
interruption interruzione
interval intervallo *m*
intervene intervenire
interview abboccamento
m; intervistare
intestine intestino *m*
intimacy intimità *f*
intimate intimo *m*; intimare
intimidate intimorire
into in; ne ; tra
intolerable intollerabile
intolerant intollerante
intone intonare; cantare
intoxicate ubbriacare
intrepid intrepido
intricate intricato
intrigue intrigo *m*
intrinsic intrinseco
introduce introdurre *[f*
introduction introduzione
introductory introduttivo
intrude intrudersi
intruder intruso *m*
intrust affidare
intuition intuizione *f*
inundate inondare
invade invadere
invader invasore *m*
invalid invalido; infermo;
invalido *m*
invalidate invalidare
invaluable inestimabile
invasion invasione *f*
invent inventare; – ion
invenzione *f*; – ive in-
ventivo; – or inventore
m; – ory inventario *m*
inverse inverso
invert invertire
invest investire
investigate investigare
investiture investitura *f*
investment investimento

invigorate rinvigorire
invincible invincibile
inviolable inviolabile
inviolate inviolato
invisible invisibile
invitation invito m
invite invitare
invocation invocazione f
invoice fattura f; fatturare
invoke invocare [are
involuntary involontario
involve involgere; compromettere; implicare
invulnerable invulnerabile
inward interno [bile
inwards all'indentro
iodine iodio m
iron ferreo; ferro m; stirare; -ical ironico;
irony ironia f
irradiate irradiare
irrational irrazionale
irreconcilable irreconciliabile [abile
irrecoverable irrecuperabile
irredeemable irredimibile
irregular irregolare [bile
irregularity irregolarità f
irresolute irresoluto
irrespective indipendente
irresponsible irresponsabile
irretrievable irreparabile
irreverent irreverente
irrevocable irrevocabile
irrigate irrigare
irrigation irrigazione f
irritable irritabile
irritate irritare
irruption irruzione f
isinglass colla di pesce f
island, isle isola f
islander isolano m
isolate isolare
isolated isolato; solitario
isolation isolamento m
issue uscita; distribu-

zione; prole f; risultato m; uscire; distribuire; emettere
isthmus istmo m
it il, la, lo; egli; esso
italics corsivo m
itch rogna f; prurito m; prudere
item articolo m; nota f
itinerary itinerario m
its suo, sua suoi, sue
itself se; sè stesso
ivory avorio m
ivy edera f

J

jabber ciarlare;
jack girarrosto; cavastivali; cricco m; – al sciacallo m; – ass somaro m; – daw cornacchia; taccola f; – et giacchetta; camiciola f
jade rozza cavallaccio; affaticarsi
jail prigione f
jam conserva; serrare
jar giara; vibrazione vibrare
jaundice itterizia f
jaw mascella f
jay ghiandaia f
jealous geloso
jealousy gelosia f
jeer beffare
jelly gelatina f
jeopardy rischio m
jerk scossa f
jessamine gelsomino m
Jesus Gesù m [pillare
jet getto; gè m; zampewel gioiello m; gemma
jewel gioiello m; gemma f; – ler gioielliere m;

- lery gioielleria *f*
job bisogna *f*
jockey fantino *m*
jocose giocoso
join unire
joint giuntura; articolazione *f*; arrosto *m*;
congiunto; in comune
joke scherzo *m*; burlare
jolly allegro; gaio
jolt trabalzamento *m*
jostle spingere
journal giornale *m*
journalism giornalismo *m*
journalist giornalista *m*
& *f*
journey viaggio *m*; viaggiare; es·ser in viaggio
journeyman giornaliere *m*
joust giostra *f*
joy gioia *f*; – **ful**, – **ous**
gioioso; – **less** tristo
judge giudice *m*; giudicare
judgment giudizio; decreto *m*
judicial giudiziale
judicious giudizioso
jug brocca; mezzina *f*
juggler giocoliere *m*
juice succo (frutti);
sugo (carne) *m*
juicy soccoso; sugoso
jumble guazzabuglio *m*
jump salto *m*; saltare
junction unione *f*
junior juniore *m*
juniper ginepro *m*
just giusto; equo; ap-
justice giustizia *f* [punto
justifiable giustificabile
justification giustificazione *f*
justify giustificare
justness giustizia *f*

jut aggettare
juvenile giovanile

K

kangaroo canguro *m*
keel chiglia; carena *f*
keen aguzzo; penetrante,
acuto; vivo
keenness acutezza *f*
keep tenere, mantenere;
– **back** ritenere; – **er**
guardiano; – **ing** guardia *f*; – **off** respingere;
key chiave *f*; – **board**
tastiera *f*; – **hole** bucco
della serratura *m*; –
kick calcio *m*
kid capretto *m*; – **gloves**
guanti bianchi *m pl*
kidnap rapire
kidney rognone *m*
kill uccidere; ammazzare
kiln fornace *f*
kin(dred) parentela; famiglia *f*; consanguineo
kind benevolo; buono;
bene; genere *m*
kindle accendere; ecci-
kindness bontà *f* [tare
king re *m*; – **dom** regno
m; – **ly** reale; da re
kinsman parente *m*
kiss bacio *m*; baciare
kitchen cucina *f*; –
kite polana *f*; cervovo-
lante *m*
kitten gattino *m*

knack destrezza; arte *f*
knapsack zaino *m*
knead impastare
knee ginocchio *m*
kneel inginocchiarsi
knicknack crepunde *f pl*

knife coltello *m*;
knight cavaliere *m*
knighthood cavalierato *m*
knit far maglie; riunirsi
knob bernoccolo *m*; maniglia *f* [urtare
knock colpo *m*; bussare;
knot nodo; gruppo *m*; annodare
knotty nodoso; difficile
know sapere; conoscere
knowing intelligente
knowledge conoscenza; sapienza *f* [under cedere
knuckle falange *f*; –

L

label etichetta *f*; cartello
labial labiale *f* [*m*
laboratory laboratorio *m*
laborious laborioso
labour laborare; lavoro
lace gallone; passamano *m*; stringa *f*; stringare
lacerate lacerare
lack bisogno *m*; mancare
lackey lacchè *m*
laconic laconico
lacquer lacca *f* [*m*
lad giovanetto; ragazzo
lady signora; dama *f*; – like di signora; – ship signoria *f* [mente
lag camminare lenta-
laggard tentennone *m*
lair tana *f*; covo *m*
lake lago *m*
lamb agnello *m*; figliare
lame zoppo; storpiare
lameness zoppicamento *m*
lament lamento *m*; lamentare
lamp lampada; lucerna *f*; – -post lampada *f*; – shade ventola *f*; para-

lume *m*
land terra *f*; regione *f*; sbarcare; – au lando *m*; – ed fondiario; – -holder proprietario di fondi *m*; – ing-place approdo *m*; – lady proprietaria *f*; – -lord proprietario *m*; – -lubber marinaio d'acqua dolce; – mark caposaldo *m*; – scape paesaggio *m*; – slip frana *f*; – -tax imposta fondiaria
lane sentiero *m*
language lingua *f*
languid languido; fiacco; – ly languidamente
languish languire
languor languore *m*
lank magro; sparuto
lantern lanterna *f*
lap grembo *m*; falda *f*; lambire
lappel rovescio *m*
lapse lasso; errore *m*;
larceny latrocinio *m*
lard lardo *m*
large largo; grosso
lark allodola; burla *f*
larynx laringe *f*
last ultimo; scorso; forma *f*; durare
lasting permanente
latch saliscendo *m*; allacciare
late tardo; recente
lately ultimamente
latent latente
lateral laterale
lather saponata *f*; insaponare
latin latino
latitude latitudine *f*
latter ultimo
laugh riso; ridere; – able ridevole; –ing

ridente; **-ing** **stock** risata; **-ter** risata *f*

launch scialuppa *f* lanciare

laundress lavandaia *f*

laundry lavanderia *f*

laurel lauro *m*

lava lava *f*

lavatory lavatoio *m*

lavender lavanda *f*

lavish prodigo; prodigare

law legge *f*; decreto *m*

lawful legale

lawn erbaio *m*; rensa *f*

lawsuit lite *f*; processo *m*

lawyer avvocato *m*

lax molle; fiacco

laxative lassativo *m*

lay laico; porre; mettere

layman laico *m*

laziness pigrizia

lazy pigro

lead piombo *m*; **--pencil** matita *f*

lead condurre; guidarre

leaden di piombo

leader capo; conduttore;

leak apertura; falla *f*; trapelare; **- age** trapelamento *m*; infiltrazione

lean magro; scarno; appoggiare; inclinare

leanness magrezza *f*

leap salto *m*; saltare; **- frog** cavallo da canciullo; **--year** anno bisestile *m*

learn imparare; studiare

learned instruito; erudito

learning erudizione

lease contratto d'affitto; appigionare

leash guinzaglio *m*

least minimo; più piccolo; meno; **at -** almeno

leather cuoio *m*; pelle *f*

leathern di cuoio

leave permissione *f*; congedo *m*; lasciare; abbandonare

left sinistro; sinistra *f*

leg gamba *f*

legacy legato *m*

legal legale; **- ity** legalità *f* **- ize** legalizzare

legate legato *m*

legatee legatario *m*

legend leggenda *f*

legendary legendario

legibility leggibilità *f*

legible leggibile

legion legione *f*

legislation legislazione *f*

legirlator legislatore *m*

legitimate legittimo

leisure agio; ozio *m*

lemon limone *m*; **- ade** limonata *f*; **- squeezer** strizzalimoni *m*

lend prestare

length lunghezza *f*; **- en** allungare

lenient leniente

lens lente *f*

lent quaresima *f*

lessen diminuire

lesson lezione *f*

let lasciare; permettere a

lethargy letargo *m*

letter lettera; epistola *f* **--box** buca delle lettere

lettuce lattuga *f*

level livellato; livello; piano *m*; mira; livellare;

lever leva *f* [spianare

levity levità *f*

levy leva *f*

lewd dissoluto

liabilities passivo *m*

liability responsabilità *f*

liable responsabile

liar mentitore *m*

libel libello *m* diffamare
liberal liberale
liberate liberare
liberty libertà *f*
librarian bibliotecario *m*
library biblioteca *f*
license autorizzare

lick leccata *f*; leccare
lid coperchio *m*
lie menzogna *f*; giacere;
mentire

lieu in - of in luogo di
lieutenant luogotenente *m*
life vita *f*; - boat battello
di salvimento *m*; - less
senza vita; - time tempo
della vita *m*

lift ascensore *m*; mano *f*;
alzare; sollevare
ligament ligamento *m*
light chiaro; luminoso;
biondo; lume *m*; illum-
inare; incontrare; - en
alleggerire; illuminare;
- house faro *m*; - ing
illuminazione *f*; - ly
leggermente; - ning ful-
mine *m*;

like simile; uguale;
tale; come; da simile *m*;
amare; volere che; tro-
vare buono; - en com-
parare; -ly probabile;
- wise parimente
liking gusto *m*
lilac lilla
lily giglio *m*; - of the
valley mughetto *m*
limb membro; ramo *m*
lime calce *f*; - kiln
fornace da calce *f*; - tree
tiglio *m*
limit limite *m*; limitare
limp fiacco; molle; zop-
picamento *m*
limpid limpido

line linea; corda *f*
lineage lignaggio *m*
lineament tratto *m*
linen tela *f*; di tela
lion, lioness leone *m*;
leonessa *f*
lip labbro *m*; orlo *m*
liquefy liquefare
liquid liquido *m*
liquidate liquidare
liquor liquore *m*
lisp scilinguare
list lista *f*; catalogo;
listen ascoltare

literary letterario
literature letteratura *f*
lithographer litografo
lithography litografia *f*
little piccolo; poco
liturgy liturgia *f*
live vivo; vivere; - li-
hood sussistenza *f*;
- liness vivacità *f*; - ly
liver fegato *m* |vivace
livery levrea; pensione
livid livido [(cavalli)]
lizard lucerta *f*
load carico *m*; caricare
loam terra grassa *f*
loan prestito *m*
loath avverso
loathe detestare
loathsome odioso
lobby vestibolo *m*
lobster astaco *m*
local locale
locality località *f*
lock serratura; chiusa;
ciocca *f*; serrare a
chiave; - et medag-
lioncino *m*; - out spiaggia *f*; - smith serruriere
lodge loggia *f*; alloggiare;
- r pigionale *m & f*
lodging alloggio *m*
loft soffitta *f*
lofty alto; sublime

log ceppo; loche *m*
logarithm logaritmo *m*
logic logica *f*; – **al** logico;
lone(ly) solo; isolato *f*;
– **liness** solitudine *f*; –
some solitario; desolato
long lungo; bramare;
evity longevità *f*
longing brama *f*
longitude longitudine *f*
look sguardo *m*; aspetto
m; guardare; parere
– **for** cercare
loose sciolto; rilassato;
– **n** sciogliere; rilassare
lord signore; padrone *m*;
lose perdere; mancare
loser perditore *m*
loss perdita *f*
lot sorte; fortuna
lotion lozione *f*
lottery lotteria *f*
loud forte; – **ly** ad alta
voce [girandolare
lounge giro; sofà *m*;
louse pidocchio *m*;
love amore *m*; amare;
– **liness** amorevolezza;
vaghezza *f*; – **ly** grazioso; – **r** amante *& f*
loving amoroso; amante;
affettuoso
low basso; triste; volgare
low muggire
lower abbassare
lower offuscarsi
lowly basso; umile

loyal leale; fedele
loyalty lealtà *f*
lozenge pasticca *f*
lubricate lubricare
lucid lucido
luck fortuna *f*; azzardo
lucrative lucrativo
luggage bagaglio *m*;

– **ticket** ricevuta del
bagaglio; – **van** carro
del bagagli
lukewarm tiepido
lull momento di calma
m; calmare
lullaby canto *m*
lumbago lombaggine *f*
lumber scarti *m pl*
luminary luminare *m*
luminous luminoso
lump massa *f*; grumo *m*
lunacy demenza *f*
lunar lunare
lunatic lunatico; pazzo
m; – **asylum** manicomio
m [dare
lunch merenda *f*; meren-
lung polmone *m*
lure esca *f*; allettare
lurch barcollare
lurid lurido
lurk nascondersi
luscious sdolcinato
lust lussuria; sensualità
f; – **ful** lascivo; – **iness**
vigore *m*; – **y** vigoroso
luxuriate crescere rigog-
liosamente; vivere nel
lusso
luxurious sontuoso
luxury lusso *m*
lye ranno *m*

M

macaroni maccherone *m*
macaroon biscotino *m*
mace mazza; mace *f*
macerate macerare
machination macchina-
zione *f* [meccanismo *m*
machine macchina *f*; – **ry**
mad pazzo; matto;

– den render furioso;
– ness demenza *f*

madam signora *f*

magazine magazzino
gironale *m*

maggot vermicciolo *m*

magic magia *f*; – al
magico; – ian mago *m*

magistrate magistrato *m*

magnanimous magnani-
magnate magnate *m* [mo

magnesia magnesia *f*

magnet magnete *m*; – ic
magnetico; – ism mag-
netismo *m*; – ize mag-
netizzare

magnificent magnifico

magnify magnificare

magnitude grandezza *f*

mahogany acaiu *m* [*m*

maid vergine; serva *f*;
– en verginale;

mail maglia; valigia *f*;
corriere *m*;

maim mutilare

main principale; essen-
ziale; grosso; oceano
m; – land terra ferma;
– ly principalmente; –
tain mantenere; – ten-
ance mantenimento *f*

maize mais *m*

majestic maestoso

majesty maestà *f*

major maggiore *m*

majority maggiorità *f*

make struttura; natura
f; fare; creare; obbli-
gare; – believe far cre-
dere; maniera *f*; – r
fabbricante *m*; – shift
peggio *m*

malady malattia *f*

malaria malaria *f*

male maschio *m*

malevolence malevolenza

malice malizia *f*   [*f*

malicious malevolo

malign malignare

malignant maligno

malt malto *m*

mammoth mammut *m*

man uomo; marito *m*;
pedina (dama) *f*; equi-
paggiare

manacles manette *f pl*

manage dirigere

manageable maneggiabile

management direzione *f*

manhood virilità; natura
humana; bravura *f*

maniac, maniacal mani-
iaco; pazzo *m*

manifest manifesto; evi-
dente;   manifestare;
mostrare; – ly manife-
stamente   [zione *f*

manifestation manifesta-

manikin umetto; busto

mankind il genere umano

manly maschile   [*m*

manner maniera *f*

mannerly cortese

manoeuvre manovra *f*

mansion casa grande *f*

manslaughter omicidio *m*

mantelpiece cappa di
camino *m*

mantle mantello *m*

manual manuale *m*

manufactory fabbrica *f*

manufacture fabbricare

manufacturer fabbricante
m   [tilizzare

manure letame *m*; fer-

manuscript manoscritto

many molti   [*m*

map carta geografica;

maple acero *m* [mappa *f*

mar guastare   [mo *m*

marble marmoreo; mar-

March Marzo *m*; marcia
f; progresso *m*; marciare

marchioness marchesa *f*
mare giumenta *f*
margarine margarina *f*
margin margina *f*; orlo *m*
mark segno *m*; segnare;
marcare
marker segnatore (giuoco)
segno (libro) *m*
market mercato *m*
marl marga *f*
marmalade marmellata
marmoset scimiotto *m*
marmot marmotta *f*
marquee tendone *m*
marquis marchese *m*
marriage martrimonio *m*
married maritata
marrow midollo *m*
marry sposare
marsh palude *f*
marshal maresciallo *m*;
ordinare
mart mercato *m*
martial marziale
martyr martire *m & f*
marvel maraviglia *f*;
ammirare
marvellous maraviglioso
masculine mascolino
mask maschera *f*; mascherare
mason muratore *m*
masonry muratura *f*
masquerade mascherata *f*
mass massa *f*
massacre massacro *m*;
massacrare
massive massiccio
master maestro; pad-
rone; direttore *m*;
superare; dominare;
mat stuoia *f*; intrecciarsi
match zolfanello; partito;
uguale *m*; accordarsi;
maritarsi; – **box** scatola

da zolfanelli; – **maker**
fabbricante di zolfanelle
m & f
mate consorte *m & f*;
compagno *m* [portante
material materiale; im-
material materiale *m*
maternal materno
maternity maternità *f*
mathematical matematico
mathematician matema-
tico   [*f*
mathematics matematica
matrimony matrimonio *m*
matron matrona *f*
matter materia; cosa *f*;
marcia (med); soggetto
m; importare; premere
mattress materasso *m*
mature maturo; mat-
urare
maturity maturità *f*
mayor sindaco *m*
maze laberinto *m*; per
me me; mi [plessità *f*
meadow prato *m*
meagre magro
meal pasto *m*; farina *f*
mean basso; medio;
mezzo *m*; media *f*;
intendere; voler dire;
– **ing** significativo;
disegno *m*;   **ness**
sordidezza *f*; – **time** nel
intervallo
meander serpeggiare
measles rosolia *f*
measure misura; dimensione *f*; misurare
meat carne *f*; cibo *m*
mechanic meccanico;
operaio *m*
mechanical meccanico
mechanism meccanismo
medal medaglia *f*   [*m*

81

meddle impacciarsi
mediate esser mediatore
mediator mediatore *m*
medical medico
medicine medicina *f*
meed ricompensa *f*; premio *m*
meek sommesso
meet incontrare; trovare
meeting incontro *m*; riunione *f*
membrane membrana *f*
memento memento *m*
memoir memoria *f*
memorable memorabile
memorandum nota *f*
memorial memoriale *m*; petizione *f*
memory memoria *f*
menace minaccia *f*; minacciare
mend raccomodare; emmenial servile [endarsi
mental mentale
mention menzione *f*; menzionare
mercantile mercantile
mercenary mercenario *m*
merchandize mercanzia
merchant negoziante
merciful clemente
mercury mercurio *m*
mercy misericordia *f*
merge immergere
meridian meridiano *m*
merit merito *m*; meritare
meritorious meritorio
merry gioviale
mesh maglia *f*
mess mensa *f*; guazzabuglio; pasticcio *m*
message messaggio *m*
messenger messaggiero *m*
Messiah Messia *m*
metal metallo *m*; – lic metallino; – **lurgy** metallurgia *f*

metaphor metafora *f*
meteor meteora *f*
meter contatore *m*
method metodo *m*
microscope microscopio *m*
midday mezzogiorno *m*
middle mezzo; centro *m*
midnight mezzanotte *f*
midshipman guardia marina *f*
midst mezzo; centro *m*
midwife levatrice *f*
might potenza *f*
migrate emigrare
mild dolce
mildew golpe *f*
mile miglio *m*
military militare *m*
militia milizia *f*
milk latte *m*; mungere; – **man** lattaio *m*; – **y** latteo; di latte; – **y way** via lattea *f*
mill mulino *m*; fabbrica *f*; macinare; follare;
milliner modista *f*
million milione *m*
mimic mimico; mimo *m*; imitare
mince sminuzzare
mind mente *f*; intelletto; *m*; osservare; fare attenzione a
mine mina *f*; minare; il mio la mia
miner minatore *m*
mineral minerale *m*
miperalogy mineralogia *f*
mingle mischiare
minister ministro; prete *m*; ministrare
ministry ministerio *m*
minor minore; minorenne *m* & *f*
minority minorità *f*
minstrel menestrello *m*

mint menta *f*; monetare
minute minuto *m*; nota *f*
minute minuto
miracle miracolo *m*
miraculous miracoloso
mirage miraggio *m*
mire fango *m*
mirror specchio *m*
miscalculation errore di
calcolo *m*   [aborto *m*
miscarriage insuccesso;
miscarry fallire; abortire
miscellaneous miscellaneo
mischance disavventura *f*
mischief male; danno *m*
mischievous malizioso
miserable miserabile
misery miseria *f*
misfortune sventura *f*
misgiving apprensione *f*
mishap disavventura *f*
mislead sviare
mismanage dirigere male
misprint errore di stampa
   m
miss signorina; svista *f*;
difetto *m*; mancare;
fallire; ommettere
missile proiettile *m*
mission missione *f*
missionary missionario *m*
mist nebbia *f*
mistake sbaglio; errore;
m sbagliare; ingannarsi
mister signore *m*
mistletoe vischio *m*
mistress padrona; am-
ante *f*   [diffidare di
mistrust diffidenza *f*

misty nebbioso
misunderstand capir male
misunderstanding con-
cetto erroneo *m*
mob folla *f*; maltrattare
mobilize mobilizzare
mock falso; contraffare;

mode modo *m*; maniera *f*
model modello; model-
lare   [erare
moderate moderato; mod-
modern moderno
modest modesto; pudico
- y modestia *f*
modify modificare
modulate modulare
mohair pelo di capra
moist umido; - en um-
ettare; - ure umidità *f*
mole talpa *f*; neo; molo
molest molestare
mollify mollificare
moment momento; - ary
momentaneo; - ous di
momento
monarch monarca *m* & *f*
monarchy monarchia *f*
monastery monastero *m*
money moneta *f*;
mongrel misto; meticcio
monk monaco *m*   [*m*
monkey scimmia *f*   [*m*
monogram monogramma *m*
monopoly monopolio *m*
monotonous monotono [*m*
monster mostro *m*
month mese *f*
monument monumento *m*
mood umore *m*
moody mesto
moon luna *f*; - light,
moor landa; brughiera
f; moro *m*; amarrare;
mop spazzatoio *m*
mope annoiarsi
morality morale *m*
morbid morboso
more più; maggiore
morning mattina *f*
morsel boccone *m*
mortal mortale; umano
mortality mortalità *f*
mortar calcina *f*; mor-

83

taio m
morgage ipoteca *f*
mosquito zanzara *f*
moss(y) musco(so) *m*
most più; molto; il più
moth falena *f*　　　[m
mother madre *f*; − -in
law suocera *f*; − -of-
pearl madreperla; nac-
chera *f*; − less senza
madre; − ly materno
motion movimento *m*;
mozione *f*; − less senza
moto
motive motivo *m* [moto
motley variopinto
motor motore *m*
motto motto *m*
mould forma; matrice;
muffa *f*; terriccio *m*;
formare; modellare; − er
formatore *m*; -y muffato
mount(ain) monte; montagna *f*; montare; − eer
montanaro *m*; − ous
montagnoso
mourn lamentare; − er
piangitore *m*; − ful
lugubre; − ing dolore *m*
mouse sorcio *m*　　[pl
moustache mustacchi *m*
mouth bocca; gola *f*;
− ful boccone *m*; − piece
imboccatura *f*
movable mobile
move movimento; muo-
vere
movement movimento *m*
mow falciare; − er fal-
ciatore *m*; − ing-mach-
ine falciatrice *f*
much molto; grande
mud fango *m*; − dy
fangoso
multiple molteplice
multiplication moltiplica-
zione *f*

multiply moltiplicare
multitude moltitudine *f*
multitudinous numeroso
mummery mascherata
mummy mummia *f*
mumps stranguglioni *m pl*
munch masticare
mundane mondano
municipal municipale
munition munizione *f*
murder omicidio *m*;
assassinare; uccidere ;
− er assassino *m*
murky tenebroso
murmur mormorio *m*;
mormorare
muscle muscolo *m*
muscular muscolare
muse musa *f*; meditare
mushroom fungo *m*
music(al) music(ale)
musician musico *m*
musk muschio *m*
musketry moschetteria *f*
muslin mussolina *f*
mussel gongola; arsella
f; muscolo *m* [dovere
must mosto *m*; muffa *f*;
mustard mostarda *f*
musty muffato
mute muto *m*
mutilate mutilare
mutilation mutilazione
mutiny rivolta *f*
mutter mormorare
mutton montone *m*;
mutual mutuo; reciproco;
− ly mutuamente
muzzle muso *m* *f*
my mio; mia; miei· mie
myself io stesso; me
stesso
mysterious misterioso
mystery mistero *m*
mystify mistificare
myth mito *m*; − ology
mitologia *f*

N

nag cavallino m; importunare [inchiodare
nail unghia f; chiodo m;
naked nudo
nakedness nudità
name nome m; riputazione f; nominare ; chiamare; – d chiamato; – less senza nome; – ly cioè; vale a dire; – sake omonimo m
nap sonnellino; pelo m
narcotic narcotico m
narrate narrare
narrative narrazione f
narrow stretto; limitato;
nasal nasale [restringere
national nazionale; – ity nazionalità f   [m
native nativo; indigeno
natural naturale [& f
naturalist naturalista m
nature natura; indole f
naught nullo; niente; zero m
naughty cattivo
nausea nausea f
nauseous nauseabondo
navel umbilico m
navigable navigabile
navigate navigare
navigation navigazione f
navigator navigatore m
navy marina; flotta f
navvy lavoratore m
nay no; anzi
neap basso; morto; – tides acque morte
near vicino; intimo; prossimo; accosto ; – ly vicino; quasi; circa; – ness prossi-

mità f
neat netto; lindo; – ness nettezza f   [mente
necessarily necessaria-
necessary necessario; –ies cose necessarie f pl
necessitate necessitare
necessity necessità f
neck collo m; gola f; – lace collana f; – tie cravatta
need bisogno m; necessità f; aver bisogno di
needful necessario
neediness indigenza
needle ago m
neglect negligenza f negligere
negligence negligenza
negotiate negoziare
negotiation negoziazione f
neighbour vicino; prossimo m; – nood vicinità
nephew nipote m.
nerve nervo m; invigorire
nervous nervoso
nest nido m; – ling uccel-
nestle cacciarsi [lino m
net netto; rete f
neuter, neutral neutro; neutrale
neutrality neutralità f
neutralize neutralizzare
never mai; giammai; – theless nullameno; tuttavia
new nuovo; novello
news notizia f; – vendor venditore di giornale; – paper giornale m
New-Year's day capo d'anno m   [dopo
next prossimo; seguente
nice gustoso; bello
nickel nichel m

niece nipote *f*

night notte *f*; – ingale
usignuolo *m*; – ly not-
turno; ogni notte;
– –nurse nottante *m & f*

nimble agile

nine nove *m*; – teen
dicianove *m*; – teenth
decimonono *m*; – tieth
novantesimo *m*; – ty
novanta *m*

ninth nono *m*

nip pizzicare

nipple capezzolo *m*;
tetta *f*

no nessuno; niuno; no

nobility nobiltà *f*

noble nobile

nobleman nobile *m*

nobody nessuno; veruno

nocturnal notturno

nod segno di testa *m*

noise rumore *m*

noisy strepitoso

nominal nominale

nominate nominare

nomination nomina *f*

nominee persona nom-
inata *f* [veruno

nonsense assurdità *f*

nonsensical assurdo

nook angolo *m*

noon mezzogiorno *m*

noose laccio; nodo scor-
nor nè [soio *m*

normal normale

north, – erly, – ern nor-
dico; settentrionale

North nord *m*

nose naso; muso *m*

nostril narice *f*

not non; no; niente

notable notevole

notary notaio *m*

notch tacca *f*; intaccare

note nota *f*; biglietto;
notare; osservare

noted noto; eminente

nothing nulla; niente *m*

notice notizia *f*; avviso
m; menzionare

noticeable percettibile

notify notificare

notion nozione *f*

nourish nutrire [*m*

nourishment nutrimento

novel novello *m*

novelist novellista *m & f*

novelty novità *f*

novice novizio *m*

now ora; al presente;
– –a-days oggi; – and
then di tempo in tempo

nude nudo

nudity nudità *f*

nugget pepita *f*

nuisance noia *f*
null nullo

numerical numerico [*f*
numerous numeroso

nun monaca; religiosa *f*

nunnery convento di
monache *m*

nurse nutrice; bambin-
aia *f*; allattare; cullare

nursery camera dei fan-
ciulli *f*; semenzaio *m*;
pepiniera *f*; – –man
pepinierista *m*

nut noce; chiocciola *f*;
– –cracker rompi noci
m; –meg noce moscata *f*

nutrition nutrizione *f*
nutritious nutritivo

nutshell guscio di noce *m*

O

O! oh!
oal scempio *m*
oak quercia *f*;
oar remo *m*
oasis oasi *f*
oath giuramento *m*
oatmeal farina di avena *f*
oats avena *f*
obedience obbedienza *f*
obedient obbediente
obese grasso
obey obbediare
obituary funerario
object oggetto; scopo *m*; obiettare
objection obiezione *f*
objective oggettivo
obligatory obbligatorio
oblige obbligare
obliging obbligante
obliterate obliterare
oblivion oblio *m*
oblong oblungo *m*
obnoxious odioso
obscene osceno
obscure oscuro
obscurity oscurità *f*
observance osservanza *f*
observant osservante
observation osservazione *f*
observatory osservatorio
observe osservare [*m*
observer osservatore *m*
obsolete disusato
obstacle ostacolo *m*
obstinacy ostinatezza *f*
obstinate ostinato
obstruct ostruire
obstruction ostruzione *f*
obtain ottenere
obtainable ottenibile

obtrusive intruso
obtuse ottuso
obviate ovviare a
obvious ovvio; chiaro
occasion occasione *f*; cagionare
occasional occasionale
occult occulto
occupant occupante *m* & *f*
occupation occupazione *f*
occupy occupare
occur occorrere
occurrence occorrenza
ocean oceano *m*
ochre ocra *f*
octagon ottagono *m*
octagonal ottangolare
octave ottava *f*
of di; del; sopra; per;
off via; lontano [da
offence offesa; delitto *m*
offend offendere
offender offensore *m*
offensive offensivo
offer offerta *f*; offerire
offering oblazione *f*
office uffizio; servizio *m*
officer official ufficiale *m*
officiate ufficiare
old vecchio; antico
olive oliva *f*
omelet frittata *f*
omen pronostico *m*
ominous sinistro
omission omissione *f*
omit omettere
omnipotent onnipotente
on sopra; su; disopra;
a; di; sotto; in; avanti
once una volta; un
tempo; at – alla volte
one uno; solo; si; uno;
alcuno
onion cipolla *f*
only solo; unico; sola-

mente
onward progressivo ;
opal opale /
opaque opaco; oscuro
open aperto; franco
open aprire; schiudere;
– **er** apritore *m*; – **ing**
apertura /
opera opera /; **--glass**
cannochiale *m*; **--house**
teatro dell'opera *m*
operate operare
operation operazione /;
effetto *m*;
operator operatore *m*

opinion opinione /
opium oppio *m*
opossum sariga /
opponent avversario *m*
opportune opportuno; a
proposito
opportunity occasione /
oppose opporre
opposite opposto; dirimpetto
opposition opposizione /
oppress opprimere
oppression oppressione /
oppressor oppressore *m*
optical, optician ottico *m*

optimist ottimista *m* &
option scelta /
optional facoltativo
opulence opulenza /
or od; oppure
oral orale
orange arancio; arancia /
orchard brolo; frutteto *m*
orchestra orchestra /
orchid orchide /
ordain ordinare
ordeal prova /
order ordine; metodo;
mandato *m*; ordinare;
comandare; **postal** –

vaglia postale /; – **ly**
regolato [decreto *m*
ordinance ordinanza /;
ordinary ordinario
ordnance artiglieria /
ore minerale *m*
organ organo *m*; – **ic**
organico; – **ist** organista *m* & /; – **ization**
organizzazione /; – **ize**
organizzare
orient oriente *m*
oriental orientale
orifice apertura /
origin origine /
original originale
originality originalità /
originate creare
ornament ornamento *m*;
ornamentare
ornithology ornitologia /
orphan orfano *m*
orthodox ortodosso
orthography ortographia /
oscillate oscillare
osier vimine *m*
ostensible ostensibile
ostentatious pomposo
ostler mozzo di stalla *m*
ostrich struzzo *m*
other altro; – **s** altri

our nostro; nostra; – **s**
il nostro   [noi
ourselves noi medesimi;
out fuori; senza; – **bid**
rincarare su; – **break**
eruzione; insurrezione /;
– **cast** espulso *m*; – **do**
soprastare; – **er** esteri-
iore; – **fit** corredo *m*;
– **going** uscita /; – **grow**
sorpassare; – **law** pros-
critto *m*; proscrivere;

oven forno *m*
over su; sopra; troppo;
di più; in; per

overbalance pesare più di
overcast offuscare [cadere
overcoat soprabito *m*
overcome vincere
overflow inondare
overgrown immenso
overhang piegare sopra
overhead in alto
overhear udire
overlay affogare
overlook sorvegliare
overpower sopraffare
oversight negligenza *f*
overtake raggiungere
overthrow rovina *f*;
rovesciare
overturn versare
overweight sorappeso *m*
overwhelm sommergere
owe dovere a
owl gufo *m*
own proprio; avere
owner proprietario *m*
ox bue; bove *m*
oxide ossido *m*
oxygen ossigeno *m*
oyster ostrica *f*
ozone ozono *m*

P

pace passo; mandar
adagio
pacify pacificare
pack pacco; mazzo
(carte) *m*; imballare;
– age balla *f*; – et
pacchetto *m*;
pad cuscinetto; des-
chetto; ovattare;
paddle pagaia *f*; remare
paddock prato *m*; pas-
tura *f*
padlock lucchetto *m*

page pagina *f*; paggio *m*
pail secchia *f*
pain pena *f*
painful doloroso
paint colore *m*; dipingere
painter pittore *m*
painting pittura *f*
pair paio *m*; coppia *f*;
appaiare
palace palazzo *m*
palate palato; gusto *m*
pale pallido; stecconе;
territorio *m*
paleness pallore *m*
palette tavolozza *f*
palisade palizzata *f*
pall drappo mortuario
m; rintuzzarsi
palliate palliare
palliation palliamento *m*
palliative palliativo *m*
pallid pallido
palm palma *f*
palmistry chiromanzia *f*
pancake frittella *f*
pander piaggiare; mez-
pane vetro *m* [zano *m*
panel quadrello *m*.
pang dolore acuto *m*
panic panico *m*
pannier paniere *m*
pansy viola *f*
pant palpitazione *f*;
palpitare
panther pantera *f*
pantile tegola *f*
pantomime pantomima *f*
pantry dispensa *f*
papal papale
paper carta *f*; giornale *m*
papist papista *m & f*
par pari *f*
parade parata; piazza
f; sfoggiare
paradise paradiso *m*
paradox paradosso *m*

89

parallel parallelo *m*;
eguagliare
paralysis paralisia *f*
paralytic paralitico
paralyze paralizzare
parch seccare
parchment pergamena *f*
pardon perdono *m*; *f*
perdonare
pare sbucciare; tondere
paregoric paregorico *m*
parent padre *m*; madre
f; – s genitori *m pl*
parentage parentado *m*
parenthesis parentesi *f*
parish parrocchia *f*
park parco *m*
parliament parlamento *m*
Parmesan parmigiano *m*
parody parodia *f*
parrot pappagallo *m*
parsley prezzemolo *m*
parsnip pastinaca *f*
parson parroco; curato *m*
part parte; porzione *f*;
dividere
partial parziale
partiality parzialità *f*
participate partecipare
particle particella *f*
particular particolare;
speciale; fastidioso;
particolare *m*
particulars informazioni
f pl
partition partizione *f*
partly in parte; parte
partner compagno; socio
party parte *f*; serata
pass passo *m*; stretta *f*;
permesso *m*; passare;
approvare
passable passabile
passage passaggio *m*
passenger viaggiatore *m*
passion passione *f*

passive passivo *m*
Passover Pasqua *f*
passport passaporto *m*
past passato; scorso
patrol sentinella *f*; pat-
tugliare   [*m*
patron padrone; patrono
patronize patrocinare
pattern modello *m*
pauper povero *m*
pause pausa *f*; riflettere
pave pavimentare
pavement pavimento;
marciapiedi *m*
pavilion padiglione *m*
paw zampa *f*; zampare
pay paga *f*; soldo; stipen-
dio *m*; pagare; saldare
payable pagabile
payment pagamento *m*
pea pisello *m*
peace pace; calma *f*;
– able, – ful pacifico
peach pesca *f*
peacock pavone *m*
peak picco *m*; cima *f*
peal scampanio; scoppio
m; scampanare
pear pera *f*
pearl perla *f*
peasant contadino *m*
peat torba *f*
pebble selce; ciottolo *m*
peck beccare
peculiar peculiare
pecuniary pecuniario
pedestrian pedestre *m*
pedigree genealogia *m*
pedler merciaiolo ambu-
lante *m*   [scorzare
peel scorza; buccia *f*;
peep sguardo furtivo *m*
peer pari *m*
pen penna *f*; pecorne *m*;
stabbiare; scrivere
penal penale

penalty penalità *f*

penance penitenza

pencil matita *f*; pennello *m*; disegnare [ante

pending pendente; dur-

penetrate penetrare

penetration acutezza *f*

peninsula penisola *f*

penniless senza denari

pension pensione *f*; pensionare

pensive pensieroso

people popolo *m*; nazione; gente *f*; popolare

pepper pepe *m*; impepare

per per; al; allo

perceive vedere; percepire

percentage percentuale *f*

perception percezione *f*

perch pertica *f*; appollaiarsi

perennial perenne; perpetuo [zionare

perfect perfetto; perfe-

perfection perfezione *f*

perforate perforare

perform fare; operare

performance esecuzione; rappresentazione *f*

performer esecutore *m*

perfume profumo *m*; profumare

peril pericolo *m*

period periodo *m*; epoca *f*

perish perire

perishable caduco; avariabile (merce)

peritonitis peritonite *f*

perjure spergiurare

perjury spergiuro *m*

permanent permanente

permeate permeare

permissible permissibile

permission permesso *m*

permit permesso *m*;

permettere

perpendicular perpendicolare

perpetrate perpetrare [*m*

perpetrator perpetratore

perpetual perpetuo

perpetuate perpetuare

perplex confondere

perplexity perplessità *f*

persecute perseguitare

persecution persecuzione *f*

persecutor persecutore *m*

perseverance perseveranza *f*

persevere perseverare

persist persistere

persistent persistente

person persona *f*; individuo *m*   [prio

personal personale; pro-

personate contraffare

personify personificare

perspective di prospettiva; prospettiva; vista *f*; sudore *m*

perspiration traspirazione

perspire sudare

persuade persuadere

persuasion persuasione *f*

persuasive persuasivo

pert impertinente

pertinacious pertinace

pertinent a proposito

pet favorita *m & f*

petal petalo *m*

petition petizione *f*; supplicare

petrify petrificare

petroleum petrolio *m*

petticoat gonella *f*

pettifogger avvocataccio

petty piccolo   [*m*.

petulance petulanza *f*

pew stallo; banco *m*

pewter peltro *m*

phaeton faeton *m*

phantom spettro *m*

pharisee fariseo *m*

pharmaceutical farmaceutico

phase fase *f*

pheasant fagiano *m*

phenomenon fenomeno *m*

phonograph fonografo *m*

phosphate fosfato *m*

phosphorus fosforo *m*

photograph — y fotografia *f*; – er fotografo

phrase frase *f*

phrenology frenologia *f*

phthisic(al) tisico

phthisis tisichezza *f*

physical fisico

physician medico *m*

physiology fisiologia *f*

pianist pianista *m & f*

piano pianoforte *m*; grand – piano a coda

pick piccone *m*; cogliere;

pickle salamoia *f*; salamoiare; salare

picklock grimaldello; ladro *m*

pickpocket borsaiolo *m*

picture pittura *f*; quadro *m*; dipingere;

picturesque pittoresco

pie pasticcio *m*; torta *f*

piece pezzo; frammento

pier pila *f*; molo *m*

pierce forare; penetrare

piety pietà *f*

pig porco; verro *m*;

pigeon piccione *m*

pike picca *f*; luccio *m*

pile mucchio *m*; pila *f*; palo *m*; ammucchiare

piles emoroide *f pl*

pilgrim pellegrino *m*

pilgrimage pellegrinaggio

pill pillola *f*

pillar pilastro *m*; colonna

pillow guanciale *m*

pillow-case federa *f*

pilot pilota *m*; governare

pimple pustola *f*

pin spillo *m*; caviglia *f*; rinserrare

pinch pizzico *m*; pizzicare

pine pino; abete *m*; languire; – -apple ananasso *m*

pink rosa; garofano *m*; tagliare

pinnacle pinnacolo *m*; cima *f*

pioneer pioniere *m*

pious pio; devoto

pipe pipa *f*; tubo; zampognare

pirate pirata *m*

pitch pece *f*; grado; tono *m*; gettare; precipitare; immergere; cadere; – er brocca *f*;

pivot perno *m*   [m

placard cartellone; affisso

place luogo; posto *m*; piazza *f*; collocare; mettere

placid placido   [tare

plague peste *f*; tormen-

plaid plaid *m*; stoffa scozzese *f*

plain piano; brutto; campagna *f*; piano *m*

plaint lamento *m*

plaintiff querelante; attore *m*

plaintive lamentevole

plait piegatura; piega *f*; pieghettare   [nare

plan disegno *m*; diseg-

plane pialla *f*; platano *m*;

planet pianeta *f*; [piallare

plank tavola *f*

plant pianta *f*; materiale *m* piantare; – ation piantagione *f*; – er

piantatore *m*
plaster gesso; impiastro
m; impiastrare; ingessare
plastic plastico
plate piatto *m*; piastra
argentiera *f*; placcare;
inargentare
platform piattaforma *f*
play giuoco *m*; ricreazione *f*; teatro *m*; giuocare (a); sonare; divertirsi; — **er** giocatore;
attore *m*; — **ful** giocoso;
scherzevole; — **fully**
scherzevolmente ; —
-**house** teatro *m*; —
thing trastullo *m*
plea difesa; scusa *f*
plead litigare; scusarsi
su; allegare
pleasant piacevole; grato
pleasantry facezia *f*
please piacere (a); soddisfare [volontà *f*
pleasure piacere *m*;
pledge pegno *m*; impegnare; garantire
plentiful abbondante
plenty abbondanza *f*
pleurisy pleurisia *f*
pliable pieghevole
pliers mollette *f pl*
plight stato; pegno *m*;
impegnare
plot trama *f*; intrigo;
pezzo di terra *m*;
cospirare
plough aratro *m*; arare;
pluck tiramento; coraggio *m*; cogliere
plug turacciolo *m*; turare
plum prugna *f*
plumber piombaiolo *m*
plump grassotto
plumpness grassezza *f*

plunder bottino *m*; spogliare [gere
plunge tuffo *m*; immerplural** plurale *m*
plush felpa *f* [mente
ply lavorare assiduamente; affogare (uova);
poach cacciare furtivamente; affogare (uova);
pocket tasca *f*; buco
(biliardo) *m*; intascare;
— -**book** portafogli *m*;
poem poema *m*
poet poeta *m & f*
poetry poesia *f*
point punta *f*; punto
m; puntare; indicare
pointed appuntato
poise pesare
poison veleno *m*; avvelenare
poisonous velenoso
poke spinta *f*; spingere;
attizzare;
pole polo *m*; pertica *f*;
timone *m*
police polizia *f*; — **man**
sbirro; questurino *m*
policy politica *f*
polish lustro *m*; pulire
polite cortese; — **ness**
cortesia *f*
political politico
politician politico *m*
politics politica *f*
poll elezione; lista elettorale *f*; votare
pollute contaminare
polyglot polyglotta
pomade pomata *f* [*f*
pomegranate melangrana
pommel pomo *m*; battere
pomp pompa *f*
pompous pomposo
pond stagno *m*
ponder meditare

93

ponderous pesante
poniard pugnale
pontiff pontefice *m*
pony cavallino *m*
poodle barbone *m*
pool pozzanghera; posta (giuoco) *f*
poor povero
poorly indisposto
pop scoppietto *m*; scoppope papa *m*   [piare
popery papismo *m*
poplar pioppo *m*
poppy papavero *m*
populace popolaccio *m*
popular popolare
porch portico; vestibolo
pore poro *m*   [*m*
pork carne di porco *f*;
porridge minestra *f*
port porto *m*; − **wine** vino di Oporto *m*
portable portabile
portrait ritratto *m*
portray dipingere
position posizione
positive positivo
possess possedere; − **ion** possessione *f*; − **or** possessore *m*
possibility possibilità *f*
possible possibile

posporre; − **ponement** posposizione *f*
pot vaso *m*; pentola;
potato patata *f*
potent potente
pottery terraglia *f*
pouch saccoccia *f*

post posta *f*; posto; palo *m*; postare; impostare; andare in posta; − **age** porto *m*;
− **-card** cartolina postale
− **man** porta-lettere *m*;
− **office** posta *f*; **pone**

poultry pollame *m*
pound libbra (peso); lira sterlina *f*; pestare
pour versare
pout fare il broncio
poverty povertà *f*
powder polvere *f*; polverizzare
power potere *m*; facoltà *f*
− **ful** potente; − **less** impotente
practical pratico
practice pratica *f*
practise praticare
practitioner esercente *m*
praise lode *f*; elogio *m*; lodare;
prank scappata *f*
pray pregare; supplicare;
− **er** preghiera *f*; − **er-book** libro di preghiere *m*
preach predicare
preacher predicatore *m*
preamble preambolo *m*
precarious precario
precaution precauzione *f*
precede precedere
precedent precedente *m*
precept precetto *m*
precinct precinto
precious prezioso
precipitate precipitato; precipitare
precise preciso
precision precisione *f*
preclude precludere
precocious precoce   [*m*
predecessor predecessore
predict predire; presagire
prediction predizione *f*
predispose predisporre
predominate predominare
prefix prefisso *m*; prefiggere
pregnancy pregnazza *f*
pregnant incinta; pregno (di)   [pregiudicare

prejudice pregiudizio *m*;
prelate prelato *m* [*m*
preliminary preliminare
prelude preludio *m*
premature prematuro
premeditate premeditare
premier primiero; primo
ministro *m*
premises locali *m pl*;
premesse *f pl*
premium premio *m*
preparation preparazione *f*
preparatory preparatorio
prepare preparare
prepay pagare anticipatamente [are
preponderate preponderare
preposition preposizione *f*
prepossession preoccupazione *f*
preposterous preposter
prerogative prerogativa *f*
prescribe prescrivere
prescription ricetta; prescrizione *f*
presence presenza *f*
present presente; corrente; dono; regalo *m*
present presentare
presentation presentazione *f* [mento *m*
presentiment presentimento
presently quanto prima
preservation preservazione *f* [serva *f*
preserve preservare; conserva *f*
preserves (game) bandita
preside presedere [*f*
president presidente *m*
press torchio; armadio *m*; stampa *f*; premere; stringere; — urgente
— ure pressione *f*
presume presumere
presumption presunzione *f*
presumptuous presuntuoso
pretence finta *f*

prey preda *f*; predare; rodere
price prezzo; valore *m*;
— less inestimabile
prick puntura *f*; pungere
pride orgoglio *m*
priest prete; sacerdote *m*
prim affettato
primary primiero; primitivo
primitive primitivo
prince principe *m*; — ly principesco; — ss principessa *f*
principal principale ;
mastro; principale;
padrone; capitale *m*
principle principio *m*
print stampa; impressione *f*; stampare;
imprimere; — er tipografo *m*; —ing stampa *f*
prior precedente; priore
prison prigione *f*
prisoner prigioniero *m*
privacy retiratezza *f*
private privato; particolare; segreto
privilege privilegio *m*
prize premio *m*; preda *f*;
apprezzare
probable probabile
probation noviziato *m*
probe tenta *f*; tentare
problem problema *m*
procedure procedura *f*
proceed procedere
proceeding procedimento
process processo *m*
procession processione
proclaim proclamare
proclamation proclama
procrastinate procrastinare

procreate procreare
prodigal prodigo m
prodigy prodigio m
produce prodotto m;
produrre; – **r** produttore m
product prodotto m;
– **ion** produzione f; – **ive** produttivo   [fanare
profane profano; profanity profanità f
profess professare
profession professione f
professional professionale
professor professore m
proffer proporre
proficiency talento m
profile profilo m
profit profitto m; profittare (a); – **able** profittevole
profligate libertino m
profound profondo
profuse profuso
profusion profusione f
progeny progenie f pl
programme programma
prognostic pronostico [m
progress progresso m; progredire
prohibit proibire
prohibition proibizione f
project progetto m; progettare
projectile proiettile m
promenade passeggio m; passeggiare in
prominent prominente
promiscuous promiscuo
promote promuovere
promotion promozione f
prompt pronto; lesto;
prong rebbio m; punta f
pronoun pronome m
pronounce pronunziare
pronunciation pronunzia f
proof prova; bozza f;

saggio
prop puntello; palo m; puntellare; sostenere
propagate propagare
propel propulsare
propensity tendenza f
proper proprio
property proprietà
prophecy profezia f
prophesy predire
proportion proporzione f
proposal proposta f
propose proporre
proposition proposizione f
proprietor proprietario m
propriety convenevolezza
prorogue prorogare   [f
prosaic prosàico
prose prosa f
prosecute proseguire
prosecution prosecuzione
prosecutor accusatore m
prospect prospetto m; ispezionare
prosper prosperare
prosperity prosperità f
prosperous prospero
prostitute prostituta f
prostrate prostrato; prostrare
protect proteggere
protection protezione f
protector protettore m
protest protesta f; protestare; – **ation** protestazione f
protract protrarre
protrude avanzare
proud fiero
prove provare
proverb proverbio m
proverbial proverbiale
provide provvedere
provision provvisione f
provisional provvisorio
provocation provocazione
provoke provocare   [f

prow prua *f*
prowess valore *m*
prowl cercar la preda;
girar intorno
proximity prossimità *f*
proxy deputato *m*
prudence prudenza *f*
prudent prudente
prune prugna *f*; potare
prussic acid acido prussico *m*
pruriency pizzicore *m*
prurient pizzicante
psalm salmo *m*
psalter saltero *m*
psychology psicologia *f*
public pubblico; pubblico *m*
publican vinaio; oste;
pubblicano *m*   [*f*
publication pubblicazione
public-house taverna *f*
publicity pubblicità *f*
publish pubblicare
publisher editore *m*
pudding torta *f*
puddle guazzo *m*
puff soffio *m*; ciarlatanata *f*; soffiare;
sbuffare
pull tirata; lotta *f*;
tirare
pulse polso; legume *m*
pulverize polverizzare
pumice pomice *f*
pump pompa; tromba *f*;
pompare
pumpkin zucca *f*
pun bisticcio *m*; giuochi
di parole
punch pulcinella; punzone; ponce *m*
punctilious puntiglioso
punctual puntuale   [*f*
punctuation puntuazione
punish punire; - able

punible; - ment punizione
punt earchetta *f*
puny piccino; sparuto;
meschino   [pupilla *f*
pupil alunno; scolare *m*;
purchase acquisto *m*;
comprare; - r compratore *m*
pure puro; chiaro; mero
purgative purgativo; purgante *m*
purgatory purgatorio *m*
purge purgare; purificare
purification purificazione*f*
purify purificare
purity purità *f*   [morio
purl smerlatura; morpurloin involare [pora *f*
purple porporino; porporato senso; tenore *m*
purpose intenzione *f*;
disesno *m*; utilita *f*;
on - a posta; to no - in vano *f*
purse borsa *f*; - r computista; - y bolso
purslain porcellana *f*
pursuant conforme a
pursue proseguire
pursuit inseguimento *m*;
occupazione *f*
purvey provvedere; - or
provveditore; fornitore *m*
pus pus *m*; puzza *f*
push colpo; impulso *m*;
spingere
pushing intraprendente
pusillanimous pusillanime
put mettere; porre;
posare; proporre; portare; obbligare; - down deporre; - off
differire; svestire; - on

97

vestire mettere ; – out
spegnere ; tormentare ;
– together metter in-
sieme ; – in entrare ;
(mar) approdare ; – to
sea spiegare la vela ;

Q

quadrangle quadrato m ;
corte interna f
quadrille quadriglia f
quadroon quartone m
quaint ricercato [tarsi
quake tremare
quaker quacquero m
qualification qualifica-
zione
qualified qualificato ;
atto ; moderato
qualify qualificare
quality qualità f
qualm schifo ; scrupolo m
quandary incertezza f
quantity quantità f
quarantine quarantena f
quarrel rissa f; altercare ;
– some irascibile
quarry cava di pietre ;
preda f
quart boccale ; quarto m ;
– er quarto ; trimestre ;
quartiere m ; grazia f;
dividere in quarti ;
alloggiare ; – erly in
quarto ; quartale ; ogni
tre mesi ; – ermaster
quartiermastro m ; – ern
loaf pane di quattro
libbre ; – ers quartiere m ;
–ette quartetto m ; – z
quarzo m
queen regina ; dama f ;
queenly da regina
queer strano ; bizzarro
quell reprimere ; domare

quench spegnere ; estin-
guere
query domanda f [ente
querulous querulo ; dol-
query, question questione
f ; interrogare ; – able
dubbioso ; incerto
quibble arguzia f
quick vivo ; rapido ;
presto ; – en vivificare ;
– lime calce viva f ;
– ness prestezza ; rapid-
ità ; – silver mercurio m
quiet quieto ; calmo ;
calma f ; calmare
quill penna f
quit pagare ; abbandon-
are ; lasciare
quite interamente ; affatto

quits quitanzato ; pace !
quiver faretra f ; trem-
olare ; vibrare
quoin canto ; cuneo m
quoit disco m
quotation citazione f ;
corso m
quote citare ; quotare

R

rabbet incavatura f
rabbi rabbino m
rabbit coniglio m
rabble canaglia f
rabid rabbioso
race razza ; corsa f ;
correre con velocità ;
– iness forza f
rack ruota f ; rastrello m ;
tortura f ; arrotare ; tor-
turare ; spremere ; – et
schiamazzo m ; rac-
chetta f
radiance splendore m
radiant radiante

radiate radiare
radical radicale *m*
radish ravanello   *m*;
  horse - · ramolaccio *m*
radius raggio *m*
raffle tombola *f*
raft zattera *f*
rafter trave *f*
rag cencio *m*
rage rabbia; collera
rail sbarra *f*; cancello *m*;
  rotaia *f*; - lery motteg-
  gio *m*; **- road**, **- way**
  ferrovia *f*
rain pioggia *f*; piovere;
  - bow arcobaleno *m*;
  - y piovoso
raise alzare; levare;
  coltivare; aumuntare
raïbon uva passa *f*
rake rastrello; libertino
  m; rastrellare
rally raccolta *f*; raccogliere; ricuperare
ram ariete; montone *m*;
  impinzare
ramble giro *m*; vagare
rambling errante [zione *f*
ramification ramifica-
rampart bastione *m*
rancid rancido
rancour rancore *m*;
random caso *m*; **at - a**
  caso
range ordine; giro *m*;
  fila; catena; ordinare
rank grosso; rango *m*
rankle inviperarsi
ransack frugare
ransom riscatto *m*

rape ratto *m*
rapid rapido; celere
rapture estasi *f*
rare raro; esimio
rasp grattugia *f*; grattugiare
raspberry lampone *m*

rat topo; ratto *m*
rate prezzo *m*; tariffa;
  velocità *f*
rather piuttosto
ratify ratificare
ratio ragione *f*
rational razionale
rattle sonaglio *m*; strep-
  itare; **- snake** serpente
  a sonagli
reach portata; estensione
  f; giungere (a); esten-
read leggere   [dere
readable leggibile
ready pronto; lesto;
  - -made clothes abiti
  fatti *m pl*
real reale; vero
reality realtà *f*
realize realizzare
really realmente
realm reame *m*
ream risma *f*
reap raccogliere
reaper mietitore *m*
rear indietro; di dietro;
  retroguardia *f*; innal-
  zare; coltivare
reason ragione *f* motivo;
  m; ragionare; **- able**
  ragionevole
reassure riassicurare
rebel ribelle *m & f*;
  insorgere
rebellion rivolta *f*
rebuke riprensione; riprendere
rebus rebus *m*
recall revocare
recant ritrattare
recantation ritrattimento
recede recedere   [*m*
receipt   *m*; quitanza
  ricetta *f*
receive ricevere
receiver ricevitore *m*
recent recente; fresco

receptacle ricettacolo m
recite recitare; citare
reckless temerario
reckon contare
reckoning conto m
reclaim riformare
recline inclinarsi
recognition ricognizione f
recognize riconoscere
recoil indietreggiare
recollect riconoscere
recollection ricordanza f
recommend raccomand-
are [andazione f
recommendation raccom-
record registrare; inscrivere; raccontare; rappor-
to; registro m; memoria
f; - s archivi m pl
recourse ricorso m
recover ricuperare
recovery ricupero
recreant poltrone
recreation ricreazione f
recriminate recriminare
recruit recluta f
recumbent giacente
recur ricorrere
recurrence ritorno m
red rosso m; - breast
pettirosso m; - den
arroisre; -ish rossatro;
- -hot rovente; - ness
rossezza f
redeem redimere; liber-
are; mantenere; - able
redimibile [riscatto m
redemption ridenzione f;
reduce ridurre
reduction riduzione f
reed canna f
reel aspo; rocchetto m;
annaspare; barcollare
re-elect rieleggere
re-establish ristabilire
refectory refettorio m
refer riferire; - ee arbitro

m   [erenza f
reference menzione; ref-
refine raffinare; - ry
raffineria f
refresh rinfrescare
refreshment rinfresco m
refrigerator refrigeratore
m
refuge rifugic; asilo m
refusal rifiuto r.
refuse rifiutare; rifiuto m
refute confutare
regenerate rigenerare
regeneration rigenera-
zione f
regent reggente m & f
regiment reggimento m
region regione f
register registro m;
registrare
registrar registratore m
regret rincrescimento m;
rincrescere
regular in regola
regularity regolarità f
regulate regolare
regulation regolamento m
rehearsal prova f
rehearse provare
reign regno m; regnare
reimburse rimborsare
rein redina f
reindeer renna f
reinforce rinforzare
reiterate reiterare
reject rigettare
rejoice giubilare
rejoin raggiungere
relapse ricaduta f; rica-
relate raccontare [dere
related affine; parente
relation relazione f;
parente m & f
relative relativo m
relax rilasciare; mitigare
relaxation m; ricreazione
relay posta f   [f
release liberare; libera-

zione *f*
relegate relegare
relent rallentare
relentless inflessibile
relevant applicabile
reliance fiducia; fede *f*
relief sollievo; aiuto *m*
relieve alleviare; soccor-
religion religione *f* [rere
religious religioso
relinquish rinunziare (a);
  abbandonare
relish gusto *m*; gustare
reluctance riluttanza *f*
reluctant avverso
rely fidarsi
remain restare; rimanere
remainder resto *m*
remark osservazione *f*;
  osservare
remarkable rimarchevole
remedy rimedio *m*; rimi-
  ediare
remember riconoscere
remembrance ricordo *m*
remind rimembrare
reminiscence reminis-
  cenza *f*
remiss negligente
remission remissione *f*
remissness negligenza
remit rimettere
remittance rimessa *f*
remote rimoto
removal trasporto *m*
remove rimuovere
render rendere
renew rinnovare
renewal rinnovamento *m*
renounce rinnegare
renovate rinnovare [*m*
renovation rinnovamento
renown rinomanza; fama
  f [affittare
rent pigione *f*; affitto *m*;
renunciation rinuncia *f*
repair ripara *m*; riparare

repeal revoca *f*; rivocare
repeat ripetere; – edly
  ripetutamente
repel reepingere
repent pentirsi
repentance pentimento *m*
repentant penitente
repetition ripetizione *f*
repine gemere
replace rimettere; sostituire
reply replica; risposta *f*;
  replicare; rispondere
report rapporto; rumore;
  scoppio *m*; rapportare;
  raccontare
repose riposo *m*; riporre
reprehensible riprensibile
represent rappresentare
representation rappresentazione *f*
representative rappresent-
  ante *m* & *f*; rappre-
  sentativo
repress reprimere
reprieve dilazione *f*
reprimand riprensione *f*
  riprendere [tampare
reprint ristampa *f*; ris-
reproach rimprovero *m*;
  rimproverare
reproduce riprodurre
reproof rimprovero *m*
reprove rimproverare
reptile rettile *m*
republic repubblica *f*
republican repubblicano
reputation reputazione *f*
repute reputazione *f*
request richiesta; domanda; richiedere
rescue riscossa; liberazione *f*; salvare; liberare
research ricerca *f*
resemblance rassomigli-

anza *f*

resemble rassomigliare
resent risentire
resentful vendicativo
resentment risentimento
reservation riserva *f* [*m*
reserve riserva *f*; conservare
reservoir serbatoio *m*
reside risedere; abitare
residence residenza *f*; domicilio *m*
resident residente *m & f*
resign rassegnare
resignation rassegnazione *f*
resort ridotto; luogo frequentato *m*; frequentare
resource risorsa *f*
respect rispetto; riguardo; rapporto *m*; guardare; concernere; − **ability** rispettabilità *f*; − **able** rispettabile; − **ful** rispettoso; − **ive** rispettivo
respiration respirazione *f*
respond rispondere
respondent convenuto *m*
response risposta; replica *f*
responsibility responsabilità *f*
responsible responsabile
rest riposo; resto *m*; pace; pausa *f*; riposare; restare
restaurant ristorante *m*
restitution restituzione *f*
restless inquieto
restoration ristoramento *m*; restituzione *f*
restore rendere; restituire; ristorare
restrain reprimere
restraint freno *m*
restrict restringere

restriction restrizione *f*
result risultato *m*; risultare; seguire
resume ripigliare
resurrection risurrezione *f*
retail minuto; dettaglio *m*; vender al minuto; spacciare; − **er** dettagliante *m & f*
retain ritenere
retaliate contraccambiare ; **:etaliation** pariglia
retard ritardare
retire ritirarsi
retirement ritiratezza *f*
return ritorno; rinvio *m*; ritornare; rendere
reveal rivelare
revel festa *f*; festeggiare; **ation** rivelazione *f*;
revenge vendetta *f*; vendicare; − **ful** vendicativo
revenue reddito; fisco *m*
reverend reverendo
reverent riverente
reverse rovescio; disastro *m*; rovesciare; rivocare
review rivista; critica *f*
revise rivedere
revision revisione *f*
revival ravvivamento *m*
revive ravvivare
revoke rivocare
revolt rivolta *f*; rivoltarsi
revolution rivoluzione *f*
revolve rivolgere
revolver rivoltella *f*
reward ricompensa *f*; ricompensare
rheumatic reumatico
rheumatism reumatismo
rhyme rima *f*; rimare
rib costola; balena (ombrello) *f* [cia *f*

ribbon nastro *m*; lettuc-
rice riso *m*
rich ricco; fertile
riches ricchezza *f*
ride cavalcata; passeggiata *f*; cavalcare; passeggiare   [cillo *m*
rider cavallerizzo; codi-
ridge cima *f*; dorso *m*
ridicule ridicolo *m*
rife comune
rifle carabina *f*; spogliare
rigging sartiame *m*
right retto;   diritto;
destro;   bene;   assai;
diritto *m*; giustizia;
– **eous** giusto; – **ly**
bene; giustamente; –
ful legittimo
rind scorza; crosta *f*
ring anello;   cerchio;
suono;   tintinnio   *m*;
suonare;   circondare;
– **leader** caporione *m*
rinse sciacquare   [tuare
riot baccano *m*; tumul-
ripe maturo
ripen maturare
ripple increspatura   *f*;
increspare
rise ascensione; eminenza
f; avanzamento   *m*;
levarsi; sorgere
risk rischio *m*; avven-
rite rito *m*   [turare
rival emulo; competitore
m; rivaleggiare
river fiume *m*   [dire
rivet ribaditura *f*; riba-
road strada;   via *f*;
cammino *m*
roam percorrere
roar ruggito; rombo *m*;
roast arrostire   [ruggire
rob rubare
robber ladro *m*
robbery ruberia *f*

robe toga; roba *f*;
vestire
robust robusto
rock roccia;   rocca *f*;
dondolare; – **er** culla *f*;
roll rotolo; ruolo; registro; rullo (tamburo);
panino *m*; rotolare;
girare; rullare;
romance romanzo *m*
romantic romantico
roof tetto *m*
rook cornacchia *f*; rocco
(scacchi) *m*
room stanza; camera *f*;
spazio *m*; – **y** spazioso
roost pollaio *m*; appollaiarsi
root radice; origine *f*;
fissare; grufolare
rope fune; corda *f*;
rosary rosario *m*
rose rosa *f*
rot putrefazione *f*; in-
fracidire; putrefare
rotate rotare
rotation rotazione *f*;
giro *m*
rotatory rotatorio
rotten putrefatto
rough aspro;   rozzo;
violento; – **ness** ruvidezza *f*
round rotondo; circolare; tondo; cerchio;
giro; rondo *m*; ronda
m; ronda *f*; arroton-
dare
rouse svegliare
rout sconfitta; rotta *f*;
metter in rotta
route via; strada *f*
routine uso *m*
rove errare; viaggiare
row fila; distesa; or-

dine *f*

row baruffa; rissa; cagnara *f*

row remare

royal reale; regale; – ist realista *m* & *f*; – ty dignità reale *f*

rub attrito *m*; fregare

rubber fregatoio *m*; gomma elastica *f*

rubbish robaccia *f*

ruby rosso; rubino *m*

ruffle manichino *m*; increspare; turbare;

rug bigello *m* [disordinare

rugged scabro; ruvido

ruin rovina *f*; desolare

ruinous rovinoso

rule regola; norma *f*; precetto *m*; governare; regolare

ruler reggitore *m*; riga *f*

rum rum *m*

rumble rombare

rumbling rombante rombo *m*

ruminate ruminare

rumour fama *f*

rummage rimuovere

run corsa; durata *f*; correre; fuggire; – away fuggitivo *m* [pere

rupture rottura *f*; rom-

rural rurale; rustico

rush slancio; urto; giunco *m*; lanciarsi; gettarsi; precipitarsi

S

sabbath Sabbato *m*; Domenica *f*

sable nero; zibellino *m*

sacrament sacramento *m*

sacred sacro; santo

sacrifice sacrificio *m*; sacrificare [religio-*m*

sacrilege, sacrilegious sacrad tristo

sadness tristezza *f*

safe sicuro; salvo; cassa forte *f*; guarda-vivande

safety sicurezza *f* [*m*

sagacious sagace

sagacity sagacia *f*

sage saggio; savio *m*; calvia *f* [giare

sail vela; ala *f*; veleg-

sailor marinaio *m*

saint(ly) santo

sake causa *f*

salad insalata *f*

salary salario *m*

sale vendita *f*

salesman venditore *m*

saliva saliva *f*

salmon salmone *m*

saloon salone *m*

salt salato; sale *m*; salare;

salute saluto *m*

salvage salvataggio *m*

salvation salvazione *f*

salve unguento; balsamo

salver vassoio *m* [*m*

same medesimo; stesso

sample mostra *f*

sanctify santificare

sanction sanzione *f*; sanzionare

sanctity santità *f*

sanctuary santuario;

sand sabbia *f* [asilo *m*

sandwich panino gravido *m*; – –man portaffissi *m*

sandy sabbioso

sanguinary sanguinario

sanguine sanguigno

sanity sanità *f*

satellite satellite *m*

satiety sazietà *f*

satin raso *m*

satire satira *f*

satisfaction soddisfazione;

riparazione f
satisfactory soddisfacente
satisfy soddisfare
saturate saturare
sauce salsa f; condimento m; – pan cazzarola f; – r sottocoppa f
saucy impertinente
saunter girandolare
sausage salsiccia f
savage selvaggio
save salvare
saving economo; risparmio m; – s-bank cassa di risparmio f
saviour salvatore m
savoury aporito
saw ega f; proverbio m; segare
scallop petonchio m
scaly squamoso
scamper correre
scandal scandalo m
scandalous scandaloso
scanty scarso
scar cicatrice f
scarce scarso; raro
scarcity scarsezza f
scare spaventare
scarecrow spauracchio m
scarf ciarpa f; velo m
scarlet scarletto m; – fever febbre scarlatina f
scatter spargere
scavenger letamaiolo m
scene(ry) scena f; scenario m   [odorare
scent odore; profumo m;
sceptical scettico
sceptre scettro m
schedule cedola
scheme schema f
scholar scolare m
school scuola f; – fellow compagno di scuola f; – master maestro m

science scienza f
scientific scientifico
scissors forbici m pl; cesoie f pl
scoff beffeggiare
scold sgridare
scoop votazza f
scope scopo m
scorch bruciarsi
score scotto; conto m; segnare
scorn sdegno m; sdegnare; – ful sdegnoso
scoundrel scellerato m
scout spia f
scramble contesa f; sforzo m; arrampicarsi
scrap frammento m
scrape raschiatura; difficoltà f; raschiare
scratch graffio m; graffiare   [scarabocchiare
scrawl scarabocchio m;
scream strido; grido acuto m; stridere
screen parafuoco; paravento m
screw vite f; spilorcio m; invitare; torcere
scribble scarabocchio m; scarabocchiare
scrip sacchetto m; cedola f; azioni f pl
Scripture Scrittura f
scroll ruolo m
scrub fregare fortemente
scruple scrupolo m
scrupulous scrupoloso
scrutinize scrutinare
scrutiny scrutinio m
scuffle zuffa f
scull cranio; remo piatto m; remare
sculptor scultore m
sculpture scultura f
sea mare; oceano m

105

seal foca *f*; sigillare
search ricerca *f*; cercare
sea-sickness mal di mare
season stagione *f*; tempo *m*; stagionare; abituare condire; – able opportuno; – ing condimento
seat sede *f*; banco   [*m*
sea-weed alga *f*
secede separarsi
secluded ritirato
second secondo; secondo *m*; – ary secondario; – -hand di seconda mano; d'occasione; – ly in secondo luogo
secrecy segretezza
secret segreto *m*
secretary segretario *m*
secrete nascondere
secretion secrezione *f*
sect setta *f*
section sezione *f*
secular secolare
secure sicuro; certo
seduction seduzione *f*
seductive seducente
see vescovato *m*; vedere
seed seme *m*
seek cercare
seem sembrare
seemly convenevole
seethe bollire
seize afferrare
seizure presa *f*
seldom raramente
select scelto; eletto; scegliere
selection scelta *f*
self stesso; medesimo; – -denial abnegazione di se stesso *f*; – ish egoista;
send mandare
senior seniore *m*
sensation sensazione *f*
sense senso; intelletto *m*; – less insensato

sensibility sensibilità *f*
sensible sensibile
sensitive sensitivo
sensual sensuale
sensuality sensualità *f*
sentence sentenza *f*
sentiment sentimento *m*
separate separato; separare
separation separazione *f*
sequel sequela *f*
serenade serenata *f*
serene sereno
serenity serenità *f*
series serie; sequela *f*
serious serio
sermon sermone *m*
serpent serpente; serpe *m*
servant domestico *m*
serve servire
service servizio *m*

set fisso; fermo; assortimento; servizio *m*
set mettere; porre
settle panca *f*; sedile *m*; fissare; decidere
settlement regolamento; colonia *f*
seven sette *m*; – fold settuplo; **teen** diciassette *m*; –teenth diciassettesimo *m*; –th settimo *m*; –tieth settantesimo *m*; – ty settanta *m*
sever staccare
several parecchi
severe severo
severity severità *f*
sew cucire
sewer fogna *f*; condotto sotteraneo *m*; – age fognatura *f*
sex sesso *m*
sexton beccamorti *m*
sexual sessuale
shabby mal vestito

shackle incatenare

shad cheppia; laccia *f*

shade ombra; tinta *f*; ombrare

shadow ombra *f*

shake scossa; stretta *f*; trillo *m*; scuotere; agitare

shame vergogna *f*; pudore *m*; svergognare;

shape forma *f*; modello *m*; formare; modellare

share porzione; parte *f*; partecipare (a); distribuire; –holder azionista

sharp acuto; tagliente; acido; – en affilare; mostra;

shatter fracassare

shave radere

shawl scialle *m*

she essa; ella; femmina (d'animali)

sheaf covone; fascio *m*

shear tondere

shears forbici grosse *f pl*

sheath fodero *m*; guiana *f*

shed tettoia *f* [m

sheep pecora *f*; montone

sheet lenzuolo; foglio; specchio (d'acqua) *m*

shelf palchetto; scaffale; scoglio *m*

shell nicchio *m*; bomba *f*; sbaccellare; bombardare

shining rifulgente

ship nave *f*; imbarcare; –ment imbarco *m*; –per speditore *m*; – wreck naufragio *m*

shirt camicia *f*; – ing tela da camici

shiver scheggia *f*; frammento *m*; tremare

shoal poco profondo; frotta; folla *f*

shock cozza *f*; urto *m*; urtare; offendere; – ing ributtante; orrido

shoe scarpa *f*; ferro *m*; ferrare; – –black lustrino *m*; – maker calzolaio *m*

shoot gettone; rampollo *m*; fucilare; lanciare; tirare; – ing tiro *m*

shop bottega *f*; – keeper mercante *m & f*

shore lido *m*; riva *f*

short corto; breve; – coming insufficienza;

shove spinta *f*

shovel pala *f*

show mostra; esposizione *f* mostrare

shower rovescio; nembo

shrewd fino; sagace; –ness astuzia *f*

shriek strido *m*; stridere

shrill acuto

shrimp squilla *f*

shrine reliquario *m*

shrink raggricchiare

shrug stretta di spalle *f*

shudder tremito *m*; fremere [colare

shuffle inganno *m*; mes-

shun evitare

shut chiudere; serrare

shutter anta *f*

shy timido

sick malato; –en rendere infermo; – le roncola *f* – ly malsano; – ness malattia *f*

side lato; canto *m*; – board credenza; – walk marciapiede

sigh sospiro *m*; sospirare

sight vista; veduta *f*; spettacolo *m*; – less cieco

sign segno *m*; segnare

signal segnale; segnalare

signature firma; segnatura *f*;
signify significare
silence silenzio; tacere *m*; far tacere
silent silenzioso
silk seta *f*; – en di seta; serico; – –worm baco *m*
silly sciocco; goffo
silver argento *m*; argenteria *f*; inargentare;
similar simile; similare
similarity similarità *f*
simile similitudine *f*
simple semplice
simplify semplificare
simultaneous simultaneo
sin peccato *m*; peccare
since da; dopo; da chè
sincere sincero
sincerity sincerità *f*
sing cantare; lodare; – er cantante *m* & *f*
singe bruciar leggiermente [celibe *m*
single solo; semplice;
singular singolare
singularity singolarità; rarità *f* [affondare
sink fogna *f*; acquaio *m*;
sinner peccatore *m*
sip sorso *m*; sorseggiare
siphon sifone *m*
sister sorella; monaca *f*; – -in-law cognata *f*;
sit sedere [– ly di sorella
site sito; luogo *m* situazione *f*
situate(d) situato
situation situazione *f*
six sei *m*;
– -teen sedici *m*; – teenth sedicesimo *m*; – th sesto *m*; – thly in sesto *m*; – tieth sessantesimo *m*; – ty sessanta *m*

size grandezza; colla *f*
skate pattino *m*; pattinare
skeleton scheletro *m*
sketch abbozzo; schizzo *m*; abbozzare; schizzare
skewer brocco *m*; schidionare
skid incastratura *f*
skiff palischermo *m*
skilful versato; abile; esperto
skill perizia; destrezza *f*
skim schiumare
skin cute *m*; pelle; buccia *f*; scorticare
sky cielo; firmamento *m* – -light lanterna *f*
slab lastra; tavola *f*
slack allentato
slacken allentare
slake annacquare
slam chidure con violenza
slave schiavo *m*
slavery schiavitù *f*
sleep sonno *m*; dormire;
sleet nevischio *m*
sleeve manica *f*
slender esile
slice fetta; placca *f*; affettare [ciolare
slide sdrucciolo *m*; sdrucciolare
slight tenue; sfregio *m*; negligenza *f*; spregiare
slim svelto
slip passo falso; sbaglio *m*; striscia; scivolare; – shod negletto
slipper pantofola *f*
slippery sdrucciolevole
slit fessura *f*; fendere; fendersi
slope pendio *m*; pendere
sloping pendente
slow lento; tardo

108

sluggard dormiglione *m*
sluggish pigro [nacchiare
slumber sonno *m*; son-
slur afregio *m*
sly astuto; malizioso
smack schiafeo; bacio *m*
small piccolo; minuto;
– **pox** vaiolo *m*
smart vivo; bello
smash fracasso *m*; fran-
tumare
smear imbrattare
smell odore *m*; sentire
smelt eperlano *m*; fondere
smile sorriso *m*; sorridere
smith fabbro *m*   [*m*
smock camicia *f*; saione
smoke fumo *m*; fumare
smoking - compartment,
– **-room** fumatoio *m*
smoky fumoso
smooth piano; liscio;
lisciare
smother soffocare
smuggle contrabbandare;
– **r** contrabbandere *m*
smut fiocco di fuliggine *m*
snail lumaca *f*
snake serpe *m*
snap rottura *f*; fermaglio
m; rompere   [polare
snare trappola *f*; trap-
snarl ringhiare
snatch presa *f*; sforzo
sneak sornione *m*
sneer sogghigno *m*
sneering beffardo
sneeze starnuto *m*; starnutare   [*m*; russare
snore, **snort** russamento
snout grugno; muso *m*
snow neve *f*; nevicare;
– **ball** palla di neve; –
drop foraneve *f*; – **y**
nevoso

snuff tabacco da naso *m*;
smoccolare; fiutare
snuffers smoccolatoio *m*
so cosi; sì; sia
soak ammollare; bagnare
soap sapone *m*
soar alzarsi   [hiozzare
sob singhiozzo *m*; sing-
soft molle; tenero; dolce;
– **en** ammollare; – **ness**
morbidezza *f*
soil suolo *m*; macchiare
sojourn soggiorno *m*
solace sollievo *m*; con-
solder saldare   [solare
soldier soldato *m*
sole pianta; soglia *f*;
solo; unico
solemn solenne
solemnity solennità *f*
solicit sollecitare
solicitor avvocato *m*
solid solido
soliloquy soliloquio *m*
solitary solitario; isolato
solution coluzione *f*
solve risolvere
solvency solvibilità *f*
some qualche; alcuno;
certi *pl*; circa; del;
– **body** qualcuno; – **how**
in qualche modo; –
thing qualche cosa *f*;
un che *m*; – **times**
qualche volta; – **what**
un poco; alquanto *m*;
– **where** in qualche
luogo   [genero *m*
son figlio *m*; – **-in-law**
song canto *m*
soon tosto; presto
soot fuliggine *f*
sorcery stregoneria *f*
sordid sordido
sore doloroso; ulcera *f*
sorrow dolore *m*;

sorry tristo; dolente;
sort sorta; specie *f*;
 classificare
soul anima *f*; spirito *m*
sound sano; valido;
 suono *m*; snoare
soup zuppa *f*
sour agro; acido
source fonte; origine *f*
south sud *m*; – erly del
 sud; meridionale
souvenir ricordo *m*
sovereign sovrano
space spazio *m*
spacious spazioso
spade vanga; picca (carte)
span spanna *f* [*f*
spaniel cane spagnuolo *m*
spar pertica *f*; alberetto
 m [magro
spare parco; frugale;
sparing economico
spark scintilla *f*
sparkle scintillare
sparrow passero *m*
spasm spasmo *m*
spawn fregola *f*; uova *f pl*
speak parlare [tore *m*
speaker favellatore; ora-
spear lancia ; asta *f*
special speciale
speciality specialità *f*
specie moneta contante *f*
species specie; classe *f*

specific specifico *m*
specification specifica-
 zione *f*
specify specificare
specimen esemplare *m*

speculate speculare
speech parola; favella *f*;
 – **less** senza parola
peed fretta; rapidità *f*;
 affrettare; – **y** rapido;
 pronto; celere
spell incanto; tempo *m*;

compitare
spend spendere
spendthr It prodigo *m*
sphere sfera *f*; globo *m*
spice spezie *f pl*
spider ragno *m*
spike spiga *f*; inchiodare
spill versare
spin filare
spinach spinaccie *f pl*
spindle fuso *m*
spine spina *f*
spinster zitella *f*
spiral spirale
spire guglia *f*
spirit spirito; coraggio;
 brio *m*; – **ed** spiritoso;
 – **less** senza spirito;
 – **ual** spirituale; – **uou**
 spiritoso
spit schidione *m*; sputare
sponge spugna *f*
spongy spugnoso
spontaneous spontaneo
spoon cucchiaio *m*
spoonful cucchiaiata *f*
sport trastullo; giuoco *m*
 – **ive** festevole; – **sman**
 amatore delle corse
spot macchia *f*; punto *m*;
 macchiare
spotless immacolato
spout doccia; tromba *f*
sprain storta *f*; storcere
sprat palamita *f*
sprawl stendersi
spray fresca; schiuma *f*
spread stendere
spring fontana; sorgente;
 molla *f*; lancio; sbalzo
 m; scaturire; proce-
 dere; sorgere; – **y** elas-
sprinkle spargere [tico
sprout germoglio; broccolo *m*; germogliare
spy spia *f*; spiare
squadron squadra *f*

square quadrato; pari. quadro *m*; piazza *f*; quadrare; bilanciare
squeak strillo *m*; cigolare
squeamish fastidioso
squeeze serrare
squint esser guercio
squirrel scoiattolo *m*
squirt siringa *f*; siringare
stab stillettare
stability stabilità *f*
stable stabile; scuderia *f*
stack mucchio *m*; am-mucchiare
staff bastone *m*
stag cervo *m*
stage palco; treatro *m*
stagger barcollare
stain macchia; tinta *f*; macchiare; tingere;
staircase, stairs scala *f*
stake palo; premio *m*; posta *f*
stale stantio; vecchio
stamp stampa; marca *f*; francobollo; punzone *m*; stampare; imprimere
stand posto; banco *m* resistenza *f*; stare; sostenere [bandiera *f*
standard di norma;
staple principale; ram-pone
star stella *f*; astro *m*
starch amido *m*; inami-dare [dentemente
stare guardare impu-
start scossa *f*; motto involuntario
start trasalire; partire
startle trasalire
starvation inedia; fame;
starve affamare
state stato ; *m*; con-dizione; pompa *f*;

111

dire; constatare; – **ly** maestoso; – **ment** rap-porto *m*; – **sman** sta-tista; politico *m*
stay soggiorno *m*
stay soggiornare; stare
stead vece *f*; luogo *m*; – **fast** fermo; – **iness** fermezza *f*; – **y** fermo
steak fetta di carne *f*
steal rubare [di soppiato
stealth segreto *m*; by – **stealthy** furtivo; fatto di soppiatto
steam vapore; fumo *m*; fumare; – **boat** battello a vapore *m*; – **-engine** macchina a vapore *f*
steel acciaio *m*
steep erto; scosceso
steep immollare
steeple campanile *m*
steer manzo *m*; gover-nare; – **sman** timoniere
stem stelo; ceppa; tron-co *m*; prua *f*; arrestare
step passo; gradino *m*; – **-brother** fratellastro *m*; – **-daughter** figlia-stra *f*; – **-father** patrigno *m*; – **-mother** matrigna *f*; – **ping-stone** passa-toio *m*; – **-sister** sorel-lastra *f*; – **-son** figlia-stro *m*
stern severo; poppa *f*
stew stufato *m*; stufare
steward fattore *m*
stick mazza; bacchetta *f*; aderire; incollare; – **y** glutinoso
stiff rigido; ostinato; – **en** indurire; – **ness**
stifle soffocare [rigidezza *f*
stile barriera *f*
still sereno; immobile,

pertanto; lambicco *m*;
quetare; calmare
stimulant stimolante *m*
stimulate stimolare
sting morsicatura *f*
stingy meschino
stink fetore *m*; puzzare
stipulate stipulare
stir moto *m*; muovere;
stock tronco; blocco;
capitale *m*; fornire;
– **broker** agente di cam-
stocking calza *f* [bio *m*
stomach stomaco *m*
stone pietra *f*; sasso *m*;
lapidare; – **y** pietroso
stool scranna; seggetta *f*
stoop inclinazione *f*;
piegare
stop fermata; posa *f*;
fermare; arrestare
stopper turacciolo *m*
store provvigione; riserva
f; magazzino *m*; ap-
provvigionare; accu-
mulare
stork cicogna *f*
storm temporale *m*;
burrasca *f*; – **y** tempestoso [*m*; bugia *f*
story storia *f*; racconto
stout grassotto
stove stufa *f*; fornello *m*
straight diritto
strain sforzo *m*; tensione *f*; sforzare; colare;
strange strano
stranger straniero *m*
strangle strangolare
strawberry fragola *f*

stray smarrire; vagare
streak screziatura *f*;
screziare
stream corrente; corso *m*
street via; strada *f*
strength forza *f*; vigore *m*
– **en** rinforzare

strenuous vigoroso
stress forza *f*
stretch tensione; estensione *f*; stendere
strike battere; colpire
string corda *f*; stringa *f*
stringent stringente; duro
strip denudare
stripe striscia *f*; rigare
strive contendere
stroke botta *f*
stroll girata *f*; girare
strong forte; vigoroso
stubborn ostinato
stud bottoncino *m*
student studente *m*
studious studioso; stu-
study studio *m* [diare
stuff stoffa; imbottire
stumble inciampare
stump moncone *m*
stun stordire
stupefy stupefare
stupendous stupendo
stupid stupido
stupor stupore *m*
sturdy tarchiato
stutter balbettare
style maniera *f*; stile *m*
subdue soggiogare
subject soggetto
sublime sublime
submerge sommergere
submersion sommersione
submission sommessione

subside abbassarsi
subsidy sussidio *m*
subsist sussistere
subsistence sussistenza
substance sostanza *f*
substantial sostanziale
substantiate provare
substantive sostantivo *m*
substitute sostituto *m*;
sostituire
subtle sottile
subtract sottrarre

112

subtraction sottrazione *f*
suburb sobborgo *m*
subvert sovvertire
succeed succedere
success successo; – ful
felice; fortunato; – ion
successione; serie *f*;
– ive successivo; con
secutivo;
suck succhiare
sucker pollone; rampollo
suckle allattare [*m*
sudden subito
sue processare
suet grasso (bove) *m*
suffer soffrire; – er vittima *f*; – ing pena *f*
suffice bastare
sufficient sufficiente
suffocate soffocare
sugar zucchero *m*
sugary zuccheroso
suggest suggerire
suggestion suggestione *f*
suicide suicidio *m*
suit assortimento *m*;
convenire; adattare;
– able convenevole; – or
postulante *m*
sum somma *f*; sommare;
– mary sommario *m*;
– mer estate; state; *f*;
– mit cima *f*; – mon
convocare; citare; –
mons chiamata *f*;
– ptuous suntuoso
sun sole *m*
sundry diversi
sunny solatio
sunrise il levar del sole *m*
sunset tramonto del sole
m
sunshine luce del sole *f*
superintend sorvegliare
superintendent direttore
m

superoir superiore *m & f*
– ity superiorità *f*
superlative superlativo
supernatural sopranatu-
rale
supersede sostituire [*f*
superstition superstizione
superstitious superstizioso
supervise sorvegliare
supervisor sopraintend-
supper cena *f* [ente *m*
supplant soppiantare
supple flessibile
supplement supplemento
m; aumentare
supplementary supple-
mentare [*& f*
supplicant supplicante *m*
supplicate supplicare
supply provvigione *f*;
assortimento *m*; prov-
vedere; approvvigion-
are
support sostegno *m*;
sostenere; – able sup-
portabile
suppose supporre
supposition supposizione *f*
suppress sopprimere
suppression soppressione
f
supremacy supremazia *f*
supreme supremo
surcharge sopraccaricare
sure sicuro; certo
surety sicurezza *f*; gar-
ante *m & f* [spuma *f*
surf cavalloni *m pl*;
surmise congettura *f*;
congetturare
surmount sormontare
surname cognome *m*
surpass sorpassare
surplus soprappiù *m*
surprise sorpresa *f*; sorprendere

113

surround circondare
survey eǎame *m*; vista *f*
  esaminare; misurare
surveyor agrimensore *m*
survive sopravvivere
susceptibility suscettibili-
  tà *f*
susceptible suscettibile
suspect sospettare
suspend sospendere
suspense sospensione *f*
suspicion sospetto *m*
suspicious sospettoso
sustain sostenere
sustenance alimento *m*
suzerainty signoria *f*
swagger vantarsi
swallow rondine *m*; gola
  f; inghiottire
swamp palude *f*
sway brandire; dominare
swear giurare; testificare
sweat sudore *m*; sudare
sweep spazzacamino *m*;
  spazzare; – ings spaz-
  zatura *f*
sweet dolce; amabile;
swell enfiare; gonfiare;
  crescere; ingrandire; en-
  fiarsi
swelling gonfiamento *m*
swerve sviarsi
swift rapido; celere
swiftness rapidezza *f*
swim nuotare
swindle truffa *f*; truffare
swing oscillamento; dondolo *m*; branda *f*; dondolare
sword spada *f*
sworn giurato
sycamore sicomoro *m*
syllable sillaba *f*
symbol simbolo *m*
symmetry simmetria *f*
sympathetic simpatico
sympathise simpatizzare

sympathy simpatia *f*
symphony sinfonia *f*
symptom sintomo *m*
syndicate sindicato *m*
synthesis sinthesi *f*
syphilis sifilide *f*
syphon sifone *f*   [ase
syringe siringa *f*; siring-
syrup sciroppo *m*
system sistema *m* – atical
  sistematico; – atically
  sistematicamente

T

tabernacle tabernacolo *m*
table tavola; lista *f*
  -cloth   tovaglia *f*;
tack bulletta; amura;
  bordata: attaccare;
  appiccare
tackle girella *f*; attiraglio
  m; attaccare; pigliare
tact tatto *m*
tail coda *f*
tailor sarto *m*
taint macchia; infettare
take prendere
talent talento *m*
talented dotato
talk parlare *m*; parlare
talkative loquace
tall alto; grande
tame domestico; domare
tamer domatore *m*
tamper subornare
tan concia *f*; bruciare
tangible tangibile
tank cisterna *f*
tanner conciaiolo *m*
tantalize tantaleggiare
tap chiave; cannella *f*;
  colpo leggiero *m*
tape cordellina *f*; – r cero
  m; terminarsi in punta;
  – ring conico; – stry tap-

pezzeria *f;* – **worm**
verme solitario *m*
tar catrame *m;* pece *f;*
catramare
tarantula tarantola *f*
tardy lento; tardivo
tare tara *f*
tardiness lentezza *f*
target bersaglio *m*
tariff tariffa *f*
taste gusto; sapore *m;*
inclinazione *f;* gustare;
– **ful** gustoso; elegante;
– **less** senza gusto
tasty di buon gusto
tatter straccio *m*
tattle ciancia *f;* cianciare
tattoo ritirata *f;* screziare
taunt insulto *m;* insultare
tavern osteria; taverna *f*
tawdry di lustro falso
tawny olivastro
tax tassa *f;* imposta *f;*
tassare; accusare –
ation tassazione *f*
tea tè *m;* – **kettle** cogoma
f; – **things** servizio da tè
teach insegnare; istruire;
– **er** maestro; istitutore
m; – **ing** insegnamento
team fila *f* . [*m*
tear lagrima *f;* – **s** pianto
m; stracciatura *f;*
stracciare; lacerare
tease seccare; importunare
telegram telegramma *m*
telegraph telegrafo *m;*
telegrafare
telephone telefono *m;*
telefonare
telescope telescopio *m*
tell dire; raccontare
temper tempera; collera
f; temperare; mescolare
temperance temperanza *f*
temperate sobrio [*f*

temperature temperatura
tempest tempesta *f*
tempestuous tempestoso
temple tempio *m*

tempt tentare
temptation tentazione *f*
tempter tentatore *m*
ten dieci *m*
tend custodire; tendere
tendency tendenza *f*
tender tenero; dolce;
offerta *f;* offerire; – **ness**
tenerezza; cura *f*
tennis – **court** palla-
corda *f*
tenor tenore; senso' *m*
tense rigido; tempo *m*
tension tensione *f*
tent tenda *f;* padiglione
tenth decimo *m* [*m*
term termine; semestre
m; durata *f*
terminate terminare [*f*
termination terminazione
terrace terrazzo *m*
terrible terribile
terrier bassotto *m*
terrific spaventevole
terrify atterrire
territory territorio *m*
terror terrore *m*
terse terso; lindo
test saggio *m;* prova *f;*
provare
testament testamento *m*
testicle testicolo *m*
testify attestare [*f*
testimonial testimonianza
testimony testimonianza *f*
testy ringhioso
tether pastoia *f;* impas-
text testo *m* [toiare
textile fessile
texture tessitura *f;* tes-
than che; di [suto *m*
thank ringraziare; – **ful**

grato; – **fulness** riconoscenza *f*; – **less** ingrato; – **s** grazie *f pl*

that quello; quella; ciò; sia; che; perche; che; il quale; la quale; chi; quegli; colui

the il; lo; la; i; gli; le

theatre teatro *m*; scena *f*

theatrical teatrale

thee te; ti

theft furbo *m*

their. – **s** il loro; la loro; i loro; le loro

them li; le; loro; essi

themselves si; se stessi

theme tema *m*

then allora; poi; dunque

there li; là; vi; ci; ivi: – **is** c'è; ecco – **about** là intorno; – **after** dopo ciò; – **by** da ciò; – **fore** quindi; perciò; – **from** da ciò; – **in** in ciò; entro; – **on** su di ciò; – **with** con ciò   [*m*

thermometer termometro

these questi; queste

they essi; esse; loro

thick spesso; grosso

thicken spessire; raddoppiare; oscurarsi

thief ladro *m*

thieve rubare

thievish da ladro

thigh coscia *f*

thimble ditale *m*

thin sottile; magro; assottigliare

thine il tuo; la tua ; i

thing cosa *f* [tuoi; le tue

think pensare

third terzo *m*

thirst sete *f*

thirsty assetato

thirteen tredici *m*

thirty trenta *m*

this questo

thorough fondato; completo;

though sebbene; benchè

thought pensiero *m*; idea *f*; – **ful** pensieroso; – **less** spensierato; –

thousand mille *m*

thrash trebbiare

thrashing bastonata *f*;

thread filo; refe *m*; infilare;

threat minaccia *f*

threaten minacciare

three tre *m*

thrift economia *f*

thrifty frugale   [tare

thrill sussulto *m*; sussu-

thrilling toccante

thrive prosperare

throat gola; strozza *f*

throb palpitare

throne trono *m*

through attraverso; per – **out** in ogni parte

throw getto; colpo *m*; gettare; lanciare

thrush tordo *m*

thrust spinta *f*; spingere

thumb pollice *m*

thunder tuono *m*; fulminare; – **bolt** fulmine

thus cosi; in questo modo

thwart attraversare

tide marea *f*

tidy pulito

tie legame *m*; cravata *f*;

tier rango *m*   [legare

tiger tigre *m*

tight tirato; serrato; – **en** stringere; – **ness** strettezza *f*; – **s** calzoni

tile tegola *f*   [*m pl*

till cassa *f* coltivare

timber legname *m*;

time tempo *m*; epoca *f*

timely opportuno

timid timido

tin stagno m; latta f; stagnare

tincture tintura; tinta f

tinge tingere

tingle pizzicare [tinnire

tinkle tintinno ; tin-

tinsel orpello m

tint tinta f; tingere

tiny piccino

tip punta f; regalo m:

tire cerchio m; stancare

tiresome seccante

tissue tessuto m

tissue paper carta velina f

tit ronzino m

tithe decima f

title titolo; nome m; intitolare [nare

titter risolino m; sogghig-to a; verso; su; per

toad rospo m

toast pane abbrustolita f; brindisi m; abbrustolire;

to-day oggi

toe dito (del piede) m

together insieme

toil pena f; travagliare

toilet toeletta f

token segno m

tolerable tollerabile

tolerant tollerante

tolerate tollerare

toleration tolleranza f

toll pedaggio m; rintoc-care

tomato pomidoro m

tomb tomba f

tomb-stone lapide m

ton tonnellata f [= 1015 kilogrammes)

tone tono; suono m

tongs molle f pl

tongue lingua f; linguag-tonic tonico m [gio m

to-night stanotte

tonsil tonsilla f

tonsure tonsura f

too troppo; anche

tool arnese; strumento m

tooth dente m; --ache mal di denti m;

torch torcia f

torment tormento m; tormentare [m

tormentor tormentatore

tornado uragano m

torpedo torpedine m

torture tortura f; tor-turare

toss trabalzare; lanciare

total totale m

touch tatto; contatto m; toccare; - stone pietra di paragone

touching toccante

tough tenace

toughness durezza f

tour giro; viaggio m; - ist viaggiatore m [m

tournament torneamento

tow stoppa f; rimorchiare

towards verso; per; a

towel tovagliolo m

tower torre f; torreggiare; dominare

town città f; borgo m; --hall casa della città f

toy giocattolo m; giocol-are

trace traccia f; vestigio m; tirella f; tracciare

track traccia; marca f; tracciare [regione f

tract trattatello m

trade commercio; nego-zio; m; negoziare; - ing mercantile; mercatura f -r mercante m

tradition tradizione f

traffic traffico m; traffi-care

tragedy tragedia f

tragic(al) tragico

117

trail traccia *f*; strascinare
train treno *m*; addestrare; istruire
trait tratto *m*
traitor traditore *m*
tranquil tranquillo
tranquillize calmare
transact negoziare
transaction transazione *f*
transcribe trascrivere
transfer trasporto *m*; trasferire
transferable trasferibile
transformation trasformazione *f*   [violare
transgress trasgredire;
transgressor trasgressore; peccatore *m*
transient passeggiero
transitory transitorio
translate tradurre
translation traduzione *f*
transmission trasmissione *f*
transmit trasmettere   [*f*
transparent trasparente
transpire traspirare
transplant trapiantare
transport trasporto *m*; trasportare; deportare
transpose trasporre
trap trappola *f*; carozza *f*; trappolare; - -door botola; *f* – pings livrea *f*
travel viaggio *m*; viaggiare; – ler viaggiatore; commesso *m*
traverse taversare
tray vassoio *m*
treacherous perfido
treachery tradimento *m*
treason tradimento *m*
treasure tesoro *m*; tesoreggiare; ammassare; – r tesoriere *m*
treasury tesoreria *f*
treat regalo *m*; cosa squisita *f*; trattare;

tree albero *m*
tremble tremare; fremere
tremendous tremendo
tremor tremore *m*
trench trincea *f*; fosso *m*; trincerare
trepidation trepidazione *f*
trespass peccato; trapasso *m*; trasgredire
triangular triangolare
tribe tribù; orda *f*
tribunal tribunale *m*
tributary tributario *m*
tribute tributo *m*
trick tiro *m*
trickery birbonata *f*
tricycle triciclo *m*
trigger grilletto *m*
trill trillo *m*; trillare
trim lindo; parare; guarnire
trinity trinità *f*
trinket ciondolo *m*
trip inciampo *m*; gita *f*; inciampare
tripe trippa *f*
triple triplo
triumph trionfo *m*;
trivial triviale
trombone trombone *m*
troop truppa; banda *f*; – er soldato di cavalleria *m*
trophy trofeo *m*
tropical tropicale
tropics tropici *m* *pl*
trot trotto *m*; trottare
trouble pena *f*; molestare; – some seccante
trough truogolo *m*
trousers pantaloni *m* *pl*
trousseau scherpa *f*
trout trota *f*
trowel cazzuolo *f*
truant pigro *m*
truce tregua *f*
truck carretta *f*

118

truculent truce; feroce

trudge marciare con fatica [cero

true vero; verace; sin-

trunk tronco m; pro-boscide f (d'elefante)
— **-maker** cofanaio m

trust fiducia; fede f; credito m; fidare; credere a; — **ee** deposi-tario m; — **worthy** fido; fidato [verace

truth verità f; — **ful**

try tentare; provare

tub tino m

tube tubo m

tug stiracchiamento m; rimorchiatore m; stir-richiare

tune tono m; aria f; accordare; — **ful** armo-

tunnel galleria f [nioso

turbot rombo m

turbulent turbolento

turf erba; torba f

turkey tacchino; pollo d'India m

turmoil imbroglio m

turn giro m; girare; volgere; — **er** tornitore m; — **ing** giro m; — **ing**-

turquoise turchese f

turret torricella f

turtle tortora f

tusk zanna f

twang suono acuto m; pronunzia nasale f

tweezers pinzette f pl

twelfth duodecimo m

twelve dodici m

twentieth ventesimo m

twenty venti m

twice due volte; doppia-

twig virghetta f [mente

twilight crepuscolo m

twin gemello m [chiare

twine spago m; avvitic-

twinge spasimo m

twinkle scintillare

twirl girar rapidamente

twist torcitura f; tor-

twitter garrire [cere

two due m

typhus tifo m

typical tipico

typography tipografia f

tyrannize tiranneggiare

tyranny tirannia f

tyrant tiranno m

U

ubiquitous onnipresente

ubiquity ubiquità f

udder tetta; poppa (animale)

ugliness laidezza f

ugly bruto; laido

ultramarine oltremarino

umbrage ombra f [m

umber terra d'ombra f

umbrella ombrella f; — **-stand** posaombrelle m

umpire arbitro m

unabashed non confuso

unable incapace [bile

unacceptable inaccetta-

unaccountable inespli-cabile [tuato

unaccustomed poco abi-

unacquainted ignaro (di)

unadorned disadorno

unadvisable imprudente

unaffected sincero

unaided senz'assistenza

unalterable inalterabile

unaltered non alterato

unanimity unanimità f

unanimous unanime

unanswerable incon-

unapt inetto [testabile
unarmed senza armi
unashamed senza vergogna
unasked non richiesto
unassuming senza pretesa
unattainable fuori mano
unattended solo [ente
unattractive poco attra-
unavailing inefficace
unavoidable inevitabile
unaware non avvertito;
 – s all'improvviso
unbecoming disdicevole
unbelief incredulità f
unbeliever infidele m & f
unburden scaricare; aprisi
unbutton sbottonare
unceremonious senza cer-
monie
uncertain incerto
uncertainty incertezza f
unchangeable immutabile
unchristian poco cristiano
uncivil incivile
uncivilized barbaro
uncle zio m
uncomfortable incomodo
uncommon non comune
unconcern indifferenza f
unconcerned indifferente
unconnected non connesso
unconscionable irragione-
vole
unconscious inconscio
unconstrained libero
uncontrollable incontrol-
uncork stappare [labile
uncouth goffo; bizzarro
uncover scoprire; svelare
undefinable indefinibile
undefined indefinito
undeniable innegabile
under sotto; al di sotto
underbid offerire meno
underdone poco cotto

undergo subire
underground sotterraneo
underhand sottomano
underline sottolineare
understanding compren-
sione f; accordo m
undertake intraprendere
undertaker impresario (di
pompe funebri) m
undertaking intrapren-
denza f [di
undervalue far poco conto
underwrite assicurare m
underwriter assicuratore
undeserved immeritato
undesirable da non
desiderarsi
undetermined indeciso
undignified senza dignità
undisciplined indiscipli-
nato [cherato
undisguised non mas-
undisturbed tranquillo
undivided indiviso
undo disfare
undoubted indubbio
undress abito di camera
m; svestirsi
undressed non vestito
undue indebito
undulation ondulazione f
uneasiness inquietudine f
uneasy inquieto
uneducated non educato
unemployed disoccupato
uneven ineguale
unexpected inaspettato
unfailing infallibile
unfair non equo
unfaithful infido
unfasten slegare [bile
unfathomable impenetra-
unfavourable sfavorevole
unfeeling insensibile
unfeigned sincero
unfinished incompleto
unfit inetto

120

unfold spiegare
unforeseen impreveduto
unforgiving implacabile
unfortunate sfortunato
unfounded infondato
unfriendly non amichevole
unfruitful infruttuoso
unfurl spiegare   [ato
unfurnished non mobiliungenerous ingeneroso
ungrateful ingrato
unguarded sconsiderato
unhappiness miseria f
unhappy infelice
unharness levaregli arnesi
unhealthy malsano
unheard inaudito
uniform uniforme; uniforme f
unimaginable inimmaginabile   [tante
unimportant poco importunion unione
unique unico
unison unisono m
unit unità f
unite unire
unity unità f
universal universale
universe universo m
university università f
unjust ingiusto
unjustifiable ingiustificabile
unkind non benigno
unknown incognito
unlace slacciare
unlawful illegale
unlearned illetterato
unless meno chè; fuorché
unlike dissimile
unlikely improbabile
unlimited illimitato
unload scaricare
unlock aprire

unloose slegare
unlucky sfortunata
unmanageable intrattabile
unmanly effeminato
unmannerly mal creato
unmarried celibe
unmeaning insensato
unmerciful inumano
unmindful immemore
unmixed puro
unmoved immoto
unnatural non naturale
unnecessary non necessario
unnoticed inosservato
unoccupied disoccupato
unoffending innocente
unpack sballare
unpaid non pagato [gusto
unpalatable sgradevole al
unparalleled incomparabile   [abile
unpardonable imperdonunpleasant spiacevole
unpolished rozzo
unpopular impopolare
unprepared impreparato
unprincipled senza principii
unproductive infruttuoso
unprofitable inutile
unreasonable irragionevole   [ciliabile
unreconcilable irreconunrelenting inesorabile
unreliable indegno di fiducia   [franco
unreserved senza riserva;
unsalable invendibile
unsatisfactory non soddisfacente
unsavoury non saporito
unscrew svitare
unseasonable fuori di stagione; intempestivo

unserviceable inutile
unsettle dissestare
unsettled disestato
unshaken fermo
unsightly difforme
unskilful inesperto
unskilled imperito
unsociable insociabile
unsold invenduto
unspeakable indicibile
unstable instabile; incostante
unsteady mal fermo
unsuccessful non riuscito
unsuitable disadatto
untidy non pulito
untie snodare [che
until sino a che; tanto
untrained inesercitato
untried non provato
untrue falso; sleale
untwist strigare
unusual insolito
unveil rilevare [rizzato
unwarranted non autounwary incauto
unwearied indefesso
unwelcome mal accolto
unwell non bene
unwholesome malsano
unwieldy pesante
unwilling mal disposto
unwind annaspare
unwise mal accorto
unwonted insolito
unworthy indegno
unwrap scoprire
unyielding inflessibile
up su; sopra; sopra di;
uphill difficile [in alto
uphold sostenere
upholsterer tappezziere m
uplift elevare
upon sopra
upper superiore; più alto
uproar tumulto m
uproot sradicare

upset capovolgere
upside-down sossopra
upstart spaccone m
upwards su; in su; in alto; più (di)
urge stimolare
urgency urgenza
urgent urgente
urine urina f
urn urna f
us ci; ce; ne; noi
usage uso
use uso m; usare; - ful utile; - fulness utilità f; - less inutile; - lessness inutilità f
usual usuale
utensil utensile m
utility utilità f
utmost estremo [ciare
utter assoluto; pronunutterance pronunzia f
utterly totalmente

V

vacancy vacanza f; spazio vuoto m
vacant vacante
vacate lasciar vacante
vacation vacanza f
vaccinate vaccinare [f
vaccination vaccinazione
valet valetto; giovano servitore m
valiant valoroso
valid valido
validity validità f
valour valore m
valuable prezioso
valuation valutazione f
value valore; prezzo m; valutare; - d valutato; - less senza valore
valve valvola f
vamp rappezzare

122

vampire vampiro
van carrettone m; avan-
guardia f
vane banderuola f
vandalism vandalismo m
vanilla vaniglia f

vanish svanire
vanity vanità f
vanquish vincere
vantage vantaggio m
variable variabile
variableness variabilità f
variance variazione f
variation variazione f
varied variato
variegate variare
variety varietà f
various vario; diverso
varnish vernice f; verni-
ciare
vary variare
vase vaso m
vault volta f; salto m;
volteggiare
veal vitello m
veer girare   [gume m
vegetable vegetabile; le-
vegetate vegetare
vegetation vegetazione f
vehemence veemenza f
vehement veemente
vehicle veicolo m
veil velo m; velare
vein vena f
velocity velocità f
velvet velluto m
vendor venditore m
venereal venereo
vengeance vendetta f
vengeful vendicativo
venison selvaggina f
venom veleno m
venomous velenoso
vent vento; sbocco m;
sfogare; - ilate ventilare
- ilation ventilazione f;

– riloquist ventriloquo m
venture ventura f; av-
venturare;
verb verbo m
verbal verbale; orale
verdict verditto m
verdigris verdame m
verdure verdume m
verge bordo; orlo m;
tendere verso
verification verificazione f
verify verificare
verily in verità
veritable vro; attuale
verity verità f
vespers vespri m pl
vessel vaso; vascello m
vest camiciola f; veste f

vestige vestigio m
vestment vestito m
vestry vestiario m; sac-
ristia f
veteran veterano m
veterinary veterinario m
veto veto m
vex irritare   [f
vexation vessazione; noia
vexatious vessante
vial caraffina f
viands vivanda f
vibrate vibrare
vibration vibrazione f
vicar vicario m
vice vizio m; morsa f;
– -admiral vice-ammir-
aglio m; – roy vicerè m
vicious vizioso
vicissitude vicissitudine f
victim vittima f
view vista f; guardare
vigilance vigilanza f
vigilant vigilante
vigorous vigoroso
vigour vigore m
vile vile
vilify avvilire
villa villa f

village villaggio *m*
villager villico *m*
villain scellerato *m*
villainous villano
villainy scelleratezza *f*
vindicate difendere   [*f*
vindication giustificazione
vindictive vendicativo;
 − **ness** carattere vendicativo *m*
vine vite; vigna *f*
vinegar aceto *m*
vineyard vigna *f*
vinous vinoso
vintage vendemmia *f*
viol viola *f*
violate violare
violation violazione *f*
violence violenza *f*
violent violento
violet viola *f*
violin violino *m*
violinist violinista *m & f*
violoncello violoncello *m*
viper vipera *f*
virago virago *f*
virgin vergine *f*
virginity verginità *f*
virtual virtuale
virtue virtù *f*
virtuous virtuoso
virulent virulento
visage viso *m*
viscera viscere *f. pl*
viscount visconte *m*
viscous viscoso
visible visibile
vision visione; vista *f*;
 − **ary** visionario
visit visita *f*; giro *m*;
 visitare;
vital vitale
vivacious vivace [zione]
vivacity vivacità *f*
vivid vivo
vocabulary vocabolario *m*
vocal vocale

voice voce *f*
void vuoto; vacuo *m*
volatile volatile
volcanic vulcanico
volcano vulcano *m*
volley scarica; salva *f*
volt vólta *f*
volubility volubilità *f*
voluble volubile   [*f*
volume volume *m*: massa
vomit vomitare *f*
vote voto; suffraggio *m*;
 votare; − **r** votante
vouch attestare;
vow voto *m*; giurare
vowel vocale *f*
voyage viaggio *m*
vulgar volgare
vulgarity volgarità *f*
vulnerable vulnerabile

voluminous voluminoso
voluntary volontario
volunteer volontario *m*;
 offrire
voluptuous voluttuoso,
 − **ness** voluttà *f*

W

wabble esitare; vacillare
wad fascio di paglia;
 mettere lo stopaccio;
 − **ding** ovatta *f*; − **dle**
 ciondolare
wade guadare
wafer cialda; ostia *f*
wag piacevolone *m*; scuotere
wage scommettere; − **r**
 scommessa *f*; scommettere; − **s** salario *m*
waist vita *f*; busto *m*;
 − **band** cintura *m*;
 − **coat** gilè *m*
wait aspettare; − **er**
 garzone *m*; − **ing** attesa

124

wake seguito *m*; veglia *f*;
funerale *m*; svegliarsi;
– **ful** vigilante; – **n** svegliare   [*f*; camminare
walk camminata; strada
wail muro *m*
waltz valzer; *m* ballar il
wan smorto   [valzer
wand bacchetta *f*
wander vagare; – **er** gir-
ovago *m*; – **ing** errante
wane decadenza *f*; declinare
want mancanza *f*; bisogno *m*; indigenza *f*;
mancare; aver bisogno
di   [zioso
wanton sboccato; licen-
war guerra *f*; far guerra
warble trillare
ward guardia *f*; rione;
pupillo *m*;   parare;
proteggere; – – **er** guardiano *m*; – **robe** guarda-
roba *f*
ware mercanzia *f*
warehouse magazzino *m*;
immagazzinare
warm caldo; vivo; scaldare
warmth caldo; ardore *m*
warn avvertire
warning avviso; avverti-
mento *m*   [torcere
warp far piegare; con-
warrant mandato *m*;
garanzia *f*; autorizzare;
garantire;
wart porro *m*
wary avveduto
wash lavatura; lozione *f*;
lavare; bagnare; – **up**
rigovernare; – **erwoman**
lavandaia *f*;   – **ing**
bucato *m*; lavanda *f*;
wasp vespa *f*

waste incolto; inutile;
sciupio; scialacquo *m*;
perdita; spesa inutile;
terra incolta *f*; deserto;
scarto   *m*;   sciupare;
prodigare; devastare;
sperperare;
watch veglia *f*; orologio
m; vigilare; sorvegliare;
– **ful** vigilante; – **fulness**
vigilanza; – **maker** oro-
logiaio *m*; – **man** guardia notturna *f*; – **word**
parola d'ordine *f*
water acqua *f*; adacquare
– **fall** cascata *f*; – **fowl**
uccello acquatico; – **ing-
place** i bagni *m pl*;
– **ing-pot** annaffiatoio *m*;
– – **jug** mesciacqua *f*;
– – **lily** ninfea *f*; – **proof**
impermeabile   *m*;   –
wave onda *f*; flutto *m*;
far fluttuare;   ondeg-
giare
waver fluttuare; vacillare
wavering esitante
wavy ondoso
wax cera *f*; crescere
way via; strada *f*; modo
m – **lay** sorprendere;
we noi
weak debole; – **en** indebolire:– **ness** debolezza *f*
wealth richezza *f*
wealthy ricco; opulento
wean svezzare
weapon arma; difessa *f*
wear logoro;   servizio;
uso *m*; portare; aver
addosso
wearied stanco, infasti-
weariness fatica *f* [dito
wearisome faticoso
weary   lasso;   stanco
f; faticare

weasel donnola *f*

weather tempo *m*; temperatura *f*; resistere;

web tela *f*

wed sposare; maritarsi; sposarsi; – **lock** matrimonio *m*

wedding nozze *f pl*; sposalizio *m*

wedge zeppa *f*; zeppare

wee piccolo [chiare

weed malerba *f*; sar-

week settimana *f*; otto giorni *m pl*; – **day** giorno feriale *m*; – **ly** settimanale

weep lacrimare

weigh pesare; ponderare

weight peso; pondo *m*

weighty pesante; grave

welcome benevenuto *m*; dare il ben venuto (a)

weld saldare

welfare ben essere; bene *m*; felicità *f*

well pozzo *m*; fontana *f*; bene; – **-bred** ben educato – **-wisher** amico

west occidentale; verso l'ovest; occidente; ovest *m*; – **erly**, – **ern** d'occidente; – **ward** a ponente

wet umido; piovoso; umidità *f*; inumidare;

what cio che; quel che; quale; che; – **ever**: – **soever** tutto cio che, qual si sia; qualunque

wheat frumento; grano *m*

wheel ruota *f*; rotare; – **barrow** carriola *f*;

when quando; allorchè; mentre; ove; allora

where dove; ove; – **about** in che luogo; di cui; – **as** mentre; mentre che; invece di; – **at** al che; su di che; – **by** per cui; pel qual mezzo; – **fore** per ció; quindi; onde; – **in** in che; nel quale; – **of** del quale; di cui; – **on**, – **upon** su di che; sopra di che; – **soever** in qualunque luogo; – **with** con che; con quale; di cui

whet aguzzare; affilare

whether se; sia; che; quale dei due

whey siero di latte

which che; il che; quale; chi

whichever qualunque; quello; quale

whiff soffio; buffo *m*

while tempo; attimo *m*; passare [che; finchè

whine gagnolamento; gemito *m*; gagnolare; gemere [frustare

whip frusta; sferza;

whirl giro rapido *m*; rotare rapidamente; – **pool** vortice *m*; – **wind** buffera *f*

whiskers fedine *f pl*; baffi *m pl* (di gatto)

whiskey acquavite (d'orzo) *f* [bisbigliare

whisper sussurro *m*;

whist wist *m*

whistle fischietto *m*; fischiare

white bianco; – **n** imbiancare; – **ness** bianchezza

who che; il quale; la quale; i quali; le quali; chi [chessia

whoever chiunque; **chic-wuole** intero; totale; tutto m; **- sale** all' ingrosso; grosso m;

whom che; il quale; cui; a chi; chi

whomsoever chiunque

whoop urlo m; urlare

whopping-cough tosse canina f

whore prostituta f

whose di cui; del quale; dei quali; delle quali;

why perché   [di chi

wick lucignolo m

wicked malvagio; cattivo; **- ness** malvagità f

wicker di vinco; vinco m

wide largo; vasto

widen allargare

widow vedova f

widower vedovo m

width larghessa f

wife moglie; sposa f

wig parrucca f

wild selvaggio; furioso

wilderness deserto m

wilful testardo

will volontà f; testamento m; volere; legare; **- ing** disposto (a); **- ingly** volentieri; **- ingness** buona volontà f

willow salice m

wily furbo; fino

win vincere; guadagnare

wind vento; fiato m; avvolgere; torcere; **- up** li:quidare; caricare (orologio); **- ing** avvolgimento m; sinuosità f;

wine vino m; **—merchant** vinaio m; **—press**

wing ala f   [follatoio m

winged alato

wink batter d'occhio m;

ammiccare

winner vincitore m

winnings vincita f

winnow spagliare   [are

winter inverno m; svern-

wisdom saggezza; sapi-

wise savio; saggio [enza f

wish desiderio m; voglia f; desiderare; volere

wisp pagliola f; pugnon m

wistful attento

wit spirito m; sagacia f

witch strega; maga f

witchcraft stregoneria f

with con; per; contro; fra; presso; di; **- draw** ritirare; levare; **- drawal** retiro m; **- er** appassire; **- ered** appassito; **- hold** ritenere; **- in** indentro; in casa; **- out** fuori; senza; fuori; **- stand** resistere (a)

witness testimonio m; testimonianza f; testificare; esser testimonio di

wizard stregone; mago m

woe guaio; dolore m

wolf lupo m

woman femmina; donna; serva f; **- ish**, **ly** donnesco; **--kind** bel sesso

womb seno m; matrice f

wonder maraviglio f; prodigio m; maravigliarsi; **- ful** maraviglioso

wood bosco; legno m;

woof trama f   [ante m

wool lana f; **- len** di lana; lano; **- lens** laneria f; **- ly** lanuto; lanoso

word parola f

work lavoro m; opera f; lavorare; operare; **- er**

lavorante *m* & *f*;
operaio *m*; – **house** casa
di lavoro *f*; – **ing-day**
giorno di lavoro *m*;
world mondo; universo
m; – **liness** mondanità

worry agitazione *f*; tormentare

worse peggiore; più male

worship sculto *m*; adorazione *f*; adorare

worst il peggio; il peggiore *m*; peggio

worst vincere

worsted filo di lana *m*

worth che vale; degno
di; uguale a; valore;
merito *m*; – **less** senza
valore; – **lessness** mancanza di valore; bassezza *f*; – **y** degno

wrap inviluppare

wrapper fascia; veste
da camera *f*

wrath collera; ira *f*

wrathful irato

wreak vendicare

wreath ghirlanda *f*

wreathe coronare

wreck naufragio *m*;
naufragare

wren reatino; liù *m*

wrench strappo *m*; chiave inglese *f*; strappare

write scrivere

writer scrittore *m*

writhe scontorcersi

writing scrittura; mano *f*

wrong malo; cattivo;
inesatto; torto; male;
danno *m*; ledere; nuocere; – **ful** ingiusto

wry di traverso; – **neck**
torcicollo; – **ness** torsione

X

xylographic zilografico

xyster rastiatoio *m*

xystus zisto; portico *m*

Y

yacht iachetto; yacht *m*'

yahoo selvaggio *m*

yankee Americano degli
Stati Uniti

yard cortile *m*; iarda
('914 metri) *f*

yarn filo *m*

yawn sbadiglio *m*; sbadigliare

yea si; già   [gliare

year anno *m*; – **ling**
d'un anno; – **ly** annuale

yearn sospirare dietro

yeast lievito *m*

yell urlo *m*; urlare

yellow giallo *m*

yellowish gialliccio

yelp latrato *m*; latrare

yeoman piccolo proprietario *m*; guardia reale

yes si   [a piedi *f*

yesterday ieri

yet ancora; anche; pure;
eppure: nondimeno

yield raccolto *m*; rendenza *f*; produrre;
rendere

yoke giogo *m*; aggiogare

yolk tuorlo; rosso d'uovo

you voi; vi; ve; te; a te

young giovane; giovani
m pl   [ragazzo *m*

youngster giovanotto;

your vostro; tuo; – **s**
il vostro; – **self**, – **selves**
voi stesso

youth gioventù *f*; – **ful**
giovanile; – **fulness** gio

vanezza *f*
Yule Natale *m*; – log

Z

zebra zebra *f*
zero zero *m*

zest fetta *f*; sapore *m*
zodiac zodiaco *m*
zone zona; cintura *f*
zoographer zoografo *m*
zoography zoografia *f*

zoological zoologico
zoologist zoologo *m*
zoology zoologia *f*

ITALIAN-ENGLISH
DICTIONARY

abbacare embroil; confuse

abbacchista *m* arithmetician

abbacinamento *m* blindness

abbagliamento *m* blindness; mistake [error

abbaglianza *f* illusion;

abbagliare deceive

abbaglio *m* mistake; blunder; error [dow

abbaiamento *m* barking

abbaiare bark; bore

abbaiatore *m* barker (*met.*) brawler [dow

abbaino *m* dormer-window

abballare pack [tate

abbalordire *va* stun; irri-

abbambagiare trim; stuff

abbandonamento *m* abandonment

abbandonare abandon

abbaruffare mix; embroil

abbassamento *m* abasement [ate

abbassare lower; humili-

abbasso under; below

abbastanza enough; sufficiently

abbattere overthrow; demolish; deduct

abbattimento *m* ruin; dejection; chance

abbattitore *m* destroyer

abbattuffolare jumble

abbecedario *m* abecedarian

abbellare embellish

abbellimento *m* embellishment; ornament

abbiettare disgrace

abbiettezza *n* abjection

abbietto low; abject

abbiezione *f* abjection

abbigliamento *n* clothes; furniture [adorn

abbigliare dress; trim;

abbindolamento *m* dodge; fraud [cheat

abbindolare deceive;

abbindolatore *n* deceiver

abbiosciare fall down; – si lose courage

abbisognante needy

abbisognare be necessary; want

abbiurare *va* to abjure

abbiurazione *f* abjuration

abboscamento *n* intervie; colloquy

abboccare seize with the teeth; fill up; – si *n* have an interview

abboccato agreeable; deli-

abbocconare hash [cate

abbombarsi get drunk

abbominabile abomin-

abbominsre hate

abbonacciamento *n* calm

abbonacciare calm; pacify

abbonamento *n* amelioration; subscription

abbonare ameliorate; improve; subscribe for

abbondante abundant

abbondantemente abundantly

abbondanza *f* abundance

abbondare di abound in

abboracciare bungle; botch

abbordare accost; board

abbozzare sketch [line

abbozzo m sketch; out-

abbracciamento m; abbracciare, abbracciata f embrace [tight

abbrancare clasp; hold

abbreviare abridge

abbreviatura f abbrevia-

abbrividiro shiver

abbrustolare toast

abbuiare darken

abbuono m improvement

abdicare abdicate

abete m fir

abietto abject

abile able; clever

abilità cleverness

abilitare qualify

abisso m abyss

abitabile habitable

abitante m inhabitant

abitare inhabit; dwell

abitatore m inhabitant

abitazione f dwelling

abito m habit; dress

abituale customary

abituarsi get accustomed

abluzione f ablution

abolire abolish

abolizione f abolition

abominare, aborrire detest

abominevole abominable

aborto m abortion

abrogare abrogate

abside f apsis

abusare misuse

abusivo abusive

abuso m abuse

accadere happen [cuse

accagionare impute: ac-

accarezzare caress

accasamento m marriage

accasarsi marry

accatarrare catch cold

accedere approach

accelerare accelerate

accelerazione f accelera-

accendere kindle [tion

accenditore m lighter

accennare beckon; hint

accenno m notice; hint

accento m accent; word

accentuare accentuate

accertare ascertain; affirm

accessibile accessible

accesso m access

accessorio accessory

accettabile acceptable

accettare accept

accettazione f acception

acchetare calm

acchiappare catch; grasp

acchiocciolarsi squat

acciabattare botch, daub

acciacco m insult; indisposition

acciaiare steel, harden

acciaieria f steel-works

acciaio m steel

acciaiuolo m fire-steel

acciappinarsi fatigue oneself

accidentale accidental

accidente m accident; apoplexy

acciglиarsi knit the brows

accio, acciocchè in order that [hair

acciuffare seize by the

acciuga f anchovy

acclamare applaud [tion

acclamazione f acclama-

acclimare acclimat(iz)e

accludere enclose

accoccolarsi squat

accoglienza f reception

accogliere welcome

accollare lade

accolta f assembly

accoltellare stab [ment

accomodamento m agree-

accomodare settle; arrange; – **si** sit down

acconcio m advantage;
arranged

acconto m part-payment

accoppiare match

accorciare shorten

accordare grant; tune;
reconcile; agree

accordo m accord; con-

accorgersi perceive [cord

accorrere run; hasten

accorr'uomo help! help!

accorto prudent

accostare approach

accosto near, beside

accostumare accustom

accozzare heap; gather

accreditare accredit

accrescere increase

accrescimento m increase

acido sour; m acid

acino m grain; grape-
stone

acqua f water; – **cedrata**
lemonade; – **di latte**
whey; – **forte** aqua for-
tis; – **dolce** fresh water;
– **di mare** sea-water

acquapendente f water-

acquartierare lodge [shed

acquatico aquatic

acquavite f brandy

acquazzone m shower

acquerellare paint in
water-colours

acquerellista m water-
colour painter

acquerello m water-col-
our painting

acquidotto m acqueduct

acquiescenza f acquiescence

acquisizione f acquisition

acquistare acquire

adamante m diamond

adattare adapt

adatto convenient

addarsi apply one's self

addentro inside; within

addestrare teach; drill

addetto attached

addietro behind

addio farewell

addirsi suit; become

addirizzare direct; correct

addizionale additional

addizione f addition;
supplement

addobb(ament)o m ornament; furniture

addobbare adorn

addolcire soften

addolorato afflicted

addome m abdomen

addomesticare tame

adempiere perform

aderente adherent

aderire adhere

adescare bait; allure

adesione f adhesion

adesso now

adiacente adjacent

adiposo adipose; fat

adirare irritate; make
angry

adoperare employ; exert

adorabile adorable

adorare adore

adoratore m adorer

adorn(ament)o m orna-

adornare adorn [ment

adottare adopt

adott(at)ivo adoptive

Adriatico m Adriatic

adulare flatter

adulatore m flatterer

adulazione f flattery

adulterare adulterate

adultero adulterous

adulterio m adultery

adulto adult
adunanza *f* meeting
adunare assemble
aere *m* air; aereo aerial
affaccendato very occupied
affacchinarsi drudge
affacciare show
affamare famish
affannare grieve; provoke
affanno *m* grief
affare *m* affair
affascinare fascinate
affaticare tire
affatto quite; entirely
affettazione *f* affectation
affetto *m* love [self
affezionarsi attach one's
affezionato affectionate
affezione *f* affection; love
affibbiare buckle [hole
affibbiatoio *m* button-
affidare confide; trust
affilare sharpen
affinare refine
affinchè in order that
affinità *f* affinity
affissione *f* posting
affisso *m* placard, poster
affittare let; hire
affitto *m* rent
affliggere afflict
afflizione *f* affliction
affluente abundant; affluent
affluenza *f* abundance
affocare set fire to
affogare suffocate; drown; be drowned
affollare tread; press; crowd
affrettare hasten
affrontare attack
affronto *m* insult
affum(ic)are smoke
affusto *m* gun-carriage
agata *f* agate

agente *m* agent
agenzia *f* agency
agevole easy
aggiustare adjust, settle
aggomitolare wind up
aggradevole agreeable
aggradire agree with, like
 'grandimento *m* increase
aggrandire increase; enlarge [tion
aggravamento *m* aggrava-
aggravare aggravate; overload
aggregare aggregate
aggressione *f* aggression
aggressore *m* aggressor
aggrinzare wrinkle
aggrottare frown
agguagliare compare
agguaglio *m* comparison
agiato comfortable; rich
agile agile; nimble
agilità *f* agility
agio *m* ease
agire work; operate
agitare agitate; shake
agitatore *m* agitator
agitazione *f* agitation
aglio *m* garlic
agnello *m* lamb
ago *m* needle
agonia *f* agony
agonizzare agonize
Agostino Augustine
Agosto August
agricoltura *f* agriculture
agro sour; – dolce sweet and sour
agrume *m* fruits like oranges, lemons, etc.
aguzzare sharpen
aia *f* governess
aio *m* tutor [floor
aiuola *f* small threshing-
aiutare aiuto *m* aid; help
ala *f* wing; – to winged

alabastro *m* alabaster
alacrità *f* alacrity
alba *f* dawn; day-break
albagia *f* pride
albeggiare dawn
albergare live; lodge
albergatore *m* host; landlord
albergo *m* hotel; inn
albero *m* tree; mast
albicocca *f* apricot
albicocco *m* apricot-tree
albino albino
albo white
alitare pant
alito *m* breath; breeze
allacciare lace; tie
allagare inundate
allargare enlarge
allarmare allarme *m* alarm
allato contiguous; beside
allatare suckle; nurse
alleanza *f* alliance
alleato allied
allegare allege
alleggerire lighten; relieve
allegrare cheer; rejoice
allegrezza *f* gaiety
allegro cheerful; merry
allentare slacken
all'erta *f* alarm; alert!
allesso *m* boiled beef
allestare prepare
allettare allure
allettato bed-ridden
allevare bring up
alleviare alleviate
allievo *m* pupil
allineare range into lines
allividire turn pale
alloggio *m* dwelling
allontanamento *m* removal
allontanare remove
allora then
alluminio *m* aluminium.

allungamento *m* enlargement
allungare lengthen
allusione *f* allusion
almanacco *m* almanack
almanco, almeno at least
alpestre, alpino alpine
alquanto a little
altalena *f* swing; see-saw
altana *f* balcony
altare *m* altar
alterabile alterable
alterare alter; incense
altercare quarrel
alterezza alterigia *f* haughtiness
alternare alternate
alternativo alternative
altero haughty
altezza *f* height; highness
altitudine *f* altitude
alto high; loud; *m* height, high sea
altrettanto as much
altrove elsewhere
altrui other people
alzare raise; – si rise
amabile amiable
amabilità *f* amiableness
amaca *f* hammock
amante *m* lover
amare love; like
amareggiare embitter
amarezza *f* bitterness
amaro bitter; painful
amatore *m* lover
ambasciata *f* embassy
ambasciatore *m* ambassador
ambedue both; the two
ambire desire ardently
ambizione *f* ambition
ambizioso ambitious
amicare reconcile; make friends
amichevole friendly
amicizia *f* friendship

136

amico m friend
amido m starch
ammaccare bruise
ammaestrare teach
ammalare fall ill
ammalato sick; ill
ammansare tame; do-
mesticate
ammassare accumulate
ammasso m heap [bricks
ammattonare floor with
ammazzamento m slaugh-
ammazzare kill   [ter
ammazzatoio m slaugh-
terhouse
amministrazione f ad-
ministration
ammirabile admirable
ammiragli(at)o m ad-
miral(ty)
ammirare admire
ammiratore m admirer
ammirazione f admiration
ammissibile admissible
ammutinarsi mutiny
ammutire become dumb
amnistia f amnesty
amo m hook
amore m love
amoreggiare court; woo
amorevole amiable
amorino m little Cupid
amoroso amorous; lover
amovibile removable
ampio ample; copious
amplificare amplify
ampolla f phial
ampolliera f cruet-stand
amputare amputate
amputazione f amputa-
amuleto m amulet [tion
anagramma m anagram
analisi f analysis
analogo analogous
ananasso m pine-apple
anarchico anarchical;
anarchist

anche too
ancora f anchor [though
ancora yet; still; - chè
ancoraggio m anchorage
andare go; suit; an-
darsene go away
andata f step, walk; - e
ritorno there and back
andito m lobby [corridor
androne m antechamber;
aneddoto m anecdote
anelare be out of breath
anello m ring
anemia anaemia   [less
anemico anaemic; blood-
anfiteatro m amphiteatre
angelico angelical
angelo m angel
angolo m angle
angoloso angular
angoscia f anguish; grief
anguilla f eel
anguria f water-melon
angusto narrow
anice m anise
anima f soul
animale (m) animal
animo m mind; courage
animosità f animosity
animoso partial
anitra f duck

annata f year
annebbiato cloudy
annegare drown
annettere annex
annichilire annihilate
annidarsi nestle   [sary
anniversario m anniver-
anno m year; Cape d'-
anno New year's day
annodare tie; knot
annoiare annoy
annotare annotate [dark
annottarsi be night, get
annuale annual
annullare annul

137

annunziare announce
annunzio *m* announcement
annuvolare get cloudy
ano *m* anus
anonimo anonymous
ansietà *f* anxiety
ansioso anxious
antartico antarctic
antecedente antecedent
antecessore *m* antecessor
antenato *m* forefather
anteriore anterior
anticaglia *f* antiquities; rubbish
anticamera *f* antechamber
antichità *f* antiquity [ber
anticipare anticipate
antico antique, ancient
anzi before; rather
apatico insensible
ape *f* bee
aperto opened; open air
apertura *f* opening
apoplessia *f* apoplexy
apostata *m* apostate
apostolico apostolic
apostolo *m* apostle
apoteosi *f* apotheosis
appagare satisfy
appaiare match
appaltare let; farm
appalto *m* leasing [nish
appannare obscure tar-
apparecchiare prepare
apparente apparent
apparenza *f* appearance
apparire appear
apparizione *f* apparition
appartenere belong
appassionato passionate
appassire fade; wither
appello *m* call; appeal
appena scarcely
appendere hang on
appendice *m* appendix; feuilleton

appetito *m* appetite
appetitoso appetizing
appetto in front; in comparison
appianare level
appiccare attach; hang
appicciare tie; stick to
appiede at the foot of
appieno entirely
apportare bring
apposta expressly
apprendere learn
apprendista *m* apprentice
apprensione *f* apprehension
appresso near; after
apprestare prepare
apprezzare appraise; val- [ue
approdare approach
approdo *m* boarding
approfittare profit by
approfondare deepen; investigate
appropriare appropriate
approssimativo approximative
approvare approve
appuntamento *m* agreement
appuntare sharpen
apuntellare prop [time
appunto precisely; in
appuzzare infect
aprire open
arancia *f* orange
aranciata *f* orangeade
arancio *m* orange-tree
arare plough
aratro *m* plough
arazzo *m* tapestry
arbitrario arbitrary
arbitrio *m* will; free will
arbitro *m* arbiter
arbusto *m* shrub
arca *f* chest; ark
arcangelo *m* archangel
arcano secret; arcanun

archeologo m archæologist
archetto m fiddlestick
architetto m architect
architettura f architecture
arcobaleno m rain-bow
ardente ardent
ardere burn; be ardent
ardire dare
arditezza f boldness
ardito bold
ardore m ardour
arduo arduous
area f area
arganello m turnstile
argano m crane; capstan
argentato silvered
argenteo of silver
argenteria f silver plate
argentino silvery
argento m silver; – vivo
quick-silver
argilla f clay
argilloso clayey
argine f dyke
argomento m argument
arguire argue
arguto able; clever
arguzia f smartness
aridità f aridity
arido arid
aringa f herring
arioso airy; graceful
arista m pig's fillet
aristocratico aristocratic
aristocrazia f aristocracy
aritmetica f arithmetic
armellino m ermine
armeria f arsenal
armistizio m armistice
armonia f harmony
arnese m equipment, har-
arnione m kidney [ness
arrampicarsi climb up
arrecare bring; cause
arredare equip; furnish
arredo m equipment
arrenare strand

arrendere surrender; yield
arrestare arrest
arresto m arrest
arricchire enrich
arricciare curl; crisp
arringa(re) harangue
arrischiare risk; venture
arrivare arrive; reach
arrivista m ambitious
person; place-hunter
arrivo m arrival
arrochire grow hoarse
arrogante arrogant
arroganza f arrogance
arrogare arrogate
arrolare enlist
arrossire redden; blush
arrostire roast; toast
arteria f artery
artesiano artesian
articolare articulate
articolo m article; joint
artificiale artificial
artificio m artifice;
fuoco d' – fire-work
artigiano m artisan
artiliere m artilleryman
artiglieria f artillery
artista m artist
artistico artistic
asbesto m asbestos
ascella f arm-pit
ascendere go up; ascend
ascensione f ascension
ascensore m lift
ascesso m abscess
ascia f axe
asciolvere breakfast
asciugamano m towel
asciugare wipe, dry
asciutto dry
asma(tico) asthma(tic)
asparago m asparagus
aspergere besprinkle
aspettare expect; wait for
aspettazione f expectation
aspetto m aspect; sala

aspirante m candidate
aspirare aspirate; aspire
aspirazione f aspiration
aspro rough; harsh
assaggiare try; taste
assai much; very
assalire attack; assault
assalto m attack; assault
assassinare, assassinio m murder
assassino m murderer
asse f plank; axle
assediare besiege
assedio m siege
assegnare assign; appoint
assegno m rent
assembiare assemble
assemblea f assembly
assente absent
assentire consent
assenza f absence
assenzio m wormwood
asserire affirm; assert
asserzione f assertion
assetato thirsty
assettare settle
assieme together
assilio m horse-fly
assise f pl assizes
assistenza f assistance
assistere assist; help
asso m ace
associare accompany
associato m partner
associazione f association
assoggettare subdue
assoluzione f absolution
assolvere absolve
assomiglianza f resemblance [compare
assomigliare resemble;
assopire make sleepy
assuefare accustom
assuetudine f custom
assumere assume
assunta, assunzione f

assumption
assurdità f absurdity
assurdo absurd
asta f stick; lance; auc-
astaco m lobster [tion
astemio abstemious
astenersi abstain
asterisco m asterisk
astinente abstinent
astinenza f abstinence
astio m envy; hatred
astraere abstract
astratto abstract
astrazione f abstraction
astringere compel
astringente astringent
astro m star
astronomia f astronomy
astronomo m astronomer
astuccio m case; box
astuto cunning
astuzia f cunning
ateista m atheist
atlante m atlas
atomo m atom
atrio m vestibule
atroce atrocious
attagliarsi suit
atteggiamento m attitude
attempato elderly
attendere apply one's self
   await; mind
attenente belonging
attentare attempt; try
attentato m attempt
attento attentive
attenuare weaken
attenzione f attention
atterrare overthrow;
   prostrate
atterrire frighten
attesa f expectation
atteso considering
attestare attest
attimo m moment
attirare attract
attitudine f attitude

attività f activity
attivo active
attizzare poke; stir up
attizzatoio m poker
atto apt; m act; deed
attonito astonished
attore m actor
attorno around
attossicare poison
attrappare deceive
attrarre attract
attrattivo attractive
attraversare cross
attraverso through; across
attrazione f attraction
attrezzo m tool
attribuire attribute
attributo m attribute
attrice f actress
attuale actual
attuare perform
attuffare submerge; dive
audace audacious
audacia f audacity
augurare wish
augurio m omen; congratulation
augusto august
aumentare increase
austerità f austerity
austero, ra austere
australe austral; southern   [trian
austriaco, ca m & f Aus
austro m southern wind
autentica f authentication   [tic
autenticare make authentication
autenticazione f authentication
autenticità f authenticity
autentico, ca authentic
autocrate m autocrat
autocrazia f autocracy
autografo m autograph
automa m automaton
autonomia f autonomy

autonomo autonomous
autopsia f autopsy
autore, trice author m; authoress f   [thority
autorevole accredited; authority f credit
autorità f credit
autorizzare authorize
autunnale autumnal
autunno m Autumn
avacciare urge; hasten
avaccio in haste
avallo m guarantee
avantichè before that
avanzamento m advancement; progress   [prove
avanzare advance; improve
avanzaticcio, cia remnant; scrap
avanzato m remainder
avanzo m remainder; profit
avaramente avariciously
avaria f damage
avarizia f avarice
avaro, ra avaricious
avello m tomb; tombstone
avena f oats; pipe
aventare grow
avere have; possess
averno m hell
aversione f aversion
avertere remove
avido, da greedy
avo, avolo m grandfather
avocare evoke
avola f grandmother
avoltoio m vulture
avorio m ivory   [age
avvallare lower; discourage
avvaloramento m courage
avvalorare encourage
avvampante burning
avvampare burn; be incensed
avvantaggio m advantage

141

avvantaggioso, sa advantageous

avvegnachè as; when

avvelenamento *m* poison-

avvelenare poison [ing

avvelenato, ta poisoned

avvenimento *m* event; arrival [*m* future

avvenire happen; arrive;

avventamento *m* impetus

avventare rush; dash

avventatagine *f* inadvertence; imprudence

avventore *m* customer

avventura *f* adventure

avventurare venture; risk

avventurato, ta, roso, sa happy; lucky

avventuriere *m* adventurer; adventurous

avverare verify; aver

avverbiale adverbial

avverbio *m* adverb

avversamente unhappily; unluckily

avversare oppose

avversario, ria adversary

avversazione opposition; contest

avversità *f* adversity

avverso, sa adverse

avverso against

avvertente warned

avvertenza *f* warning;

avviare prepare; credit

avviato, ta attracted

avvicendare alternate

avvicendevole alternate

avvicinamento *m* proximity

avvicinare approach

avvilimento *m* humiliation

avvilire degrade [tion

avvilitivo, va degraded

avvilito, ta humiliated

avviluppare confuse; embroil

avvinacciato, ta drunk

avvinare mix with wine

avvinazzarsi get drunk

avvincere, vinchiare twist; tie [collision

avvisaglia *f* dispute;

avvisare inform

avvisatamente prudently

avvisatore *m* adviser

avviso *m* advice; advertisement

avvistare observe

avviticchiare twist; knot

avvivare revive

avvizzare, ire wither

avvocare practise; plead

avvocato *m* advocate

azione *f* act; deed; share

azoto *m* azote

azzampato, ta clawed

azzannare snap up; nal

azzardare risk

azzardo *m* hazard; chance

azzardoso, sa hazardous

azzeccare strike; beat

azzicare move

azzimare adorn; dress

azzimina *f* coat of mail

azzoppare become lame

azzuffamento *m* fight; collision

azzuffarsi dispute; fight;
– colvino drink hard

azzuolo *m* dark blue

azzurro *m* blue

B

babbo *m* father

babbuino *m* baboon

babele babel; confusion

baccelliere *m* bachelor

baccello *m* pod; shell

baccheo a; chico, ca bacchic

bacchetta *f* wand; drumstick

bacchettone, .na bigot; hypocrite

bacchio *m* stick; pole

bacco; per – by jove!; **poffarbacco** by jove!

bacheca *f* show-case

baciamento *m* kiss; kissing   [bigot

baciapile *m* hypocrite;

baciare kiss; *m* kiss

bacile, no *m* basin; water-

bacio *m* kiss   [tax

baciozzo *m* kiss

baco *m* worm; **– da seta** silkworm

bacocco *m* imbecile

bacucco *m* hood; cowl

baffi *pl* moustache

bagaglia, glio *f & m* luggage

bagaglione *m* camp-follower

bagascia *f* prostitute

bagascione *m* bully

bagattella trifling

bagattelliere *m* mounte-

baggeo *m* booby   [bank

baggianata *f* trifle

baggiano *m* blockhead

baggiolare support

baggiolo *m* support; prop

bagliore *m* lightning

bagnaiuolo *m* bather; bath-keeper

bagnare bathe; water

bagnato, ta bathed;

bagno *m* bath   [watered

bagordo *m* seducer

baia *f* trick; bay; gulf

baiata *f* trifles; joke

baietta *f* taming; small

bailo *m* bailiff   [bay

baio, ia bay   [jester

baionaccio, baione *m*

baionnetta bayonet

balausta, tra, tro *f & m*

---

pomegranate-tree blossom

balaustrata *f* balustrade

balbettante stuttering

balbettare stammer

balbo, ba stammerer

balbuzie *f* stammering

balconata *f* balcony

balcone *m* balcony

baldanza *f* courage

baldanzoso, sa daring

baldo, da audacious; bold

baldoria *f* Greek fire; bonfire

baldracca *f* prostitute

balena *f* whale

balenare be lightening

baleno *m* lightning

balia *f* nurse; power

balla *f* bale; pack

ballabile dancing

ballare dance

ballata *f* ballad; dance

ballerino *m* dancer

balsamo *m* balm

balza *f* rock; precipice

balzare jump

balzo *m* leap, jump

bambagia *f* cotton

bambinello *m* baby

bambino *m* child

bambola *m* doll

bambu *m* bamboo

banano *m* banana

banca *f* bank

bancarotta *f* bankruptcy

banchetto *m* banquet

banchiere *m* banker

banco *m* bench

banda *f* band; side

barattare exchange; barter   [switch

baratto *m* exchange

barba *f* beard

barbabietola *f* beet-root

barbaro barbarous

barbiere *m* barber

barbieria *f* barber's shop
barbone *m* water-spaniel
barbugliare stutter
barbuto bearded

barca *f* bark; boat
barcaiuolo *m* boatman
barchetta *f* small boat
barcollare vacillate; totter
bargello *m* sheriff
barile *m* barrel; hogshead
baritono *m* baritone
baroccio *m* car
barocco odd
barometro *m* barometer
barone *m* baron; sharper
barra *f* bar; cross-bar
barricata *f* barricade
barriera *f* barrier
baruffa *f* tumult; fray
basamento *m* pedestal
base *f* base; basis
Basilea Basle
basilica *f* basilica
bassezza *f* meanness
basso low; mean; *m* bass
bassorilievo *m* bas-relief
bassotto *m* terrier
basta enough! stop!
battaglione *m* battalion
batello *m* boat; - a
    vapore steamer
battere knock; beat; - le
    mani applaud
batteria *f* battery
battesimale baptismal
battesimo *m* baptism
battezzare baptize
batticuore, battito *m* pal-
Battista Baptist [pitation
battisterio *m* baptistry
baule *m* trunk
bava *f* slaver; foam
Bavarese Bavarian
bavero *m* collar
Baviera *f* Bavaria
bazar *m* bazar

bazzotto half-boiled
beatificare beatify [tion
beatificazione *f* beatifica-
beato happy, blessed
beffare joke, mock
beghino hypocrite
belare bleat
Belgio Belgium
belladonna *f* nightshade
belletto *m* paint (face)
bellezza beltà *f* beauty
bellico warlike; *m* navel
bellino pretty
bello beautiful
belvedere *m* belvedere
benché though
benda *f* band; - re bind
    up
bene well; *m* good;
    property
beneficenza *f* benevolence
beneficio *m* benefice
benefico beneficent
benessere *m* well-being
benevolenza *f* benevol-
    ence
benevolo benevolent
benigno benign; kind
bensi certainly
beone *m* drunkard
bere, bevere drink
bersaglio *m* mark; target
bertuccio *m* monkey
bestemmia *f* blasphemy
bestemmiare blaspheme
bestia *f* beast; - le bes-
bestiame *m* cattle [tial
bettola *f* tavern
betula *f* birch-tree
beva, bevanda *f* beverage
beveraggio *m* tip
bevitore *m* drinker
biacca *f* whitelead
biancheria *f* linen
bianchezza *f* whiteness
bianchire bleach
bianco white

144

biasciare mumble; munch
biasimare blame
bicchiere m glass; cup
bicicletta f bicycle
ciclista m bicyclist
bidello m beadle
bieco squinting
bietola f beet
bietta f wedge
biforcarsi fork
bigamo m bigamist
bigatto m silk-worm
bigio grey
bigliardo m billiards
biglietto m ticket
bigoncia f tub
bilanciare balance; weigh
bilanciere m beam; bal-
  ance-wheel
bile f bile; anger
bilioso bilious
bimbo m baby
binario m track
bindolo m sharper
binocolo m binocle
biografia f biography
biografo m biographer
birreria f brewery
bis! encore' [father
bisavo(lo) m great-grand-
bisbigliare whisper
bisca f gambling-house
biscazzare gamble
biscia f snake
bisogna f business; affair
bisognare be necessary;
  want
bisogno, m need; aver
  – di want; – so poor;
bisticciare dispute
bisticcio m pun
bistrattare ill-treat
bitume m bitumen
bivaccare bivacco m
  bivouac
bivio f cross-road

bizzarro capricious; odd
blandire flatter
blando soft; bland
blenoraggia f gonorrhœa
blocco m blockade; block
blu blue
boa m boa
boaro m cow-herd
bocca f mouth
boccale m jar; mug
boccata m mouthful
boccetta f small bottle
boccia f bud; decanter;
boccone m bit; mouthful
boia m executioner
bolgia m pocket; bag
bolla f bubble; blister
  bull (papal)
bollare seal; stamp
bolletta f bill (of health)
bollire boil
bollo m stamp
bomba f bomb
bonaccia f calm
bonaccio good-natured
bonificare improve
bontà f goodness [ble
borbottare grunt; grum-
bordello m brothel
bordo m edge; board
bordone m pilgrim's staff
borea m north-wind
borghese m burgess;
borgo m borough [citizen
boria f vanity
borrico m ass
borsa f purse; pocket
borsaiuolo m pickpocket
borzacchino m buskin
boscaiuolo m woodman
boschett(in)o m grove
bosco m forest; wood
botte f tub; cab
bottega f shop
bozza f sketch; proof
bozzo f free-stone

145

braca f trousers
braccare search; scent
bracciale m brassard; armlet
braccialetto m bracelet
braccio m arm [chair
bracciuolo m arm of a
brachiere m truss
brama f longing, eager
bramare long for [ness
branca f claw
branchie f & pl gills
branco m herd; flock
brandire brandish
Brasile m Brazil
bravaccio m braggart
bravo brave; bravo!
bravura f bravery
breccia f breach
breve brief
brevetto m patent
breviario m breviary
brevità f brevity
brezza f breeze
briaco drunk
briacone m drunkard
bricco m ass
brigare seek; strive
brigata f brigade
briglia f bridle
brillante brilliant, bright
brindisi m toast
brio m vivacity
brioso lively; fiery
brivido m shivering
brocca f jug
broccolo m brocoli
brod(ett)o m broth
broncio m anger
brontolare grumble
bronzo m bronze
bruccio m cream-cheese
bruciare burn [nut
bruciata f toasted chest-
bruco m caterpillar
brulicare swarm [ish
brunetto brownish, dark-

brusco rude; blunt
bruscolo f straw
brutale brutal
bruto m brute
bruttura f dirtiness
bruzzaglia f mob
buaggine f foolishness
buca f hole; cave
bucare perforate
bucato m lye; wash
buccia f bark; peel
buccina f trumpet
buccinare trumpet
buccioso thick-skinned
buccolica f bucolic
bucherare bore
bucinamento m buzzing
bucinare buzz; whisper
budellame m entrails
budello, della m & f
bue m ox; beef [bowel
bufera f hurricane
buffa f child's play
buffalo m buffalo
bugiare bore
bugigatto, tolo m hole; hiding-place
bugna f bump; basket
bugno m bee-hive
buio m darkness
buio, ia dark; obscure
bulbo m bulb
bulboso, sa bulbous
bulicame m spring
bulicare boil; bubble
bulima f crowd
bulimo m hunger
bulino m graver [port
bulletta f ballot; pass-
bullettino m note; safe
conduct [cord
buonaccordo m harpsi-
buonamente certainly
buonavoglia m volunteer
buondì m good day; good morning
buono, na good; proper;

alla buona simply; sincerely
buonpresso *m* bowsprit
burbero, ra *a* & *n* surly; grumbler
burchia, burchio *f* & *m* row-boat
burchiello *m* small boat
burello *m* woollen cloth
burla *f* joke
burlare joke [burlesque
burlesco, ca, burlevole
burletta *f* joke
burrasca *f* squall; storm
burrascoso, sa stormy
burro, butirro *m* butter
burrone *m* precipice
busca *f* quest; inquest
buscare cheat
busecchia, secchio, chione *f* & *m* bowels
bussa *f* grief
bussare strike
busse *fp* blows
bussola *f* compass
busta *f* case
busto *m* bust
buttare dart; throw

C

cacare evacuate
cacatoio *m* water-closet
cacazibetto *m* coxcomb; dandy [ies; grimaces
caccabaldole *fp* cajoler-
caccao *m* cocoa-nut [ing
caccia *f* hunting; shoot-
cacciaffanni entertaining
cacciagione *f* hunt; game
cacciapassere *m* scarecrow
cacciare expel; hum
cacciatoia *f* nail-driver
cacciatore, trice *m* & *f*

hunter
cacciavite *f* screw-driver
caccio *m* cheese
cacio *m* cheese
cacume *m* top; summit
cadauno each; every
cadavere, ro *m* corpse
cadaverico, ca cadaverous
cadente falling; decaying
cadenza *f* cadence
cadere fall; happen
cadetto *m* cadet; junior
cadevole old; fragile
cadimento *m* fall: fault
caducità *f* weakness; decay
caduco decaying
caduta *f* fall
caduto, ta fallen; ruin
caffè *m* coffee
caffettiera *m* coffee-pot
cagionevole sickly; weak
cagliare abate; coagulate
cagna *f* bitch [titute
cagnaccia *f* hussy; pros-
cagnaccio *m* big dog; bad
caimane *m* alligator
cala *f* hold (ship); slip; dock-yard [drone
calabrone *m* hornet;
calafatare calk
calamaio *m* inkstand
calamita *f* magnet
calamità *f* calamity
calamitare magnetize
calamitoso, sa calamitous
calandra *f* weevil
calandrella *f* lark
calappio *m* snare; trap
calare take down; go down [stonecutter
calastra *f* stonecutting;
calata *f* descent, fall
calca *f* crowd
calcagnare fly; run away
calcare tread upon;

crush [chalky
calcareo calcareous;
calcatura f pressure
calce f lime, chalk
calcestruzzo p cement
calcetto m sock; pump
calcina f lime
calcinare calcinate
calcio m heel; kick
calcistruzzo m cement
calcitrante recalcitrant
calcitrare kick
calcitroso kicking; recalcitrant
calcolare calculate
calcolatore m calculator;
accountant [tion
calcolazione f calcula-
caldana f heat; pleurisy
caldanino m small stove
caldano m stove
caldaro m boiler [seller
caldarrostaio m chestnut-
caldeggiare protect
calderaio m brazier
calderone m boiler
calderuola f small caldron
caldezza f heat; warmth
caldo, da m warm; m heat
calduccio lukewarm
calere signify
calessino m cab

calice m chalice
calido, da warm; hot
califfo m calif
caligine f obscurity
caliginoso obscure; dark
calla f opening; gap
calle f road; street
callido, da astute
calma m calmness
calmare calm; – si com-
pose one's self
calmo, ma calm
calore m warmth
caloria f improvement;

manure
calorico m caloric
calorifico calorific
caloroso warm
calotta f cap
calpestare tread upon
calpestio m treading upon
calterire graze; raze
calunnia f calumny
calunniare calumniate
calunniatore, trice m & f
calumniator
calunnioso, sa slanderous
calvare make become bald
calvario m calvary
calvezza f baldness
calvinista m calvinist
calvizie f baldness
calvo m bald man
calza f stocking
calzaiuolo m hosier
calzamento, turn m & f
covering for the feet
(boots; shoes etc.).
calzare m shoe
calzare put on one's shoes
calzetta f stocking
cambiamento m change
cambiare change; vary
cambiario, via change;
exchange
cambio m change;
change; in – instead of
cambista m money chan-
ger; tanker [lia
camelea, camelia f camel-
camello m camel
camera f chamber; room
camerata m comrade
cameriera f chamber-
maid
cameriere m waiter
camerino m closet; bath-
camicia f shirt [room
camiciuola f undervest
camino m chimney(-piece)

cammello *m* camel
camminare walk
camminata *f* walk [ney
cammino *m* road; jour-
camoscio *m* chamois
campagna *f* country;
campaign

campagnuolo *m* peasant
campana *f* bell
campanaio *m* bellringer
campanello *m* bell
campanile *m* steeple
campare save; live
campestre rural
Campidoglio *m* Capitol
campionario *m* book of
samples [ship
campionate *m* champion-
campione *m* champion;
sample [cemetery
campo *m* field – santo
camuso flat-nosed
canaglia *f* rabble
canale *m* canal
canapa *f* hemp
canapè *m* sofa
cánapo *m* cable
cancrena *f* gangrene
candela *f* candle
candelabro *m* chandelier
candelliere *m* candlestick
candidato *m* candidate
candido white; candid
candito candied
cane *m* dog
canestro *m* basket
canfora *f* camphor
cangiare change; vary
canicola *f* dog-days
canile *m* dog-kennel
canino canine [barrel
canna *f* reed; cane;
cannella *f* cinnamon
cannocchiale *m* spy-glass
cansare remove
cantabile ·cantabile

cantante *m* singer
cantare sing
cantina *f* cellar
canto *m* song; corner
cantonata *f* corner
cantone *m* angle; corner
cantoniere *m* road-sur-
veyor; watchman
cantore *m* singer
cantuccio *m* biscuit
canuto grey-haired
canzone *f* song
canzonare jest; laugh at
canzoniere *m* song-book
caos *m* chaos
capace capable
capacità *f* capacity
capanna *f* cottage; bran
caparbio stubborn

capello *m* hair
capelluto hairy
capestro *m* cord
capezzale *m* pillow
capire understand
capitalista *m* capitalist
capitano *m* captain
capitello *m* capital
capitolare capitulate
capitolo *m* chapter
capitombolare tumble
capo *m* head; chief;
cape; – d'anno New-
year's day; da – once
more
capogiro *m* giddiness
capolavoro *m* master-
piece
capovolgere turn upside
cappa *f* cloak; cape [down
cappella *f* chapel
cappellano *m* chaplain
cappelliera *f* hat-box
cappellinaio *m* hat-stand
cappello *m* hat
cappero *m* caper
cappio *m* knot

149

cappuccio *m* hood
capra *f* she-goat
capraio *m* goat-herd
capriccio *m* caprice
capriccioso capricious
caraffa *f* decanter
carato *m* carat
carattere *m* character
caratteristico character-
  istic
carbone *m* coal
carbonio *m* carbon
carbonico carbonic
carbonizzare carbonize
carcerare imprison
carcere *m* prison
carciofo *m* artichoke
cardare card
carezza(re) caress
carica *f* load; office
caricare load; attack
caricatura *f* caricature
carie *f* caries
carino dear; darling
carità *f* charity
carmelitano *m* carmelite
carminio carmine
carnagione *f* carnation;
  complexion
carnale carnal; sensual
carne *f* flesh; meat
carreggiare cart; carry
carreggiata *f* cart-road
carretta *f* cart
carriera *f* run; career
carro *m* cart; waggon
carrozza *f* carriage; coach
carruba *f* carob
carrucola *f* pulley
carta *f* paper; deed;
  map; card; − sugante
  blotting paper; − mon-
  eta paper-money;
cartella *f* bill; portfolio
cartello(ne) *m* placard
cartiera *f* paper-mill

cartilagine *f* cartilage
cartoccio *m* cartouche;
  oup of paper
cartoleria *f* paper-trade
cartone *m* pasteboard
cartuccia *f* cartridge
casa *f* house; home
casale *m* hamlet
casalingo domestic
casata *f* family name
cascare fall
cascata *f* water-fall
cascina *f* dairy
casella *f* cell
caserma *m* barracks
caso *m* case; chance
casotto *m* watch-box
cassa *f* chest; box; coffin
cassare cancel
cassetta *f* casket; box
cassettone *m* chest of
  drawers
cassiere *m* cashier
castagna *f* chestnut
castagneto *m* grove of
  chestnut-trees
castagno *m* chestnut-tree
castello *m* castle
castigare chastise
castigo *m* punishment
castità *f* chastity
casto chaste; modest
castoro *m* beaver
catastrofe *f* catastrophe
catechismo *m* catechism
categorico categorical
catena *f* chain
catinella *f* basin
catramare, catrame *m* tar
cattedra *f* chair; pulpit
cattedrale *f* cathedral
cattivare captivate
cattivo wicked   [ism
cattolicismo *m* catholic-
cattolicità *f* catholicity
cattolico catholic

cattura *f* capture
causare, causa *f* cause
caustico caustic
cautela *f* caution
cauto cautious
cauzione *f* bail; security
cava *f* pit
cavadenti *m* dentist
cavalla *f* mare
cavallaro *m* muleteer
cavalleresco chivalrous
cavalleria *f* cavalry;
    gallantry   [school
cavallerizza *f* riding-
cavalerizzo *m* riding-
    master
cavalletta *f* locust
cavalletto *m* easel
cavallo *m* horse
cavare dig; draw out
caverna *f* cavern; den
caviale *m* caviare
cavicchia *m* peg
cavità *f* cavity
cavo hollow
cavolfiore *m* cauliflower
cavolo *m* cabbage
cazzottare box
cece *m* pea
cedere cede; yield
cedola *f* schedule; bill
cedrare season with lemon
cedro *m* cedar
ceffata *f* box on the ear
ceffo *m* muzzle
ceffone *m* cuff; slap
celare hide
celebrare celebrate
celebre celebrated
celebrità *f* celebrity
celere speedy
celerità *f* speed
celeste celestial
celia *f*, celiare jest; joke
celibato *m* celibacy
celibe unmarried; bache-

cella *f* cell   [lor
cencio *m* rag; – so rag-
cenere *f* ash   [ged
cenerino ash-coloured
cenno *m* signal; nod
censo *m* census; tax
centigrado centigrade
centimetro *m* centimetre
centinaio *m* hundred
cento hundred
centrale central
centrifugo centrifugal
centro *m* centre
centuplo hundredfold
ceppo *m* trunk
cera *f* wax; air; mien
cerca *f* cercare search
cerchio *m* circle; hoop
cerco *m* circus

cereale cereal
cerebrale cerebral
cessare cease; leave
cesso *m* water-closet
cesta *f* basket
cetra *f* cithern
cetriuolo *m* cucumber
che which? what? that
checche whatever
cherica *f* tonsure
chericato *m* clergy
cherico *m* priest
chetare, cheto quiet
chi who
chiacchiera *f*; – re chat;
    prattle
chiamata *f* call; appeal
chiamare call; name
chiappare snatch; catch

chiara *f* white of egg
chiarire clear up

chiaro *m* clearness; light
chiaro clear; illustrious
chiaroscuro chiaroscuro
chiasso *m* great noise
chiave *f* key

151

chiavistello *m* bolt
chicca *f* sweetmeats
chicchera *f* cup
chicco *m* grain; seed
chiedere demand; ask
chiesa *f* church
chiglia *f* keel [metre
chilogramma *m* kilogram-
chilometro *m* kilometre
chimera *f* chimera
chimica *f* chemistry
chimico chemical; chem-
China *f* China [ist
china *f* slope
chinachina *f* quinquina
chinare bend; incline
chincaglieria *f* hardware
chinina *f* quinine
chiocciola *f* snail; scala
a - winding staircase
chicdo *m* nail
chiostro *m* cloister
chiotto silent
chirurgo *m* surgeon
chitarra *f* guitar
chiudere enclose; shut up
chiusa *f* enclosure; fence
ciarla *f*; - re chat; talk
ciarlatano *m* mountebank
ciascheduno each
cibare feed
cibo *m* food; aliment
cicala *f* grasshopper
cicatrice *f* cicatrice
cicerone *m* guide
cicisbeo *m* lover; gallant
ciclista *m* cyclist
ciclo *m* cycle
cicogna *f* stork
cicoria *f* chicory
cicuta *f* hemlock
ciecità *f* blindness
cieco blind
cialo *m* heaven
ciera *f* mien; looks
cifra *f* cipher; figure
ciglio *m* eye-lashes

cignere gird; surround
cigno *m* swan
ciliegia *f* cherry
ciliegio *m* cherry-tree
cilindro *m* cylinder
cima *f* top; summit
cimentare risk
cimice *f* bug
cimitero *m* cemetery
cinabro *m* cinnabar
cingere gird; surround
cinghia *f* girth
cinghiale *m* wild boar
cinquantina *f* about fifty
cinque five
cinta *f* enclosure
cintura *f* girdle
ciò this; that
ciocca *f* bunch; tuft
cioccolata *f* chocolate
cioccolattiera *f* chocolate-
pot
ciocia *f* kind of sandal;
- re inhabitant of the
Campagna
cioè that is; namely
cioncare tipple
ciondolare sway; dangle
ciottolo *m* pebble
cipolla *f* onion
cipresso *m* cypress
circolo *m* circle
circoncidere circumcise
circoncisione *f* circum-
cision
circondare surround
circondario *m* district
circostanza *f* circum-
stance
circuito *m* circuit
cislonga *f* couch
città *f* city
cittadinanza *f* citizenship
cittadino *m* citizen
ciuco *m* ass
ciurma *f* gang; rabble

civaia *f* vegetable
civile civil; polite
civilizzare civilize
clamore *m* clamour
clandestino clandestine
clarinetto *m* clarinet
classe *f* class
classico classic
clausola *f* clause
clavicola *f* collar-bone
clemente clement
clemenza *f* clemency
clero *m* clergy
cliente *m* customer
clientela *f* customers
clima *m* climate
cloaca *f* sink; sewer
cloro *m* chlorine
cloroformio *m* chloroform
coagulare coagulate
coalizione *f* coalition
cocchiere *m* coachman
cocchio *m* carriage; coach
coccodrillo *m* crocodile
cocomero *m* water-melon
cocuzzo *m* top; crown of
  the head
coda *f* tail; train
codardo coward
codesto that
codice *m* code
codino *m* pigtail
coerente coherent
coevo, coetaneo contem-
cofano *m* box [porary
cogliere gather
cognato brother-in-law;
  related
cognizione *f* knowledge
cognome *m* family name
coiaio *m* tanner
coincidenza *f* coincidence
colà there
colaggiù down yonder
colare a fondo sink
colassù there above

colazione *f* breakfast
colera *m* cholera
colica *f* colic
colla *f* paste; glue
collaborare collaborate
colle *m* hill
collega *m* colleague
collegio *m* college
collera *f* anger
colletto *m* collar; – ritto
  stand-up collar; – ro-
  vesciato double collar
collezione *f* collection
collina *f* hill
collisione *f* collision
collo *m* neck
collocare place
colmo full
colomba *f* pigeon
colombaia *f* pigeon-house
colonia *f* colony
coloniale colonial
colonizarre *va* colonize
colonna *f* column
colorare colour
colore *m* colour
colorito *m* colouring
colossale colossal
Colosseo *m* Coliseum
colpevole guilty
colpire strike; hit
colpo *m* stroke; blow
coltellinaio *m* cutler
coltello *m* knife
coltivare cultivate [man
coltivatore *m* husband-
colto caught; cultivated
coltre *f* coverlet
coltrice *f* featherbed
comandare command
comare *f* gossip
combattere fight
combattimento *m* fight
combinare combine
combinazione *f* combina-
  tion; chance [how?

153

come like; as; why?
comecchè though; however [tary
comentario m commen-
cometa f comet
comico comical
cominciare begin
comino m cumin
comitato m committee
commedia f comedy
commediante m comedian
commemorare remember
commemorazione f com-
memoration
commendare recommend
commerciare trade
commercio m commerce
commettere commit
commiato m leave
commozione f commotion
commuovere move; affect
commutare commute
comodino m night-table;
comodo convenient; m
comodità f convenience
compagnia f company
compagno equal; m
companion
comparabile comparable
comparare compare
comparativo comparative
comparazione f compari-
comparire appear [son
compressa f compress
comprimere (com)press
compromesso m com-
promise

comunicare communicate
comunione communion
con with
conca f tub; shell
concavo concave; hollow
concedere grant
concentrare concentrate
concepire conceive
concernere concern

concertare concert
concerto m concert
concetto m idea; pun
concessione f concession
concezione f conception
conchiglia f shell
concia f tan; tannery
conciare adorn; tan
conciatore m tanner
conciliare conciliate
concilio m council
concime m manure
conciso concise
concittadino m citizen
conclave m conclave
concussione f extortion
condannare condemn
condensare condense
condimento m condiment
condire season; preserve
condiscendere condescend
condizionale conditional
condizione f condition
condoglianza f condolence
condolersi condole
condonare pardon
condotta f conduct
condottiere m leader
condurre conduct
confabulare chat
confarsi agree; suit
confederarsi confederate
confederazione f confed-
eracy
conferenza f conference
conferire confer
confermare confirm
confessare confess
confess(at)ore m confes-
sor
confessionario m confes-
sional
confessione f confession
confetta m preserve
confettare preserve
confidare confide
confidente m confident

154

confidenza *f* confidence
confidenziale confidential
confinare, confine *m* confine; border
confiscare confiscate
conforme conform
confortabile comfort(able)
confortare comfort; strengthen
confrontare confront
confusione *f* confusion
confuso confused
confutare confute
cougedare dismiss
congedo *m* leave
congestione *f* congestion
congiura *f* conspiracy
congiurare conspire
congruente congruous
coniare coin
conico conical
coniglio *m* rabbit
conio *m* die; coin
coniugale conjugal
connessione *f* connexion
conoscenza *f* knowledge; acquaintance
conoscere know [seur
conoscitore *m* connoissconquista *f* conquest; -re conquer; *m* - tore conqueror
consacrare consecrate
consanguineo consanguineous
conscio conscious
consecutivo consecutive
consegnare consign; deposit [quently
per conseguente conseconseguenza *f* consequence
conseguire obtain; result
consenso *m* consent
consentire consent
conserva *f* save; conserve

conservare conserve
conservatorio *m* conservatory
considerabile considerable
considerare consider
consigliare advise
consigliere *m* counsellor
consiglio *m* counsel; council
console *m* consul
consolidare strengthen
consonante *f* consonant
consorte *m f* husband; wife
conspirare conspire
constare sul sist
constatare ascertain
consueto accustomed
consuetudine *f* custom
consultare consult
consultazione *f* consultation [complish
consumare consume; acontagioso contagious
contaminare stain
contante cash
contare number
contatore *m* (gas-) meter
contatto *m* contact
conte *m* count
contemplare contemplate
contemporaneo contemporary
contendere dispute
contenere contain
contentare content
contento contented
contenuto *m* contents
continente *m* continent
contingente *m* contingent
continuare continue
continuazione *f* continuacontinuo continuous [tion
conto *m* account; story
contorno *m* outline

còntra against [gler
contrabbandiere *m* smug-
contrabbando *m* smug-
  gling [ange
contraccambiare exch-
contracchiave *f* false key
contraccolpo *m* counter-
  blow
contrada *f* country
contraddire contradict
contradizione *f* contradiction
contraffare counterfeit
contrariare contradict
contrario contrary
contrarre contract [sign
contrassegnare counter-
contrastare contest
contrasto *m* contrast
contrattempo di—un-
  seasonably
contratto *m* contract
contravveleno *m* antidote
contravvenire infringe
contribuire contribute
contribuzione *f* contri-
contrito contrite [bution
contro against; opposite
controllare control [order
contrordine *m* counter-
controverso doubtful
contumacia *f* contumacy
contumelioso injurious
contusione *f* contusion
convalescente convalescent [cence
convalescenza *f* convales-
convegno *m* meeting
convenevole convenient;
  decent
convenire agree; become
convento *m* convent
convenzione *f* agreement
convergere converge
convincere convince
convitare invite
convocare convoke

convoglio *m* convoy; train
convulsione *f* convulsion
cooperare co-operate
coperchio *m* lid
coprire cover
coraggio *m* courage
coraggioso courageous
corallo *m* coral
corame *m* leather
corazza *f* cuirass; armour
corazzata *f* iron-clad
corazziere *m* cuirassier
corba *f*, **corbello** *m* basket
corbellare banter; jeer
corbezzola *f* arbute-berry
corbezzolo *m* strawberry-
  plant
corda *f* cord; rope
cordaio *m* rope-maker
cordame *m* cordage
cordiale (*m*) cordial
cordialità *f* cordiality
cordiglio *m* string
cordone *m* string; band
coreggia *f* strap
coricare lay down
cornice *f* cornice; frame
corno *m* horn [plenty
cornucopia *f* horn of
cornuto horned
corredare equip; adorn
corredo *m* equipment
correggere correct
corrente *f* current
correre run; flow
corretto correct
corrispondente *m* corres-
  pondent [pondence
corrispondenza *f* corres-
corrispondere correspond
corroborare corroborate
corrodere corrode
corrompere corrupt
corrugare corrugate
corruttibile corruptible
corruzione *f* corruption
corsa *f* course; drive

corso _m_ course
corte _f_ court
corteggiare court
cortese courteous
cortesia _f_ courtesy
cortezza _f_ brevity
cortina _f_ curtain
corto short; brief
corvo _m_ raven
cosa _f_ thing
coscia _f_ thigh
coscienza _f_ conscience
così so   [tan
cosmopolitano cosmopoli-
cospetto _m_ aspect
cospirare conspire   [tor
cospiratore _m_ conspira-
cospirazione _f_ conspiracy
costa _f_ hill; rib; coast;
costà there   [side
costante constant
costanza _f_ constancy
costare cost   [tion
costellazione _f_ constella-
costernare confound
costernazione _f_ conster-
      nation
costì here   [tion
costipazione _f_ constipa-
costipare constipate
costituire constitute
costituzione _f_ constitution
costo _m_ expense; costs
costola _f_ rib
costoletta _f_ cutlet; chop
costoso expensive
costringere constrain
costruttore _m_ construc-
      tor   [tion
costruzione _f_ construc-
costume _m_ & _f_ custom
costumato well-bred
cotale such a one
cotanto so much
cote _f_ whetstone
cotenna _f_ rind

cotesto this; that
cotidiano daily

cotogna _f_ quince
cotone _m_ cotton
cottimo _m_ job
cotto cooked; baked
cottura _f_ cooking
covare brood; hatch
covile, covo _m_ den
cranio _m_ skull
crapulone _m_ dissolute
creare create
creatore _m_ creator
creatura _f_ creature
creazione _f_ creation
credente _m_ believer
credenza _f_ faith; credit;
      buffet
credere believe
credulo credulous
creduto believed
crema _f_ cream
cremisi _m_ crimson; grain
cren _m_ wild raddish
creolo _m_ creole
crepaccio _m_ crevice; chap
crepare burst out; die
crepitante crackling
crepitare crackle
crepolare crack
crepuscolo _m_ twilight
crescente increasing
crescenza _f_ growth
crescere grow
crescione _m_ water-cress
cresciuto increased
cresima _f_ chrism
cresimare confirm
crespa _f_ frown; wrinkle
crespare frown; knit;
cresta _f_ summit   [curl
criminale criminal
crimine _m_ crime; mis-
      demeanour
criminoso criminal

crinale hairy
crine *m* hair
criniera *f* mane; horse- [hair
crisalide *f* chrysalis
crise, crisi *f* crisis
crisma *m* confirmation
cristallino crystalline
cristallizzare crystallize
cristallo *m* crystal
cristeo, stere *m.* clyster; injection
cristianesimo *m* Chris- [tianity
cristiano christian
Cristo *m* Christ
criterio *m* criterion
critica *f* censure
criticare criticise; cen- sure
criticatore *m* censor; critic
critico critic
crocchiare beat; chat
crocchio *m* circle; club
croce *f* cross; torment
crocefisso *m* crucifix
crociare crucify; torment
crociata *f* crusade
crociato crossed; tor- mented; *n.* torment
crocicchio *m* cross-road
crocifiggere crucify
crocifisso *m* crucified; *n* crucifix
croio, ia rough; harsh
crollare agitate
crollo shaking
cronico chronic
cronista *m* chronicler
cronologia *f* chronology
cronologico chronological
crosciare pour (rain)
croscio *m* bubbling
crosta *f* crust
crostare to cover
crucciamento, cruccio *m* passion
crucciare irritate
crucciato tormented

cruciare torment
crudele cruel
crudeltà *f* cruelty
crudetto crudish; sourish
crudezza cruelty
crudo crude
cruento horrible
cruna *f* eye (needle)
cubatura *f* cubing
cubico cubic
cubitale cubital
cubito *p* cubit
cubo *m* cube
cuccagna *f* feast
cucchiaia *f* drag
cucchiaiata *f* spoonful
cucchiaio spoon
cuccia *f* seat
cucina *f* kitchen
cucinare cook
cuciniere, ra *m* & *f* cook
cucire sew
cucito *m* sewing
cucitore *m* stitcher
cucitrice *f* seamstress
cucullato hooded
cucurbita *f* pumpkin
cugino, na *m* & *f* cousin
cui of whom
culata *f* backside
culla *f* cradle
cullamento *m.* rocking
cullare rock
culminare culminate
culmine *m* summit
culo bottom
culto *m* worship
cultore *m* farmer
cumulare cumulate
cumulativo cumulative
cumulo *m* heap
cuna *f* cradle
cuneo *m* wedge
cunicolo, culo *m* mine
cuoca *f* cook
cuocere cook

158

cuoco *m* cook
cupola dome *f*
cura *f* care
curabile curable
curadenti *m* tooth-pick
curante careful; caring
curare to cure
curiosità *f* curiosity
curioso curious
cursore *m* policeman
curva *f* curve
curvare curve
curvità *f* curvature
curvo bent
cuscino *m* cushion
cuspide *f* point
custode *m* guardian
custodia *f* custodian
custodia *f* custody
custodire keep
cutaneo cutaneous
cute *f* skin

D

da of; by; from; in;
for; near; according to
dabbasso underneath
dabbene good
dacchè as; since
dado *m* die; *pl* dice
daga *f* dagger
daina *f* doe
daino *m* deer
dalla of the
dama *f* lady
damigella *f* young lady
damigello *m* young man
damina *f* miss
damma *f* doe
damo *m* gallant
danaio *m* money
dannabile damnable
dannare condemn
dannato *m* reprobate

dannazione *f* sentence
danneggiare damage
danno *m* damage; injury
dante *m* curried deerskin
danza *f* dance
danzare dance
danzatore *m* & *f* dancer
dappiè *ad* from below
dappoco lazy
dappoi from; after
dappoichè since
dardeggiare shoot
dardo *m* dart
dare give; grant; permit;
produce; yield; show; tell
darsena *f* wet-dock
dassezzo finally
data *f* date
datare date
dativo dative
dato given
davanzale *m* frontal
davvantaggio more
davvero truly
daziare tax
daziere *m* tax-collector
dazio tax
dea goddess
debaccare rage; rave
debellare conquer
debile weak; sickly
debito owed
debitore debtor
debolezza *f* weakness
debolmente weakly
debordare overflow
decadenza decay
decadere decline
decano *m* dean
decantare laud; decant
decapitare behead
decapitazione *f* beheading
decennale decennial
decennio ten years
decente decent
decenza *f* decency

159

decesso dead
decezione f deception
decidere decide
decifrare decipher
decima f. tithe
decimale decimal

decimare tithe
decimo tenth
decisione f decision
decisivo decisive
declive steep
declivio slope
decollare behead
decomporre decompose

decorrere overflow
decorso m overflowing
decotto decoction
decremento, crescimento m decrease

decrescere decrease
decretare decree

dedica f dedication
dedicare dedicate
dedurre deduct; deduce
deduzione f consequence; deduction
deferenza f deference
deferire condescend
deficit m deficit
definire define
definitivo decisive
definizione f definition
deformare disfigure
deforme deformed
defunto deceased
degnità f dignity
degno worthy
degradare degrade
degustare taste

delfino m dolphin
deliberare deliberate
delicatezza f delicacy
delicato delicate
delineamento m outline
delinquente m delinquent
delirare rave

delirio m delirium; raving
delitto m crime
delizioso delicious
demente mad
demenza f madness
democratico democratic
democrazio f democracy
demolire demolish
demonio m demon
denaro m money
denegare deny
denigrare slander
denominare name
denominatore m denom-
denotare denote [inator
densità f density
denso dense
dentatura f set of teeth

dente m tooth
dentista m dentist
dentizione f dentition
dentro within
denudare strip; uncover
denunziare denounce
depilatorio m depilatory
deplorabile deplorable
deplorare deplore [lation
depopolazione f depopu-
deporre deposit; depose
deportare transport
depositare deposit
deposito m deposit
depravare deprave
depredare plunder
depressione f depression
deprimere depress
deputato m deputy
descrivere describe
descrizione f description
deserto m desert

desiderabile desirable
desiderio m desire; wish
designare design
desinare dine; dinner
desistere desist
desolare desolate

desso same
destare w ke; awake
destinare destine
destinatario m addressee
destinazione f destination
destino m destiny; fate
destituire depose
desto awake
destrezza f dexterity
destra f right hand s
determinare determine
determinazione f determination
detestabile detestable
detestare detest
detettivo m detective
detonazione f detonation
detrarre deduct
devastare lay waste
deviare deviate
devoto devoted; devout
devozione f devotion
di m day
diabete f diabetes
diabetico diabetic
diaframma m diaphragm
diagnosi f diagnosis
diagonale diagonal
dialetto m dialect
dialogo m dialogue
diamante m diamond
diametro m diameter
diario m diary
diarrea f diarrhoea
dibattere debate
dibattimento m debate
dicembre m December
dicervellato crazy
dichiarare declare
dichiarazione f declaration
dieci ten
dieta f diet
dietro behind
difendere defend
difesa f defence
difetto m defect

difettoso defective
diffamare defame
differente different
differenza f difference
differire differ; postpone
difficile difficult
difficoltà f difficulty
diffidare distrust
diffidente diffident
diffidenza f distrust
difterite f diphtheria
difformità f deformity
diga f dike
digestione f digestion
digiunare fast
digiuno fasting
dignità f dignity
dilatare dilate
dilazione f delay
dilemma m dilemma
dilettante m amateur
dilettare delight
dilettevole delightful
diletto loved
diluire dilute
diluvio m flood
dimagrare grow lean
dimensione f dimension
dimenticare forget
dimentichevole forgetful
dimettere forgive
dimorare live; reside
dimostrare demonstrate
dimostrazione f demonstration
dinamite f dynamite
dinamo m dynamo
dinanzi before
dintorno arrear; m neighbourhood
Dio m God
dipartimento m department
dipendente depending
dipendenza f dependence
dipendere depend

diploma *m* diploma
diplomatico diplomatic
diretto direct
direttore *m* director
direzione *f* direction
dirimpetto opposite
diritto (*m*) right; straight
dirotto excessively
dirupare fall down
disagio *m* want
disapprendere unlearn
disapprovare disapprove
disarmamento *m* disarming
disarmare disarm
disastro *m* disaster
disastroso disastrous
disattento inattentive
discendere descent
discepolo *m* pupil
disciplina *f* discipline
disco *m* disk
discernere discern
discorso *m* speech
discreditare discredit
discrezione *f* discretion
discreto discreet
discussione *f* discussion
discutere discuss
disdetta *f* denial
disegnare draw [design
disegno *m* drawing;
diseredare disinherit
disertare destroy; desert
disfare undo; dissolve
disfatta *f* defeat
disfidare challenge
disgrazia *f* disgrace
disgraziato unfortunate
disgustare disgust
disgusto *m* disgust
disimparare forget
disinfettare disinfect
disobbedire disobey
disoccupato unoccupied
disonestà *f* dishonesty

disonorare dishonour
disordine *m* disorder
dispaccio *m* despatch
dispari odd; uneven
disparte, in – aside
dispendioso expensive
dispensa distribution;
larder   [tribute
dispensare dispense; dis-
disperare despair
disperazione *f* despair
disperato desperate
dispetto *m* anger; con-
tempt   [displeasure
dispiacere displease; *m*
dispiacevole unpleasant
disponibile disposable
disporre dispose
disposizione *f* disposition
disprezzare despise
disputa *f*, –re dispute
dissolvere dissolve
dissomigliare differ
dissonanza *f* dissonance
dissuadere dissuade
distaccare separate
distante distant
distanza *f* distance
distare be distant
distesa *f* extent
distillare distil
distilleria *f* distillery
distinguere distinguish
distinzione *f* distinction
distrarre distract
distrazione *f* distraction
distribuire distribute
distribuzione *f* distribu-
distruggere destroy [tion
distruzione *f* destruction
disubbidire disobey
disturbo *m* disturbare
trouble
divertire divert
divezzare disaccustom
dividere divide

162

divietare forbid
divieto *m* prohibition
divinità *f* divinity
divino divine [parting
divisa *f* device; uniform;
divisione *f* division
divorare devour [divorce
divorziare, divorzio *m*
dizionario *m* dictionary
doccia *f* shower-bath
docile docile
documento *m* document
dogana *f* custom-house
doganiere *m* custom-house officer
dogma, domma *m* dogma
dolce sweet; *m & pl*
dolere grieve [sweets
dolore *m* grief; pain;
doloso fraudulent

domanda *f* demand

domandare ask
domani to-morrow
domare subdue; break
domattina to-morrow; morning
donare give; – zione *f*
gift; – tore *m* giver
donde, d'onde, dondeche
whence; why
dondolare swing
dondolo *m* joke
donna *f* woman; wife;
lady; – esco womanlike
donnaiuolo *m* beau
donno kind; *m* master;
donnola *f* weazel [lord
donnona *f* stout woman
dono *m* gift; present
donora *f* wedding outfit
donzella *f* young lady
donzello *m* young gentleman; servant
dopo after; – chè when
doppia *f* pistole (coin); flounce

doppiare increase; -mente
doubly; wickedly
doppio *m* double; – piezza *f* duplicity
doppione *m* doubloon
dorare gild; – tura *f*
dramma *f* drachma
drappare, peggiare drape;
– peria *f* drapery; – piere *m* draper
drappello *m* troop; band
drappo *m* cloth; coat
drizzare raise; erect
droga *f* drug; – gheria
f drug-trade; – ghiere
m druggist
dromedario *m* dromedary
druda *f* sweet-heart; concubine
drudo gallant; loving
clever; *m* lover
dualità *f* duality; – lismo
dubbiare doubt [*m* dualism
dubbiezza, bio, biosità *f*
& *m* doubt

due two
duecento, ducento, gento
two hundred
duellante *m* duellist
duellare fight a duel
duello *m* duel
duennale biennial
duetanti double
duetto *m* duet
dumo *m* thorn; bramble
duna *f* down; sand-hill
dunque then; so [*m* grief
duodecimo twelfth; duolo
duomo *m* dome
duplicare double
duplicità *f* duplicity
durabilità, rata *f* duration; – bile durable
duramente hard; harshly
durante, turo durable
durare endure

163

E

e, ed and
ebanista *m* cabinet-maker
ebano *m* ebony
ebbrezza, brietà, bria-
  chezza *f* drunkenness;
  – bro, brioso, briaco
  drunk; mad
ebdomadario weekly
ebete weak; stupid
ebollimento, ebollizione
  m & f ebullition
ebraico hebraic; – ismo
  m hebraism
ebreo, ea *n* Hebrew
eccellente excellent; –
  tissimo very excellent
eccellenza *f* excellency
eccellere excel
eccelso high; eminent
eccentricità eccentricity;
  – trico eccentric; *n* eccentric [centric
eccepire except
eccessività, eccesso *f &*
  m excess; – vo, va excessive; – vamente ex-
  cessively
eccetera *m* etcetera
eccètto except; but
eccettuare except; – tu-
  ato excepted
eccettuazione, cezione *f*
  exception
eccidio *m* destruction
eccitare excite; – tativo
  exciting [ecclesiastic
ecclesia *f* church; – stico
eclisse *f* eclipse
ecco here is
edera *f* ivy
edificare edify; build
edificio, zoi *m* edifice
edile *m* edile

edito published
editore *m* editor
editto *m* edict
edizione *f* edition
adotto educated
educazione *f* education
aducare educate; – tivo,
  va educative; – tore *n*
  educator
edulo *m* comestible
effabile expressible
effemeride *f* ephemeris
effeminare effeminate
efferatezza *f* cruelty;
  efferato cruel
effervescenza *f* efferves-
  cence; – cente efferves-
  cent
effetto *m* effect; – tivo
  tuale effective
effettuare effect; – tua-
  f effect
effigiare make; imagine
effimero ephemeral
efflorescenza *f* efflores-
  efflusso *m* flux   [rence
effluvio *m* effluvium
effrenato unbridled
efod *m* ephod
egestione *f* evacuation

egida aegis
egli, ei, e' he
egoisme *m* egotism;
  – ista egotist
egregiamente egregious-
  ly; – gio, a egregious
egritudine *f* illness
egro sick; infirm
eguagliare equalize;
  – glianza, lità *f* equality
eguale equal
eh, ehi eh!
eiezione *f* election
elaborare elaborate; – zione *f* elaboration
elasticità elasticity

- tico elastic
elazione f pride
elce f holm-oak
elefante m elephant
elegante a & n f elegant; - za f elegance
eleggere elect; - ggibile eligible; - gibilità f eligibility
elegia f elegy; - giaco elegiac
elemento m element; - tare elementary
elemosina f alms; charity; - nare give alms;
elogio m eulogy
eloquente eloquent
eloquenza f eloquence
eludere elude
emancipare emancipate
emblema m emblem
embrione m embryo
emendare mend
emergenza f occurrence
emergere emerge
emerito retired
emetico m emetic
emettere emit
emigrare emigrate
emigrazione f emigration
eminente eminent
eminenza f eminence
emisfero m hemisphere
emolumento m emolument
emorraggia f haemorrhage
emorroide fpl haemorrhoids
emozione f emotion
empiere fill
empio impious
emporio m emporium
enfasi f emphasis
enfiare swell
enfiatura f swelling
enimma m riddle; - tico enigmatic

enorme enormous
ente m being
entrambi both
entrare enter
entrata f entrance
entusiasmo m enthusiasm
enumerare enumerate
enunciare enunciate
epico epic
epidemia f disease
epidemico epidemic
epifania f epiphany
epigramm m epigram
epilessia f epilepsy
epilettico epileptic
episcopato m episcopate
equipaggio m equipment; carriage; luggage; crew
equipaggiare equip
equivalente equivalent
equivoco equivocal
era f era, epoch   [table
erba f herb; grass; vegerbaiuolo m greengrocer
erborizzare botanise
erede m heir; eredità f inheritance; ereditare inherit
eremita m hermit
eresia f heresy
eretico heretic
eretto, erigere erect
ergastolo m prison
erica f heath
ermellino m ermine
ermetico hermetic
ernia f hernia   [heroic
eroe m hero; eroice
errato m error
erroneo erroneous
errore m error
erta all' - on one's guard
erto steep
erudito learned
esagerare exaggerate
esagerazione f exaggera-

165

tion

esalazione *f* exhalation
esaltare exalt
esaminare examine
esame *m* examination
esasperare exasperate
esattezza *f* exactness
esatto exact
esaudire grant; hear
esaurire exhaust
esca *f* bait; tinder
escavazione *f* excavation
esclamare exclaim
esecutare execute; esecutivo executive; esecuziore *f* execution
eseguire execute
esempigrazia for instance
esempio *m* example
esemplare exemplary; copy
esente exempt
esequie *f* / *pl* exequies
esercitare exercise
esercito *m* army
esercizio *m* exercise
esibire exhibit
esibizione *f* exhibition
esigere exact; demand
esiliare, esilio *m* exile
esimere free
esimio excellent
esistere exist
esperienza *f* experience; experiment [perience
esperimentare try; experto expert
espiare expiate
esplicare explain
esplodere explode
esplosione *f* explosion
esplorare explore
esploratore *m* explorer
esporre expose
esportare export
esportazione *f* exportation
esposizione *f* exhibition

espressione *f* expression
espresso express
esprimere express
espropriare expropriate
espulsione *f* expulsion

essenza *f* essence
essenziale essential
essere be; *m* being
est *m* oriente; east
estasi *f* ecstasy
estate *f* summer
estendere extend
estensione *f* extension
estenuare extenuate
esteriore exterior
esterno external
estero foreign (country)
estradizione *f* extradition
estraneo strange(r)
estraordinario extraordi-
estrarre extract [nary
estravagante extravagant
estremo extreme
estremità *f* extremity
estro *m* poetry
estrudere expel; — sione *f* expulsion
estuante boiling
esturbare drive out
esuberante exuberant; — za *f* exuberance
esule *m* exile
esultare exult; — tanza *f* exultation; — zione *f* exultation
esurire be hungry
età, etade *f* age; time
etera, etere *f* & *m* ether; air; sky; — reo, a ethereal
eterno eternal, — mente eternally; — nare eternize; — nità *f* eternity
eterogene heterogenous
euro *m* East wind; — peo European

evacuare evacuate; – **cuamento, zione** *m & f* evacuation

evadere escape

evaporare evaporate; – **zione** *f* evaporation

evasione *f* evasion; – **sivo** evasive

evento *m* event; – **tuale** eventual; – **tualità** *f* eventuality

evidente evident; – **za** *f* evidence [*f* eviction

evincere evict; – **zione** *f*

evirato enasculated; – **zione** *f* emasculation

evitare avoid; escape

evo evocation

evocare evoke; – **zione** *f* evocation

evoluzione *f* evolution

extempore directly [yet

eziandio to; also; even;

F

fabbrica *f* factory; fab-ric; – **are** manufacture – **tore** *m* manufacturer

fabbriceria *f* fabric

fabbro *m* smith; author

faccenda *f* affair; busi-ness; – **diere** *m* intri-guer

facchino *m* porter; scoun-drel

faccia *f* face; side

facciata *f* front; facade

face *f* torch

facente doing

facezia *f* jest; joke;

facilità *f* facility; – **le** easy; – **tare** facilitate; – **lmente** easily

facinoroso wicked

facitoio feasible

facitore *m* author

fagiano *m* pheasant

fagiuolo *m* kidney bean; falcare bend

falcastro *m* sickle

falce *f* scythe; – **cetto** sickle; – **ciare** mow; – **tore** *m* mower

falegname *m* carpenter

falinbello *m* booby

fallace fallacious; – **cia** *f* fallacy; – **lante** de-ceiving; – **lanza** *f* de-ceit

fallare be mistaken; fail

fallire err; fail; deceive; – **libile** fallible; – **libi-lità** *f* fallibility; – **men-to** *m* error; failure

fallo *m* fault

falsa *f* discord

falsare, sificare falsify; – **so, sa** false; – **samen-te** falsely; – **sario** *m* forger; – – **sificazione** *f* falsefication

falsetto *m* falsetto

falta *f* fault

fama *f* fame; – **moso, sa** famous

fame *f* hunger; – **lico** famishing

famigerato famous

famiglia *f* family

famigliare familiar; servant; friend; – **rità** *f* familiarity

famiglio *m* servant

fanale *m* lantern

fanatico fanatic; – **tismo** *m* fanatism

fanciulla *f* girl; maid

fanciullaggine, lezza *f* childishness

fanciullesco childish [ish

fanciullo *m* child; child-

landonia _f_ story

fanghiglia _f_ mud [muddy

fango _m_ mud; **- so , sa**

fantaccino _m_ foot-soldier

fantasia _f_ fancy; opinion

fantasima _f_ phantom

fantasmagoria _f_ phantas-
magoria

fantasticaggine, cheria _f_
fancy; whim

fantasticare rave; fancy;
 – co fantastic [soldier

fante _m_ servant; . foot-

fanteria _f_ infantry

fantesca maid-servant

fardaggio _m_ luggage

fardello _m_ lead

fare make; do; work

farfalla _f_ butterfly

farina _f_ flour

farmacia _f_ pharmacy

farmacista _m_ chemist

faro _m_ light-house

farsa _f_ farce

fascia _f_ band; bandage;
 sotto – by book-post;
 under wrapper

fasciare bind

fasciatura _f_ bandage

fastidiare annoy

fasto _m_ pomp

fata _f_ fairy

fatale fatal; **fato** _m_ fate

fatica _f_, **– care** fatigue

fatto made; _m_ fact

fattorino _m_ shop-boy

fattura _f_ doing; invoice

favoloso fabulous

favore _m_ favour

favorevole favourable

favorito _m_ favourite

fazzoletto _m_ handkerchief

fabbre _f_ fever

febrifugo febrifuge

febrile feverish

feccia _f_ dregs

fecondare fertilise

fecondo fruitful

fede _f_ faith

fedele faithful

fedeltà _f_ fidelity

federa _f_ pillow-case

fegato _m_ liver

felce _f_ fern

felice happy

feltro _m_ felt

femmina _f_ woman; female

femminile feminine

fendere cleave

fenile _m_ hay-loft

fenomeno _m_ phenomenon

feretro _m_ coffin, bier

feria _f_ holiday

ferire strike

ferita _f_ wound

fermo firm; **– in posta**
 to be left till called for

feroce ferocious

ferro _m_ iron

ferrovia _f_ railway

ferruginoso ferruginous

fertilità _f_ fertility

fertile fertile

fervente, fervido fervent

fetta _f_ slice

fiaccare break

fiaccola _f_ torch

fiala _f_ phial

fiamma _f_ flame

fiammifero _m_ match

fianco _m_ flank; side

fiasco _m_ bottle (packed
 in straw, 2.25 litre)

fiatare breathe; **fiato** _m_

fibbia _f_ buckle [breath

fibra _f_ fibre

ficcare fix; drive in

fico _m_ fig; fig-tree

fidanzare betroth; engage

fidare confide

fidanza _f_ confidence

fido faithful

fiducia *f* confidence
fiele *m* gall
fieno *m* hay
fiera *f* wild beast; fair
fiero ferocious; proud
flevole weak
fievolezza *f* weakness
figgere fix
figliastra *f* daughter-in-law
figliastro, *m* son-in-law
figlio, figliuolo *m* son
figura *f* figure; face
figurare represent
fila *f* file; row
filare spin
filatoio *m* spinning-wheel
filatore *m* spinner
filetto *m* small thread; [fillet
filiale filial
filiera *f* wire-drawing-mill;
filigrana *f* filigrane
filo *m* thread
filologia *f* philology
filologo *m* philologer
filosofo *m* philosopher
filtrare, filtro *m* filter
filza *f* file; string
finanza *f* finance
finale final
fine *f* end
finestra *f* window
fingere feign
finire finish
fino fine
finocchio *m* fennel
finora till now
finzione *f* fiction
fiocco *m* tuft
fioco hoarse
fioraia *f* flower-girl
fioraliso *m* blue-bottle
fiordaliso *m* lily
fiore *m* flower
fiorire bloom
firma *f* signature; – re
sign
firmamento *m* firmament

fischiare whisthle; hiss
fischi(etto) *m* .whistle
fisica *f* physics
fisciù *m* handkerchief
fisionomia *f* physiognomy
fisso fixed: permanent
fissare fix
flotta *f* fleet
fluido fluid
flutto *m* wave
fluttuare waver; fluctuate
foca *f* seal
focaccia *f* cake
fochista *f* fireman; stoker
foce *f* mouth
focolare *m* hearth
fodera *f* lining
foderare line
foglia *f* leaf [paper
foglio *m* sheet; news-
fogna *f* sewer
folata *f* flock of birds;
gust of wind
fondamento *m* foundation
fondare found
fondata *f* dregs
fondere melt; fonderia
f foundry [background
fondo deep; *m* bottom;
fontana *f* fountain
forare bore

forbici *f/pl* scissors
foresta *f* forest
forestiere *m* stranger
forma *f* formare form
formaggio *m* cheese
formale formal
formalità *f* formality
formalizzarsi take amiss
formazione *f* formation
formento *m* wheat
formica *f* ant; – io *m*
ant-hill
formidabile formidable
formula *f* formula
fornace *f* furnace

169

fornaio m baker
fornire furnish; fornitore m purveyor
forno m oven
foro m hole; forum
forse perhaps
forte strong   [force
fortezza f stronghold;
fortificare fortify   [tion
fortificazione f fortificafortuna f fortune
fortunato happy; lucky
forza f force; strength;
forzare force   [power
forziere m safe
fosforo m phosphorus
fossa f grave
fosso m ditch
fotografare photograph
fotografia f photograph(y)
fotografico photographic
fotografo m photographer
fra among; m friar
fracassare break; smash
fragile fragile
fragola f strawberry
franco frank
frangere break   [stand
frantendere misunderfraternità f fraternity
fraterno fraternal
fratellastro m step-brother
frattanto meanwhile
frattura f fracture
frazione f fraction
freccia f arrow
freddo freddura f cold
freddare cool
fregare rub
fregata f frigate
fregiare adorn
fremere shiver
frenare refrain
frenatore m brakesman
freno m bridle; brake
frequentare frequent
frequente frequent

fresco fresh; cool
freschezza f coolness
fretta f hurry
frettoloso in a hurry
fricassea f fricassee
friggere fry
frigido cold
frizione f friction   [band
froda f fraud; contrafrodare defraud; smuggle
frollo tender
fronda f foliage   [leaves
frondeggiare put forth
frontiera f frontier
fronte f forehead; front
frontone m gable
frottola f story; ballad
frugalità f frugality

frugale frugal
frugare search
fruire enjoy
frumento m wheat
frusta f; - re whip
frustrare frustrate
frutto m fruit; produce
fucile m gun; fucilare
fucina f forge   [shoot
fuga f flight
fugare route
fuggire fly; flee; - ga
f flight; - tivo fugitive
- gifatica idle; idler;
- giasco m fugitive
fulgere shine; - gidezza
f shine; - gido shiny
fuliggine f dusk; soot;
- noso fuliginous
fulmine m thunderbolt;
lightning;
funerale, nebre, reo funeral   [fatal
funestare afflict; - to
fungaia f mushroom-bed;
- go m mushroom
fungosità f fungosity;
- so fungous; spongy
funzione f function

170

fuoco *m* fire; love; – **chista** *f* firework-maker; – **coso** fiery

fuora, ri outside; – **fuorchè**; – **solamente** except; save

fuormisura -excessively

fuoruscito *m* exile; out-

furacchiare juggle [law

furare rob; – **race. rante** robbing; – **tore** *m* robber

furbo *m* knave; cheat; – **beria** *f* cheating; – **besco** knavish; crafty; – **betto** *m* little rogue

furente furious

furfantare cheat; – **tag** g . **teria** *f* knavery

fu . a *f* fury; – **riare** be a .gry; – **bondo, oso**

furoncolo runcolo *m* boil

furore *m* fury [-**vo** furtive

furto *m* theft; stealth; **di** – by stealth

fusello *m* tree

fusione *f* fusion; melting; – **sibile** fusible; – **so** melting; spindle

fustigare whip; – **zione** *f* whipping

fusto *m* trunk [futility

futile futile; – **lità** *f*

futuro future

G

gabbadeo *m* hypocrite

gabbare deceive; – **mento** *m* deceit; – – **tore** *m* cheat

gabbione *m* gabion

gabbo *m* joke

gabella *f* custom-duty; – **liere. lotto** *m* custom-house officer

gabinetto *m* closet; office

gaggio *m* pledge

gagliardo playful; strong;

gagno *m* sheepfold; trap

gagnolare whine; – **mento, lio** *m* howling

gaiezza *f* joy; – **io** gay

gala *f* gala

galante gallant; gay; *m* spark; – **mente** elegantly; – **teggiare** court; – **ria** *f* gallantry

galantuomo *m* gentleman

galappio *m* trap; cheat

galassia *f* galaxy

galbano *m* galbanum

galea, lera *f* galley; – **leotto** *m* convict

galeone *m* galleon

galeotta *f* gallot

galetta *f* butter-paste; sea-biscuit

galla *f* gall-nut

gallare float; revel

gallina *f* hen; – **naccio** *m* turkey; – **naio** *m* hen roost; – **nella** *f* young hen; (astr.) pleiades; – **lione** *m* capon

gallo *m* cock [lace

gallone *m* lace; – **nare**

galloria *f* joy

gallozza, lozzola, luzza, *f* gallnut; bubble

galoppare gallop; – **pata, po** *f & m* gallop

galoscia *f* galosh

galuppo *m* rude man

galvanismo *m* galvanism; –**nico** galvanic; –**nizzare** galvanize

gamba *f* leg; centipede

gambale *m* trunk; stem

gambero *m* crawfish; (astr.) cancer

gambetto *m* tripping up
gambo *m* stalk
gara *f* debate; emulation
garabullare cheat
garbare please; - **tezza** *f* good looks; - **to** well bred
garbo *m* good looks
garbuglio *m* confusion
gareggiare complete; - **tore** *m* rival; - **gioso** quarrelsome
garetto *m* ham [mur
gargagliare gurgle; mur-
gargarismo *m* gargle
gargarizzare *m* gargle
gariglione *m* chime
garofano *m* pink
garrire chirp
garzone *m* boy; servant;
gas *m* gas [waiter
gatto *m*, **gatta** *f* cat
gazza *f* magpie
gazzetta *f* gazette
gelare freeze
gelato *m* ice(-cream)
gemma *f* gem; bud
generale (*m*) general

generalizzare generalize
generare engender
generazione *f* generation
genero *m* gender
genero *m* son-in-law
generosità *f* generosity
generoso generous
genesi *f* genesis
gengiva *f* gum
genio *m* genius
genitori *m pl* parents
gente *f* people
genuino genuine
geografia *f* geography
geografo *m* geographer
geologia *f* geology
geometria *f* geometry
gerarchia *f* hierarchy

gerente *m* manager
germe *m* germ
germinare germinate
gesso *m*, **gessare** plaster
gesto *m* gesture
Gesù *m* Jesus
Gesuita *m* Jesuit
gettare cast; **getto** *m* throwing), cast
ghiacciaia *f* ice-house; ice-safe; glacier
ghiacciare freeze
già already; **giacchè** as;
giacca *f* jacket [since·
giacere lie
giallo yellow
giammai never [ese
Giapponese *m* Japan-
giardiniere *m* gardener
giardino *m* garden

ginastica *f* gymnastics
ginocchio *m* knee; -**ne** kneeling
giocolatore *m* juggler
giocondo jorose; gay
giogo *m* yoke [stone
gioia *f* joy; precious
gioiello *m* jewel

gioelliere *m* jeweller
gioioso joyous
giornalaio *m* news-vendor
giornale *m* journal
giornalista *m* journalist
giornaliero daily
giornata *f* day; day's work; day's wages;
giorno *m* day [journey
giovane *m* young man; *f* young woman

giracapo *m* dizziness
girare move round
girasole *m* sunflower
giro *m* round; turn
gita *f* going; excursion
giu down [coa·
giubba *f* mane; waist-

giubbileo *m* jubilee
giubilare rejoice
giudeo *m* jew
giudicare judge
giudice *m* judge
giudicio *m* judgment;
 -so judicious
giumenta *f* mare
giunco *m* rush
giungere arrive; join
giunta *f* arrival; increase;
 meeting
giuocare play
giuoco *m* play
giuramento *m* oath
giurare swear
giurato *m* juryman
giure *m* law; right
giuridico juridical
Giuseppe *m* Joseph
giustificare justify
giustizia *f* justice; -re
giusto just [execute
gloria *f* glory; fame; *re*
 glorify; glorioso glorious
glutinoso glutinous
gobba *f* hump
gobbo *m* hunchback
goccia *f* drop
gocciolare drip
godere enjoy; rejoice
godimento *m* pleasure
goffo silly; rude
gola *f* throat
golfo *m* gulf
goloso gluttonous
gomito *m* elbow
gomitolo *m* ball; clue
gomma *m* gum; – ara-
 bica gum arabic; –
 elastica india-rubber;
 -to gummed
gonfiare swell; blow up
gonfio swollen
gonn(ella) *f* gown
gonorrea *f* gonorrhœa

gorga, gorgia *f* throat
governante *f* housekeeper
governare govern
govern(ament)o *m* gov-
 ernment
gradevole agreeable
gradino *m* step
gradire please; approve
grado *m* liking; degree
graffiare scratch
grafite *f* black-lead
gragnola *f* hail(storm)
gramatica *f* grammar;
 -le grammatical
gramma *m* gram
granaio *m* granary
granata *f* grenade
granato *m* garnet
grande great; -zza *f*
 greatness; – ggiare play
 the lord [hail
grandine *f* grandinare
grandioso magnificent
granduca *m* grand-duke;
 -to *m* grand-duchy;
 -chessa *f* grand-duchess
granello *m* grain; nugget
granita *f* iced lemonade
grano *m* grain; – turco
 maize [grapes
grappolo *f* bunch of
grassatore *m* highway-
 man
grasso stout; fat
grato agreeable; grateful
gratitudine *f* gratitude
grattare scratch
grattino *m* razor
gratuito gratuitous
gravare grieve; burden
grave grave
gravido pregnant; panino
 – sandwich
gravità *f* gravity
grazia *f* grace; thanks
graziare absolve; pardon

173

grazioso graceful
Greco m Greek; north-
greggio raw [east
grembiale m apron
grembio m lap
greppia f manger
greppina f couch
gretto stingy
gridare shout; call
grido m cry; fame
grossa f gross [nancy
grossezza f size; preg-
grosso big
grossolano rough
grotta f grotto
groviera f gruyère
gru f crane
gruccia f crutch
grugnare grunt
gruppare group
guadagnare gain; win
guadagnato m gain; profit
guancia f cheek; – – **ciale**
  m pillow; – **lino** m
  cushion; – **ta** f buffet;
guardare look at; consider; keep;
guardamento m aspect
guardatore m spectator;
  guardian
guardia f guard
guardiano m guardian
guardingo prudent
guardo m glance; look
guarentire guarantee; –
  tia, tigia f warranty
guari (non) little; nearly
guarire cure; heal; –
  gione f cure
guarnacca f (night)gown
guarnire furnish; trim;
  – **gione, tura** f trimming
guatare look at; spy;
  – **tura** f glance
guazzabugliare embroil;
  confuse; – **glio** m con-

fusion
guazzare shake; ford;
  – **toiò** m ford; –**zzo** m
  ford; –**zoso** muddy
guazzetto m ragout; sauce
guercio squinting
guerra f war; obstacle;
  – **reggiare** fight; –
  giante belligerent; –
  reggiamento m fight;
  – **reggiatore. riere. ro**
  m warrior; – **ricciola** f
  guerrilla
gufare laugh at
gufo m owl
guida f guide
guidare guide; lead
guiderdonare reward; –
  done m reward; salary
guirminella f deceit
guisa f way; will
guitto dirty; paltry
guizzare stir; swim;
  –**zo** m stirring; swimming
guizzo faded
guscio m pod
gustare try; approve;

H

The letter **h** is used
only to harden the sound
of the letters **c** and **g**
before the vowels **e** and
i. It is used also to distinguish the words **ho,
hai, ha, hanno** from **o,
ai, a, anno**.

I

The **I** is used instead of
the **J**.
iacinto m hyacinth; –
  aspide m jasper

174

iattura f lost; disgrace
iberno wintery
ibrido hybrid
icnografia f ichnography;
-fico ichnographic
iconoclasta m iconoclast
Iddio m God
idea f idea; -le ideal; -
lismo m idealism; -
lista m idealist; -lità f
ideality; -are imagine
idem ditto
identicità f identity; -co
identical; -tity f identity
idolo m idol; - trare
worship idols; - tria
f idoltary
idoneo fit; suitable; -
neità f convenience
idra f hydra
idraulica f hydraulics;
-co hydraulic
idrofobia f hydrophobia
iena f hyena
ierarchia f hierarchy
ieri m yesterday
ier l'altro m day before
yesterday [hygienic
igiene f hygiene; -nico
ignaro, ra ignorant
ignavia f cowardice; -
vo cowardly
igneo igneous; fiery; -
gnizione f ignition
ignoranza f ignorance;
-te, tello ignorant;
-rare ignore
ignoto unknown
ignudare undress; -do
ih come [naked
il the
ilare gay; -rità f hilarity
illativo, va consequent;
-zione f consequence
illecebra f flattery
illecito unlawful; m

crime [illegality
illegale illegal; - lità
illeggibile ineligible
illegittimità f illegitimacy;
-mo illegitimate
illeso safe
illetterato illiterate
illibatezza f integrity;
-to honest
illimitato unlimited
illuminazione f illumina-
tion; - re illuminate;
-to illuminated
illusione f illusion; -sore
m deceiver; -sorio il-
lusory
illustrazione f illustration
illuvione f flood
imbaccarsi get tipsy
imbaccucare disguise
imbaldanzire be proud
imbaldire grow bold [of
imballaggio m packing;
- lare pack; - latore
m packer
imbalordire stupefy
imbalsamare embalm;
-zione f embalming
imbarazzare embarrass;
-zo m embarrassment
imbarcare embark; -co
m embarking
imbardare flatter
imbarrare bar
imbasamento m basis
imbasceria f embassy
imbastardire deprave
imbastare saddle
imbastire baste
imbasto m pack-saddle
imbattersi meet by chance
imbatto m chance; im-
pediment
imbeccare teach
imbecile silly; stupid;
-lità f imbecility

175

imbelle weak; faint
imbellettare shave; paint (face)
imbellire beautify
imbendare bind
imberbe beardless
imberciare hit (mark)
imbevere imbibe
imbonire appease
imborsare pocket
imboscare lie in ambush; -ta *f* ambush
imboschire plant woods
imbottare decant; -toio *m* funnel
imbottigliare bottle
imbracciare embrace
imbragacciare stick in mud
imbrandire brandish
imbrattare soil; damage -to *m* dirt; hog's wash
imbriacare get tipsy; -cato, co tipsy; -mento, tura *m* & *f* drunkenness
imbrigare embroil
imbrigliare bridle
imbroccare aim at
imbroglio *m* confusion
imbrunire become dark
imbruttire grow ugly
imbuto *m* funnel
imitare imitate

imitazione *f* imitation
imitatore *m* imitator
immacolato immaculate
immaginabile imaginable
immaginare imagine
immaginazione *f* imagination
immagrire grow thin
immediato immediate
immemorabile immemorable
immenso immense [able
immergere submerge
immeritato undeserved
immobile immovable

immollare moisten
immorale immoral
immortale immortal
immortalità *f* immortality
immutabile invariable
impacc(hett)are pack up
impagabile invaluable
impagliare stuff
impallidire turn pale
impalpabile impalpable
imparare learn [rable
impareggiabile incomparable
impari odd
imparziale impartial
impegnare pledge
impellere push; impel
impenetrabile impenetrabile
impensato unforeseen
imperatore *m* emperor
imperatrice *f* empress
impercettibile unperceivable [able
imperdonabile unpardonable
imperturbabile calm
impetuoso impetuous
impiagare wound
impiccare hang
impicciare trouble [point
impiegare employ; appiegato *m* official
impiego *m* office
impiombare lead; stop
implacabile implacable
implicare embroil
implorare implore

impolverare powder
impopolare unpopular
imporre order; impose
importare matter
importante important
importanza *f* importance
importazione *f* importation
importunare trouble
importuno troublesome

impossibile impossible
impostare post
impostore *m* impostor
impotente impotent [able
impraticabile impractic-
impreccare curse
imprendere undertake
impresa *f* enterprise
impressione *f* impression
imprestare lend
imprigionare imprison
imprimere stamp
improbabile improbable
improbo wicked
impronta *f* stamp
improprio improper
improvveduto unforeseen
inanimare encourage
inappetenza *f* want of
appetite [able
inapprezzabile inestim-
inargentare silver
inaspettato unexpected
inaudito unheard of
inaugurare inaugurate
inazione *f* inaction
incagliare strand
incalzare pursue
incandescente incandes-
cent [cence
incandescenza *f* incandes-
incantare enchant
incarcerare imprison
incaricare load; charge
incartare wrap up
incassare cash; enshrine
incatenacciare bolt
incatenare chain
incavare dig; hollow
incendiare set on fire

inchiesta *f* inquest
inchinare incline
inchino *m* bow
inchiodare nail
inchiostro *m* ink
inchiudere enclose

incominciare begin
incomodare trouble
incomparabile incompa-
rable
inconsolabile inconsolable
incontestabile indisput-
able
incontanente directly
incontrare meet
incontro against; andare
all' – go to meet
incoraggiare encourage
incorniciare frame
incoronare crown
incorporare incorporate
incorrere incur
incorrigibile incorrigible
incredibile incredible
increspare knit; curl
incrinare split
indarno in vain
indebitarsi run into debt
indebolire weaken
indeciso irresolute
indefinibile undefinable
indennità *f* indemnity
indennizzare indemnify
independenza *f* independ-
dence [able
indescrivibile indescrib-
indi afterwards
Indiano *m* Indian
indicare indicate [guide
indicatore *m* advertiser;
indice *m* fore-finger;index
indicibile inexpressible
indietro backward
indifferenza *f* indifference
indigeno indigenous
indigente poor
indigestione *f* indigestion
indignarsi grow angry
indignazione *f* indigna-
tion [address
indispensabile indispen-
sable

177

indisporre indispose
indisposizione f indisposizione
individuale individual
indizio m indication; sign
indolcire soften
indolente indolent
indorare gild
indovinare guess
indubitabile indubitable
indugiare, indugio m delay
indulgente indulgent
indulgenza f indulgence
indurare harden
indurre engage; induce
industria f industry
inebbriare inebriate
inedito unpublished
ineguale unequal
inerme unarmed
infallibile infallible
infallibilità f infallibility
infamare slander
infame infamous
infantile childish
infanzia f infancy
infarinare flour
infaticabile indefatigable
infatti indeed
inferiore inferior
inferire infer
infermeria f infirmary
infermiere m nurse
infermità f infirmity
infernale infernal
inferno m hell
infettare infect
infezione f infection
infiammare inflame
infilare thread
infimo very low; lowest
infine at last
infingardo idle
infinità f infinity
infinito infinite
infino till

influente influent
influenza f influence
informare inform [tion
informazione f informazione
informe deformed
infortunio m misfortune
infoscato darkened
infossato buried; hollow
infrangere break
ingabbiare put in a cage
ingaggiare pawn; pledge
ingannare deceive
inganno m deceit [try
ingegnarsi exert oneself;
ingegnere m engineer
ingegno m genius; – so ingenious
ingenuo ingenuous
ingessare plaster
inghiottire swallow
ingiallire get yellow
inginocchiarsi kneel
inginocchiatoio m kneeling-stool
ingiù down; below
ingiungere enjoin; order
ingiuria f injury; – re insult
ingoiare swallow
ingommare gum
ingrandire increase
ingrassare fatten
ingrato ungrateful
ingraziarsi ingratiate
ingrediente m ingredient
ingresso m entrance
ingrossare increase
ingrosso m wholesale
inguantarsi put on gloves
inibire inhibit
iniettare inject
iniziale initial
iniziare initiate
innamorarsi fall in love
innanzi before
innato innate

innegabile indisputable
innestare graft
inno *m* hymn
innocente innocent
innocenza *f* innocence
innominato nameless
innovare innovate
innovazione *f* innovation
insalare salt
insalata *f* salad
insano insane
insaponare soap
insaziabile insatiable
inscrivere inscribe
inscrizione *f* inscription
insegna *f* flag; arms
insegnamento *m* teaching
insegnare teach
inseguire pursue
insensato foolish
inseparabile inseparable
inserire insert
insetticida, polvere
  insect-powder
insetto *m* insect
insidioso insidious
insieme together [cant
insignificante insignifi-
insino till
insonne sleepless
insonnia *f* sleeplessness
insopportabile unbearable
insorgere revolt
insozzare stain; soil
insperato unhoped for
ins,irare inspire
installare instal
instancabile indefatigable
instantaneo instantaneous
instante *m* instant
instigare instigate
instruire instruct
instrumento *m* instru-
  ment   [sult
insultare, insulto *m* in-

insuperabile insuperable
insurrezione *f* insurrec-
intagliare engrave [tion
intaglio *m* carving; cut
intanto in the mean time
intarlato worm-eaten
intarsio *m* inlaid work
intascare pocket
intatto entire
intendere hear; under-
  stand; wish; s' intende
  of course
intenerire soften
intensità *f* intensity
intensivo intense
intenzione *f* intention
intercettare intercept
interdire interdict
interessare interest
interesse *m* interest
interiore interior
intermezzo *m* interlude
interno internal
interminabile intermin-
intero entire   [able
interprete *m* interpreter
interporre interpose
interrogare interrogate
intervista *f* interview
intesa *f* intention; con-
intestino intestine [sent
intignato worm-eaten
intimare summon
intimidire intimidate
intimo intimate
intorno(a) round; about
intraducibile untranslat-
intralciare embroil [able
intraprendere undertake
intrapresa *f* enterprise
intrattabile intractable
intrattenere entertain
intrepido intrepid
intrigare, intrigo *m* intrigue   [tion

179

introduzione *f* introduc-
introdurre introduce
introito *m* entrance
intronizzare instal
intrudere intrude
intuizione *f* intuition
inudito unheard of
inumare bury
invadere invade
invalidare invalidate
invalido invalid
invano in vain
invariabile invariable
invasione *f* invasion
invecchiare grow old
invece instead of
inventare invent
inventivo inventive
inventore *m* inventor
inventario *m* inventory
invenzione *f* invention
inverisimile unlikely
inverniciare varnish
inverno *m* winter
invero truly
invertere upset; invert
investigare search
investire invest
invetrare glaze
invettiva *f* invective
inviare send
invidia *f* envy; — bile
enviable; — re envy
invigorire strengthen
inviluppare wrap up
invincibile invincible
invio *m* sending
inviolabile inviolable
invisibile invisible
invitare invite
invito *m* invitation
invocare invoke
involgere wrap up
involto *m* parcel
involtare envelope
ipocrisia *f* hypocrisy
ipocrita *m* hypocrite

ipoteca *f* mortgage
ippodromo *m* hippodrome
ippopotamo *m* hippo-
ira *f* anger [potamus
ire go
iri. iride *f* iris; rainbow
ironia *f* irony; — nico
ironical
irradiare irradiate; — zione *f* irradiation [able
irragionevole unreason-
irrazionabile irrational
irreduttibile irreducible
irrefragabile irrefragable
irregolare irregular; —
rità *f* irregularity
irreligione *f* irreligion;
— so irreligious
irremediabile irremediable
irremissibile irremissible
irreparabile irreparable
irresistibile irresistible;
— bilmente irresistibly
irresoluto irresolute; — zione *f* irresolution
irretire embroil; net
irreverente irreverent;
— za *f* irreverence
irrevocabile irrevocable
irricordevole oblivious
irriflessivo thoughtless
irrigare irrigate; — zione
f irrigation.
irritabile irritable; — lità
f irritability; — re provoke; irritate; — zi-
one *f* irritation
irritrosire grow stubborn
irr.verente irreverent;
— za *f* irriverence
irrorare water; besprin-
irrugginire rust [kle
irrugiadare bedew
irruzione *f* irruption
irsuto, irto bristling;
hideous
islamismo *p* islamism

isola *f* island; **- no** *a* insular

istantaneo instantaneous; **- te** instant; moment

isterismo *m* hysterics; **- rico** hysteric

istesso *m* the same

istigare instigate; **- tore** *m* instigator; **- zione** *f* instigation

istinto *m* instinct; **- tivo** instinctive

istituire institute

istmo *m* isthmus

istoria *f* history; story; **- rico** historic; **- rietta** *f* novel; **- riografo** *m* historian

istrice *m* porcupine

istruire instruct; teach; **- zione** *f* instruction; information

itterizia *f* jaundice

iugero *m* acre

iuniore junior

iussione *f* order

ivi there

izza *f* anger; wrath

J

The letter 'J' does not exist in Italian, and the words beginning with 'J' will be found under the letter 'I'

L

la the; her; it

là there; yonder; **quà e là** here and here

labbro *m* lip

labe *f* stain; **- latto** stained [byrinth

laberinto, birinto *m* labile decaying; slippery; **- lità** *f* decay

laboratorio *m* laboratory

lacca *f* haunch; lac

lacchè *m* lackey

laccio *m* snare; net

lacerare lacerate; **- mento, zione** *m & f* laceration; **- ro** lacerated

lacerto *m* forearm

laco, go *m* lake

lacuna *f* marsh; defect

laddove so that; where; whereas

laddovunque everywhere

ladino fluid

ladramente disagreably

ladreria *f* leprosy; stinginess

ladro, ne *m* thief; **- neggiare** rob

laggiù, giuso below

lagno, mento *m* affliction; **- gnarsi** complain

lagrima *f* tear; **- bile, mevole, moso** deplorable; **- male** lacrimal; **- mare** cry; bewail; **- zione** *f* weeping

lagume *m* marsh; puddle [dle

laguna *f* lagoon

lai *mpl* lamentations

laico lay

lama *f* plain; blade

lambire lick

lamentare lament

lamentevole lamentable

lamina sheet; **laminare** laminate

lampada *f* lamp

lampeggiare lighten

lampione *m* lantern

lampone *m* raspberry

lampreda *f* lamprey

lana *f* wool
lancetta *f* lancet; hand
lancia *f* lance
lanciare throw; fling
lancio *m* leap
languire languish
lanterna *f* lantern
laonde therefore
lapidare stone
lapide *f* tomb-stone
lapis *m* lead-pencil
lappola *f* trifle
lardellare lard
lardo *m* lard; bacon
larghetto easy
larva *f* phantom; mask; chrysalis [mit
lasciapassare *m* pass; perlasciare leave; let
lascito *m* legacy
lascivio lascivious
lassare, lasso weary
lassù up there [stone
lastra *f* sheet; paving
lastricare pave
lastrico *m* pavement
laterale lateral
latifondo *m* landed
Latino Latin [property
latitudine *f* latitude;
lato *m* side; wide

lavanda *f* washing
lavandaia *f* washer-wolavare wash [man
lavorare, lavoro *m* work
leale loyal
lebbra *f* leprosy
leccare lick; flatter
leccio *m* holm-oak
lecito lawful
lega *f* league; allay
legale lawful
legalizzare authenticate
legame *m* tie; chain
legare bind; tie; bequeath.
legge *f* law

leggenda *f* legend
leggere read
leggiadro graceful; eleleggibile legible [gant
leggiero light
leggio *m* desk
legione *f* legion
legislativo legislative
legislazione *f* legislation
legislatore *m* legislator
legittimare legitimate
legittimo legitimate
legna *f* wood
legnaiuolo *m* carpenter
legname *m* timber
legno *m* wood; cab

legume *m* vegetable
lena *f* breath; strength
lente *f* lens
lento slow
lentezza *f* slowness
lenticchia *f* lentil
lenzuolo *m* sheet
leone *m* lion
leonessa *f* lioness
leopardo *m* leopard
lesina *f* avarice; miser
lessare boil
lesso *m* boiled beef
letizia *f* joy
lettera *f* letter; – le literal; – rio literary; – to learned; – tura *f* literature
lettiera *f* bedstead
letto *m* bed
lettore *m* reader
lettura *f* reading
leva *f* levy
levare raise; – si rise
lezzare lezzo *m* stink
libbra *f* pound
libeccio *m* S. W. wind
libello *m* libel
liberale liberal
liberare free; deliver
libero free

libertà *f* liberty
libro *m* book
libreria *f* library
licenza *f* liberty
licenziare discharge
licenzioso licentious
liceo *m* lyceum
lido *m* shore
lieto gay
lieve light
lignite *f* lignite
lila *m* lilac
lima *f* file; – **re** file
limbo *m* limb
limitare, limite *m* limit
linguaggio *m* language
lino *m* lint, flax
liquefare liquefy
liquido liquid
liquirizia *f* liquorice
liquore *m* liquor
lira *f* lyre; lira
lirico lyric
lisca *f* fish-bone
lisciare burnish; polish
liscio smooth; polished
lista *f* sash; list
litanie *f pl* litanies
lite *f* law-suit
litigare plead
litografia *f* lithography
litro *m* litre
liturgia *f* liturgy
livellare, livello *m* level
livido livid
livrea *f* livery
locale local
località *f* locality
locanda *f* inn
locandiere *m* inn-keeper
locare let
locomotiva *m* locomotive
logico logical
logorare wear out
logoro worn out
lolla *f* chaff

lombagine *f* lumbago
lombata *f* sirloin; loin
lombo *m* loin
lombrico *m* earth-worm
longitudine *f* longitude
lontananza *f* distance
lontano distant; far
lucciola *f* firefly; glow-
luce *f* light   [worm
lucertola *f* lizard
lucido bright; lucid
lucidare elucidate; – **dezza** *f* clearness; – **dità** *f*
lucidity; – **do** lucid;
ludificare deceive; – **zione** *f* deceit
lue *f* infection; pest;
– **venerea** venereal disease
lui *m* him; it; he
lumaca *f* snail; – **cone**
m snail
lume *m* light; genius;
star; – **metto** *m* candle;
– **minello** *m* wick;
– **minoso** shining
lumiera *f* torch
luminaria *f*, illuminazione illumination
luna *f* moon; – **re** lunar;
– **ria** *f* moon-wort; – **rio**
m calendar; – **tico** *a*
whimsical; – **to** moon-
shaped; – **zione** *f* luna-
tion
lunetta *f* glass
lunga *f* strap; length of
time
lungo long; *m* length;
along; long time; – **ge,
gi** far; – **gheria, ghezza**
f length; – **ghesso**
along; near
luogo *m* place; motive
luogotenente *m* lieutenant; – **za** *f* lieutenancy

183

lusinga f flattery; – **gare** caress; – **ghevole, ghiero** charming; – **tore** m flatterer

lusso m luxury

lustrare lighten; illustrate; – **le** lustral; – **tura** f mangling; – **tro** m lustre

lustre f pl grimaces

lustrino m lustrine; tinsel

luteranismo m Lutheranism; – **no** Lutheran

lutifigolo m potter

luto m mud; – **so, tulento** muddy

lutta f wrestling; debate

lutto m lute; grief; – **tuoso** painful; – **samente** painfully

M

ma but

macca f plenty; store

macchina f machine; plot; – **le** machinal; – **nista** m machinist; – **re** plot; – **zione** f plot

macchione m thicket

macco m shambles

mace f mace

macellaio m butcher; – **lare** kill; – **lo** m shambles

macerare macerate; mortify; – **mento, zione** m & f maceration; – **ro** macerated; maceration

maceratoia m retting-pool

maceria f rubbish

machiavellismo m machiavelism

macigno m stone

macilento flabby; lank

macina f grinding-stone; – **nare** grind; ruin; – **toio** m oil-mill; – **tura, zione** f grinding

macinello m grindstone

madia f kneading-trough; hutch   [Virgin

madonna f lady; the

madornale great; – **lità** f greatness

madre f mother; origin; mould

madreperla f mother-of-pearl

madreselva f honeysuckle

madrevite f screw-nut; female screw

madrigale m madrigal

madrigna f step-mother

madrina f god-mother

maestà f majesty; nobleness; – **tevole, toso** majestic

maestra f mistress (school)

maestrale m north-west-wind

maestrare teach; – **tranza** f workmen; – **trevole** industrious; – **tramento, tria** m & f art; skill; – **tro** m teacher; professor; director;

maga f sorceress

magagna f defect; – **gnare** vitiate; spoil

magari please God

magazzino m magazine; – **niere** m warehouse-keeper

maggengo of May

maggio m May; greater

maggiore of age; greater; m elder son; superior; – **renne** of age; – **ri**

m pl ancestors; – **rità** *f*
majority   [magical
magia *f* sorcery; – **co**
magione *f* house
magisterio, stero *m* skill;
mastership; – **trale, tre-**
vole magisterial
magistrato *m* magistrate;
– **tura** *f* magistracy
maglia *f* witchcraft;
mail; link
magnetizzare magnetize
magnificare magnify;
praise
magnificente magnificent
mai ever; non – never
maiolica *f* majolica
malagevole difficult
malandare ruin one's self
malandrino *m* highway-
man
malaticcio sickly
malaria *f* malaria
malattia *f* sickness; illness
malcontento discontented
male *m* evil; sickness;
–di **testa** headache;
–di mare sea-sickness
maledetto cursed
maledire curse
maleficio *m* witchcraft
malevole malevolent
malfatto *m* misdeed;
–re *m* malefactor
malgrado in spite of
malia *f* witchcraft
malignità *f* malignity
maligno. wicked; *m* devil

malo bad
malora *f* ruin
malore *m* illness; disease
malsano unwholesome
malvagio wicked
malvisto hated
malvolentieri against
once's will
malvolere *m* hatred

mamma *f* mamma;
breast   [nipple
mammella *f* breast;
mammola *f* violet
manata *f* handful
mancare fail; want
mancanza *f* defect
manchevole defective
mancia *f* tip
mancino left-handed
manco defective, **left;**
m fault
mandare send; **inform**
mandato *m* order
mandarino *m* mandarin
mandibola *f* jaw
mandorla *f* almond [cake
mandorlato *m* almond-
mandorlo *m* almond-tree
mandolino *m* mandolin
mandra *f* flock; herd
maneggiare manage
maneggevole manageable
mania *f* mania; – **co**
maniac
manica *f* sleeve
manico *m* handle
maniera *f* manner [ture
manifattura *f* manufac-
manifestare manifest
manifestazione *f* manifestation
manifesto *m* manifest
maniglia *f* bracelet
maniglio *m* handle
mano *f* hand   [script
manoscritto *m* manu-
manovale *m* labourer
manovella *f* crank
manovra *f*; – **re** man-
mansueto mild   [œuvre
mantello *m* cloak
mantenere maintain
manuale manual
manubrio *m* handle;
mappa(mondo) map (of
the world)

maraviglia *f* marvel; wonder; **a – admirably; – rsi** wonder

maraviglioso wonderful

marca *f* mark; **– re** mark

marchesa *f* marchioness

marchese *m* marquis

marcia *f* march; pus

marciapiede *m* footway

marciare march

marea *f* tide

maremma *f* marsh

margherita *f* pearl; daisy

margine *m* margin; border [shore

marina *f* navy; marine;

marinaio *m* sailor

marinare pickle

maritale marital

maritare marry

martello *m* hammer

martire *m* martyr

martirio *m* martyrdom

marzapane *m* marzipan

marzolino *m* march-cheese

mascella *f* jaw

maschera *f*; **– re** mask

mascherata *f* masquerade

maschile manly

maschio male

mascolino masculine

masnada *f* gang; troop

massa *f* mass

massaio *m* steward

massima *f* maxim

massimo greatest

masso *m* rock

massone *m* free-mason

masticare chew

mastice *m* mastic

matassa *f* hank; heap

matematica *f* mathematics

materassa *f* mattress

materia *f* matter; substance; **– le** material;

– lista *m* materialist

materno maternal

maternità *f* maternity

matita *f* pencil

matrigna *f* step-mother

matrimonio *m* marriage

matrina *f* god-mother

matrona *f* matron

mattana *f* ill-humour

mattina *f* morning

mattinata *f* forenoon

matto mad

mattonare pave with bricks

mattone *m* brick

maturare ripen

maturo ripe

meccanica *f* mechanics

meccanico mechanic

meccanismo *m* mechanism

medaglia *f* medal

medaglione *m* medallion

medesimo same; self

media *f* mean; average

mediante by means of

mediano, medio middle

mediatore *m* mediator

medicamento *m*. **medicina** *f* medicine

medico *m* physician

mediocre indifferent

mediocrità *f* mediocrity

meditare meditate

meditazione *f* meditation

meglio better

mela *f* apple

melo *m* apple-tree

melagrana *f* pomegranate

melassa *f* treacle

mele *m* honey

mellone *m* melon

melodia *f* melody

melodioso melodious

membro *m* limb; member

mendace lying; liar

mendicante *m* beggar

mendicare beg
meno less; al - at least
menomo very small; least
mensa f table
mensuale monthly
mentale mental
menta f mint
mente f mind; a - by
heart
mentire lie; mentitore
mento m chin [m liar
menzognero lying; false
mercante m merchant
mercanteggiare trade;
haggle
mercantile mercantile
mercanzia f goods
mercato m market
merce f goods [pity
mercè, mercede f reward;
merceria f hosiery
merciaio m mercer
mercurio m mercury
merenda f luncheon
meretrice f prostitute
meridiano meridian
meridionale southern
meriggiare lie down
(sleep) in the shade
meriggio m midday
meritare deserve; merit
merito m merit
mescolanza f mixture
mescolare mingle
messa f mass; stake
messaggiere m messenger
messaggio m message
mestare mingle; stir
mestiere m business;
mestola f ladle [trade
metà f half
metallo m metal
metropoli f metropolis;
- tano metropolitan
mettere put; place
mezzana f procuress;
flagstone

mezzanino m entresol
mezzano middle
mezzanotte f midnight
mezzo half; m half;
middle; mean; - busto
m half-bust; - di noon:
- giorno noon: south
mezzombra f mezzotinto
miagolare mew
mica (non) not at all
miele m honey
mietere reap
mietitore m reaper
mietitrice f mowing-
machine
migliaio m thousand
miglio m mile
migliorare improve
miglioramento m im-
provement
milionario m millionaire
milione m million
militare military
milizia f militia
millantarsi boast
mille thousand
millepiedi m millipede
milligrammo m milligram
millimetro m millimetre
milza f spleen
mimico mimic
mina f mine; - re mine
minaccia f threat; - re
threaten
minatore m miner
miniera f mine
minimo very little; least
ministero m ministry
ministro m minister
minoranza f minority
minore smaller; younger;
under age; minor
minorità f minority
minuetto m minuet
minugia f intestine
minuscolo minuscule
minuta f minute

187

minuto (*m*) minute; **al -** minuzia *f* trifle [by retail

minuzia *f* trifle [by retail

mio my; mine

miope short-sighted

miopia/short-sightedness

mira *f* aim

mirabile wonderful

miracolo *m* miracle; **- so** miraculous

mirare look at; aim

miscellanea *f* miscellany

mischia *f* fight; **- re** mix

misconoscere mistake

miscuglio *m* mixture

miserabile miserable

miseria *f* misery

misericordia *f* mercy

misericordioso merciful

misfatto *m* crime

missionario *m* mis.ionary

missione *f* mission

misterio *m* mystery; **- so** mysterious

mobiliare furnish

mobilitare mobilise

moccio *m* mucus

moccolo *m* bit of candle

moda *f* fashion

modellare mould

modello *m* model

moderare moderate

moderazione *f* modera- tion

moderno modern [tion

modestia *f* modesty

modesto modest

modico moderate

modificare modify

modista *f* milliner

modo *m* manner; mood; **di - che** soft hat

modulo *m* module; form

mole *f* mass; large build- ing

molestare molest [ing

molesto troublesome

molla *f* spring; *pl* nip- pers

molle tender; moist

mollezza *f* softness

moltiplicare multiply

moltitudine *f* multitude

molto much; very

momento *m* moment

momentaneo momentary

monaca *f* nun

monaco *m* monk

monarca *m* monarch

monarchia *f* monarchy

monastero *m* monastery

moncare maim

monco maimed

mondare cleanse

mondano wordly

mondo *m* world

monello *m* cheast; rogue

moneta *f* coin; **- re** coin

monna *f* mistress; ape

monocolo one-eyed; mo- nocle

monopolio *m* monopoly

monogramma *m* mono- gram

monologo *m* monologue

monotono monotonous

Monsignore *m* my Lord

montagna *f* mountain

montagnoso mountainous

montare ascend; amount

montanaro *m* mountain-

Moresco Moorish

morfina *f* morphine

moribondo dying

morire die

mormorare murmur ; grumble [tree

moro *m* moor; mulberry-

moroso morose

morsello *m* morsel

morso bitten; *m* bit

mortaio *m* mortar

mortale mortal

mortalità *f* mortality

morte *f* death

morto, ta dead; – *m* corpse; – **torio** *m* funeral; – **tuario** *m* tuary funereal

morviglione *m* small pox; measles *pl.*

mosaico mosaic

mosca *f* fly; – **cieca** blindman's buff

moscada *f* nutmeg

moscadello *m* muscatel

moscaiuola *f* larder

moscardino *m* sparrow-hawk; fop

moscato musky

moscherino, schino *m* mosquito; gnat

moschea *f* mosque

moschettare shoot: – **teria** *f* volley; – **tiere** *m* musketeer; – **to** *m* musket

moscio flabby; soft

moscione *m* mosquito; drunkard

Mosè *pm* Moses

mostarda *f* mustard

mosto *m* must; new wine

mostra *f* review; trial; face; – **trare** demonstrate

mostro *m* monster; prodigy; – **sità** *f* monstrosity; – **truoso** monstrous

mota *f* mud; mire; – **toso** muddy [cause

motivare *m* motive;

moto *m* movement; – **tore** *m* mover

mottetto *m* anthem

motto *m* pun; motto

movenza *f* movement; – **vere** move; – **vibile** changeable; – **vimento** *m* movement; moving; – **vitore** *m* motor

mozione *f* motion

muco *m* mucus; – **sità** *f* mucosity; – **so** mucous

muda *f* moulting; – **dare** change

muffa *f* mouldiness; – **fare** grow musty or **muffetto** *m* fop [mouldy

mugghiare, gire bellow; – **gito** *m* bellowing

mugnaio *m* miller; sea [gull

mugnere suck; milk

mugolare grunt; yelp

mula *f* mule; slipper; – **laggine** *f* obstinacy

mulacchia *f* crow; jackdaw

mulattiere *m* muleteer; – **latto** *m* mulatto

muliebre feminine

mulinare dream

mulinaro *m* miller

mulinello *m* handmill

mulo *m* mule

multa *f* fine; – **re** fine

multiforme multiform

multiplicare multiply; – **zione** *f* multiplication; – **tore** *m* multiplicator

multitudine *f* multitude

mummia *f* mummy; – **mificare** mummify

munerare reward; remunerate; – **zione** *f* reward

municipale municipal; – **lità** *f* municipality; – **pio** *m* town council

munificenza *f* munificence; – **fico** liberal

munire provide; – **zione** *f* ammunition; stores

munto milked [ade

muovere move; persu-

muraglia *f* wall; – **rale** mural; – **rata** *f* tower;

189

– **ratore** *m* mason;
– **rare** build; wall
musica *f* music; – **cale**
musical
musoliera *f* muzzle
musone scorning
mussolina *f* muslin
mutare change; – **bile**,
tevole changeable; – **lità**
f mutability; – **mento**
m change
mutande *f pl* drawings
mutilare mutilate; – **zione** *f* mutilation
muto dumb; mute; *n*
dumb person; **mutismo**
m dumbness
mutuare lend money;
– **tuante**, **tuatario** *m* bor-
rower; – **tuazione** ,re-
ciprocity; – **tuo** mu-
tual; – **tuamente** mu-
tually

N

nabissare make a noise;
destroy; bluster; – **so**
m abyss; hell
nappo *m* glass; cup;
fountain
narciso *m* narcissus
narcotico narcotic
nari, **narici** *f pl* nostrils
narrare relate; – **tiva**,
zione *f* narration;
tore *m* relater
nasale nasal
nascere be born; set;
proceed; – **cimento**, **ta**
f & *m* birth; extrac-
tion; descent; – **cituro**
future
nascondere abscond;
hide; – **diglio** *m* hiding-
place; – **samente** se-

cretly
nasello *m* haddock
naso *m* nose; **nasuto**
big-nosed
nastro *m* ribbon
natalizio *m* birthday
natale native; Christmas
natività *f* nativity
nativo native
natura *f* nature; natural;
– **lista** *m* naturalist;
– **lizzare** naturalise
naufragare be wrecked
naufragio *m* wreck
nausea *f* nausea; – **bondo**
nauseous; – **re** give
nausea
nauta *m* mariner
nautico nautical
navale naval
navigare sail; navigate
navicella *f* boat
nè nor; ne of it; of them
nebbia *f* fog; mist; cloud
nebbioso cloudy; misty
necessario necessary
necessità *f* necessity
nefando infamous
nefasto unlucky
negare deny; disown
negativo negative
negazione *f* negation
negligente negligent
negligenza *f* negligence
negoziante *m* merchant
negoziare negotiate
negoziatore *m* negotiator
negoziazione *f* negotia-
negozio *m* trade [tion
negro *m* negro; black
neonato *m* new-born
nerbo *m* nerve
nerbuto nervous
nero black
nerastro blackish
nervo *m* nerve; – **so**

nervous
nescienza f ignorance
nespola f medlar
nespolo m medlar tree
nessuno no; none
nettare clean; scour
netto clean; pure; net
Nettuno Neptune
neutrale, neutro neutral
neutralità f neutrality
nevata f snow-fall
nevicare snow
neve f snow

nidificare nestle
niente nothing
nientedimeno nevertheless; however
Nilo m Nile
ninfa f nymph
ninnolo m trifle
nipote m nephew; grand-
nissuno none [son
no no; not
nobile noble
nobilizzare ennoble
nobiltà f nobility
nocca f knuckle
nocchio m knot
nocciolo m stone; pip
nocciuola f filbert; hazel-
nut [tree
noce f walnut; walnut
noia f tediousness; – re
noioso tedious [annoy
noleggiare freight
nolo m freighting; rent
nomade wandering
nome m name; fame
nomina f nomination; fame
nominale nominal
nominare nominate
nominatamente namely
non not
non che not only
noncurante careless

nondimeno nevertheless
nonna f grand-mother
nonno m grand-father
nono ninth
nonostante nevertheless
nonsenso m nonsense
norte m North
norma f rule; – le normal
nosco with us
nostalgia ; home-sickness
nostrale of our country
nostro our(s) [notable
nota f note; – bile
notaio m notary
notare note; swim
notevole remarkable
notificare notify
notizia f news; notice
novanta ninety
novella f story; news
novello new; young
novembre m November
nulla nothing, – di don't mention it; – dimeno nevertheless
nullo null; void
numerare number
numeratore m numerator
número m number
numeroso numerous
numisma f medal
nunziare announce
nuocere hurt; harm
nuora f daughter-in-law
nuotare swim
nuova f news; notice
nuovo new
nutatore m swimmer
nutrimento m food; nourishment
nutritivo nutritive
nutrire feed; nourish
nuvola f cloud
nuvoloso cloudy
nuziale nuptial

O

o, od or
oasi *f* oasis
obbedienza *f* obedience;
 – dire obey; – dient
 obeying
obbiettare object; –
 biezione *f* objection;
 – biettivo objective; – to
 m cause; object
obbioso suspicious
obblazione *f* oblation
obbliare forget
obbligare oblige; bind;
 – gante obliging; –
obbliquare slant; de-
 cline; – quità *f* obli-
 quity; – quo oblique
obbrobrio *m* dishonour;
 shame; – so shameful
obbumbrare darken; –
 zione *f* darkness
obelisco *m* obelisk
oberato *m* indebted
obesità *f* obesity
obice, obizzo *m* mortar
obito *m* death
obliterare obliterate;
 cancel
oblungo oblong
occasionare cause; occa-
 sion; – nale occasional;
 – sione *f* occasion;
 cause; – so *m* chance
occhialaio *m* spectacle-
 maker; – le, letto *m*
 spectacles; telescope
occhiare eye; ogle; –
 chiazzurro blue eyed
occhiello *m* buttonhole;
 eyelet [will; bud
occhio *m* eye; sight;
occidente *m* west; –

tale occidental; western
occidere kill; – ditore *m*
 killer; – sione *f* killing;
 death
occipite *m* occiput
occorrenza *f* occurrence;
 need; – rere happen;
 occur; be necessary
occultare conceal; hide;
 – to hidden
occupare occupy; pos-
 sess; seize; – mento,
 zione *m & f* occupation;
 abode
oceano *m* ocean; – nico
 oceanic
ocra *f* ochre
oculare ocular
oculatezza *f* care; – to
 prudent; sharp
odorare smell
odorato *m* smelling
odore *m* smell; scent
offendere offend; hurt
offrire offer
oftalmia *f* ophthalmia
oggetto *m* object
oggi to-day
osliaro *m* oil merchant
ogni every
olio *m* oil
oliva *f* olive
oliveto *m* olive-yard
olivo *m* olive-tree
olmo *m* elm-tree
olocausto *m* holocaust
oltraccio moreover
oltraggiare offend
oltre beyond; further
oltremodo extraordinarily
omaggio *m* homage
omai now
ombelico *m* navel
ombra *f* shade; shadow
ombreggiare shadow

ombrello *m* umbrella
ombrellino *m* sunshade
ombroso shady; shy
omelia *f* homily
omeopatia *f* homœopathy
omero *m* shoulder
omettere omit
omicidio *m* man-slaughter
ommissione *f* omission
omnibus *m* omnibus
omogeneo homogeneous
omonimo homonymous
onda *f* wave; sea; billow
onde where; therefore;
onorabile, onorevole honourable
onore *m* honour
onorare honour
onorario *m* honorary
onta *f* shame; injury
onoso shameful; bash-
ontano *m* alder-tree [ful
opaco opaque
opalo *m* opal
opera, opra *f* work;
opera; deed   [do
operare work; make;
operaio *m* workman
operatore *m* operator
operazione *f* operation
opificio *m* studio
opimo abundant; rich
opinare opine; vote
opinante *m* voter
opinione *f* opinion
oppio *m* opium
opporre oppose
opportunità *f* opportunity
opportuno seasonable
opposito opposite
opposizione *f* opposition
opprimere oppress
oppure that is; or
opulento wealthy
ora *f* hour; time; now;
che –? what time is it?
oracolo *m* oracle

oragano *m* hurricane
orafo *m* goldsmith
oratore *m* orator
oratorio *m* oratory
orbe *f* orb; universe
orbene well done
orbita *f* orbit; rut
orchestra *f* orchestra
orcio *m* jug; pitcher
ordegno *m* engine; tool
ordinare order; ordain
ordinario ordinary
ordine *m* order
ordire warp; plot
ordo dirty
orrechiare listen
orezza *f* breeze
orfano *m* orphan
orfanotrofio *m* orphanage
organizzare organize
organo *m* organ
organista *m* organist
orgoglio *m* pride; – **so**
orientale oriental [proud
oriente *m* orient; east
orifizio *m* opening
originale, originario orig-
origine *f* origin   [inal
orina *f* urine; – le me
urinal; – re urinate
orizzonte *m* horizon
orrizontale horizontal
orlare hem; border
orlo *m* edge; hem
ormai now
ornamento *m* ornament
ornare adorn
orno *m* ash-tree
oro gold
orologio *m* clock
orrendo, orribile horrible
orzo *m* barley
osare dare
oscenità *f* obscenity
osceno obscene
oscillare oscillate; vacil-

osculare kiss [late
oscurare darken; defame
oscurità f obscurity
oscuro dark; vile
ospedale. ospitale m
hospital
ospitabile hospitable
ospite m guest; host
ospizio m hospice; asylum
ossame m bones
ossequio m reverence
osservare observe [tory
osservatorio m observa-
osservatore m observer
osservazione f observa-
ossesso obsessed [tion
ossidare oxidize
ossigeno m oxygen
osso m bone; stone (of
fruit)
ostacolo m obstacle
ostare oppose; resist
oste m host; guest
ostensorio m ostensory
ostentare display; boast
osteria f inn
ostessa f hostess
ostilità f hostility
ostile hostile
ostinarsi be obstinate
ostinato obstinate
ostrica f oyster
ostruire obstruct
ottarda f bustard
ottanta eighty
ottava f octave
ottavo eighth
ottenere obtain
ottica f optic
ottico optic; optician
ottimo best; perfect
otto eight
ottone m brass
ottuplo eightfold
otturare stop up; dam
ottuso stupid; obtuse

ovvio obvious
ovvolo m mushroom
ozio m leisure; idleness

P

pacca f stroke; wound
pacchebotto m steamer;
- chetto m steamer;
pace f peace; quietness;
- ciere. cificatore m
peace-maker; - fico
pacific; - cificare pacify;
appease; reconcile
padella f frying-pan;
knee-pan
padiglione m pavillon;
tent
padre m father; - drino
m god-father
padrone m master; cox-
wain; patron; - na f
mistress
paesaggio m landscape
paesano, na a & n pea-
sant
paesante, sista m land-
scape-painter [scape
paesi m country; land-
paffuto plumb; fat
paga f salary; wages
paganesimo m paganism;
- no pagan
pagare pay; punish; -
bile payable; -ghero
m promissory note; -
gamento m payment
paggio m page
pagina f page
paglia f straw; - gliaio
m straw-rick; - glieri-
ccio m straw-mattress
- gliuola f gold dust
pagnotta f small loaf

pago satisfied; *m* pay-
pagoda *f* pagoda [ment
pagonazzo violet
paio *m* pair; brace
paiuolo *m* boiler; kettle
pala *f* shovel; spade
paletta *f* shovel
paletto *m* bolt
palio *m* cloak; canopy
palla *f* ball; bullet; bow
palleggiare play tennis
pallido pale; pallid
pallidezza *f* paleness
pallini *m pl* shot; small
   shot   [ball
pallone *m* balloon; foot-
pallore *m* paleness
palma *f* palm; palm-tree
palmeto *m* palm-tree-
   grove   [branch
palpitazione *f* palpitation
palude *f* marsh; paludoso marshy
panattiera *f* bread-basket
panca *f* bench
panchetta *f* little bench
pancia *f* paunch; belly
panciotto *m* waistcoat
pancone *m* bench
pane *m* bread; loaf
panegirico *m* panegyric
panforte *m* gingerbread
pania *f* bird-lime
panico panic
paniera *f* basket; – ie *m*
   basket-maker
panino gravido sandwich
panna *f* cream
panno *m* cloth
panneggiare drape
pantofola *f* slipper
pantomima *f* pantomime
papa *m* pope; – le papa
papavero *m* poppy
papiro *m* papyrus
pappa *f* pap

pappare eat to excess
parabola *f* parable;
   parabola; – no bragger
paracadute *m* parachute
paracolpi *m* buffer
paradiso *m* paradise
paradosso paradox(ical)
parafrasi *f* paraphrase
parafulmine *m* lightning-
   conductor
parafuoco *m* fire-screen
paraggio *m* country
   shore   [comparison
paragone *m* touch-stone;
paragonare compare
paragrafo *m* paragraph
paralisi *f* paralysis
paralitico paralytic
parallelo parallel
paralume *m* lampshade;
   screen   [apparel
paramento *m* sacerdotal
parapetto *m* parapet
parare adorn; dress
parata *f* parade; show
parasito *m* parasite
paravento *m* screen
parco sober; *m* park
parecchi several
parecchio equal; like
pareggiare compare
parénte *m* kinsman
parentella *f* affinity;
   relationship
parentesi *f* parenthesis
parere appear; *m* opinion
parete *f* wall
pargolo *m* little child
pari like; equal
parità *f* equality
parroco *m* parson
parrucca *f* wig [dresser
parrucchiere *m* hair-
parte *f* part; country;
   party; da – aside
partecipare partake
partenza *f* departure

particolare particular; private
parziale partial
parzialità f partiality
pascere, pascolare graze
paseolo m pasture
Pasqua f Easter
pasquinata f satire
passabile tolerable
passaporto m passport
passare pass
passata f passage
passatempo m pastime
passato (m) past
passeggiare walk
passione f passion
passivo passive [passage
passo faded; m step;
pasta f paste; dough
pasteggiare board
pasticcio m pie
pasto m food; meal
pastore m shepherd
pastoso soft; sweet
patire suffer
patimento m suffering
patria f native country
patriarca m patriarch
patrigno m step-father
patrimonio m patrimony
patriota f patriot
patrono m patron
patteggiare agree
pattinare, pattino m skate
pattuglia f patrol
pattume m sweepings
paura f fear
pauroso timorous
pausa f; – re pause
paventare fear
pavimento m pavement
pavone m peacock
pavoneggiarsi boast
paziente patient
pazienza f patience
pazzia f madness

pazzo mad; fool
pecca f fault
peccare, peccato m sin
peccatore m sinner
pecchia f bee
peccia f paunch
pece f pitch
pecora f sheep
pecorino m lamb; cheese
peculiare peculiar
pecunia f money
pedaggio m toll
pedagogia f pedagogy
pedalare bike
pedale m pedal; trunk
pedante m pedant
pedata f track; kick
pedestre pedestrian
pedina f pawn
pedone m pedestrian
peggio worse [worse
peggiorare make (grow)
pegno m pawn
pellegrino m stranger;
pelo m hair; split; – so
    hairy
pena f punishment; pain;
    care; penal; – re suffer
pendaglio m belt [ful
pendente hanging; doubt-
pendenza f declivity
pendere hang; incline
pendice f, pendio m slope
penetrare penetrate
penetrazione f penetra-
    tion
penisola f peninsula
penitente penitent
penitenza f penitence
penitenziario m peniten-
    tiary
penna f feather; pen
pennacchio m plume
pennello m pencil; brush
pennino m steel-pen
pennone m pennon

pentimento *m* repentance
pentola *f* pot; – io *m*
penuria *f* penury [potter
penzolare dangle
pepe *m* pepper
pera *f* pear
percepire perceive
percezione *f* perception
perchè because
percorrere peruse
percuotere strike
perdere lose; ruin
perdita *f* loss
perditore *m* loser
perdonare, perdono *m*
pardon
perdonabile pardonable
peregrinare wander
perfetto perfect
perfezionare perfect
perfezione *f* perfection
perfidia *f* perfidy
perfido perfidious
perforare perforate
pergamena *f* parchment
pergamo *m* pulpit
perire perish
perito experienced
perizia *f* skill
perla *f* pearl
perlustrare explore
permanente permanent
permesso permitted; *m*
permit; permission
permettere permit
pernice *f* partridge
pernicioso pernicious
pernio *m* pivot
pernottare pass the night
pero *m* pear-tree
però therefore; – chè
pbecause   [cular
perpendicolare perpendi-
perpetrare perpetrate
perpetuare perpetuate
perpetuo perpetual
erplesso perplexed

perquisizione *f* perquisi-
tion   [tion
persecuzione *f* persecu-
perseguire pursue; per-
secute   [ance
perseveranza *f* persever-
perseverare persevere
persuadere persuade
persusione *f* persuasion
pertanto however
pertica *f* pole
pertinace obstinate
perturbare disturb
pervenire arrive
perverso perverse; de-
pesanto heavy   [praved
pesantezza *f* weight
pesare weigh
pesca *f* peach
pesca *f* fishing
pescaia *f* dike, sluice
pescare fish
pescatore *m* fisherman
pesce *m* fish
pescheria *f* fish-market
peschiera *f* fish-pond
pesciaiuolo *m* fishmonger
pesco *m* peach-tree
peso *m* weight
pessimo very bad; worst
petardo *m* petard
petizione *f* petition
peto *m* fart
petrolio *m* petroleum
pettegola *f* chatter-box;
– re chatter
pettinare comb
pettine *m* comb
pettino *m* shirt-front
petto *m* breast; – rale
pectoral
petulante arrogant
pezza *f* piece; strip
pezzato speckled
pezzo *m* piece; bit
pezzuola *f* handkerchief
piacere please; *m* plea-

piaga f wound [cure
piaggia f strand; declivity [lament
piagnere, piangere weep;
pialla f, - re plane
pianella f slipper; tile
pianerottolo m landing-
pianeta m planet [place
pianista m pianist
pianto m lament; weep-
pianura f plain [ing
piataforma f platform
piatto flat; m dish
piattola f cockroach
piazza f place; market
picchiare strike; knock
picchio m stroke; wood-
pecker
picchiotto m knocker
piccino small (boy)
piccolo little; small
piccone m pick-axe
pidocchio m louse
pie, piede m foot; a -
on foot
piedestallo m pedestal
piega m fold; - re fold;
bend; incline; yield
pieghevole flexible
piena f flood; throng
pieno full
pieta f grief; sorrow
pietà f pity; piety; love
pigliare take; receive
pignatta f pot; kettle
pignone m dike [gage
pignorare pawn; mort-
pigolare pip; chirp
pigrizia f laziness
pigro idle
pilone m pilaster
pilota m pilot
pina f pine-apple
pineto m pine-grove
pingere paint
pingue fat

piovere rain
piovoso rainy
piovigginare drizzle
pipa f pipe; - re smoke
pipistrello m bat
pira f wood-pile
piramide f pyramid
pirata m pirate
piroscalo m steamer
piscia f urine; - re
urinate; - toio m urinal
piscina f fish-pond
pisello m green pea
pispigliare whisper
pisside f pyx [nut
pistacchio m pistachio-
pistagna f furbelow;
pistillo m pistil [flounce
pistola f pistol
pistone m piston
itale m urinal
pitocare beg
pitocco m beggar
pittore m painter
pittoresco picturesque
pittura f painting; pic-
ture
più more; al - at most;
per lo - mostly; i -
most (men)
piuma f feather
piuolo m stake; peg
piuttosto rather
piva f bagpipe
pizzicagnolo m pork-
butcher [prick
pizzicare itch; pinch;
pizzo m pointed beard
placare appease
placido placid
plagio m plagiarism
plagiario m plagiarist
plasmare model
plastica / plastico plastic
platano m platane
platea f pit (theatre)

platino *m* platina
platonico platonic
plausibile plausible
plauso *m* applause
plebaglia *f* mob
plebe *f* common people
pluviale rainy
pneumatico pneumatic
pneumonia *f* pneumonia
po', poco little
podere *m* estate; power
podestà *f* power; bailiff
poema *m* poem
poesia *f* poetry
poeta *m* poet
poetico poetical
poggia *f* prop
poggio *m* hill [as; when
poi afterwards; – chè
polare polar
poledro *m* colt; foal
polemico polemical
polenta *f* polenta
poligono *m* polygon
polipo *m* polypus
polire polish
politica *f* politics
politico political; politician
polizia *f* police
polizza *f* note; bill
pollice *m* thumb
polmone *m* lung
polmonare pulmonary
polo *m* pole
polpa *f* pulp
polpaccio *m* calf (leg)
polsetto *m* bracelet
polsino *m* cuff
polso *m* pulse
poltiglia *f* mire
poltrona *f* easy-chair
pomello *m* knob
pomeridiano afternoon
pomice *f* pumice-stone
pomo *m* apple

pompa *f* pump
ponce *m* punch
ponderare weigh
pondi / *m* *pl* dysentry
ponente *m* West
ponte *m* bridge; deck
pontefice *m* pontiff; – cale pontificial
pontone *m* pontoon
popolaccio *m* mob [late
popolare popular; popu-
popolazione *f* population
popolo *m* people; nation
popoloso populous
popone *m* melon
poppa *f* breast
poppare suck
porgere offer; present
poro *m* pore; – so porous
porpora *f* purple
porre place; put
porro *m* leek; wart
porta *f* door; – bandiera
ensign-bearer; – bile
portable; – fogli port-
folio; – lettere postman;
– ta range; tonnage;
course; – tore bearer
portare bring; carry
portiera *f* door-curtain;
coach-door
portiere *m* door-keeper
portico *m* portico [riage
porto *m* harbour; car-
portolano *m* pilot; door-
portone *m* gate [keeper
porzione *f* portion
posa *f* pause
posare place; stand
posata *f* rest; cover
poscia afterwards
poscritto *m* postcript
posdomani after to-morrow
positivo positive
posizione *f* position

possedere possess
possessione *f* possession
possente powerful
possibilità *f* possibility
possibile possible
posta *f* post; ambush; stake; — **le** postal; **a** — expressly
posteri *m pl* posterity
posteriore (*m*) posterior
posterità *f* posterity
posticcio *m* sham; false
posticipare delay
postino *m* postman
posto *m* place; situation
postremo last
potente powerful
potenza *f* power
potere be able; *m* power
povero poor
povertà *f* poverty
pozza(nghera) *f* puddle
pozzetta *f* dimple
pozzo *m* well [dinner
pranzare dine; **pranzo** *m*
practica *f* practice; — **bile** practicable; — **re** practise
practico practical
precedere precede
precedenza *f* precedence
precetto *m* precept; — **re** preceptor; tutor
precidere remove; shorten
precipitare precipitate
precipizio *m* precipice
precisamente precisely
precisione *f* precision
preciso precise
precoce precocious
precogitare premeditate
preconio *m* praise
precursore *m* precursor
predestinare predestinate
predellino *m* step
predellone *m* bench

predica *f* sermon; — **re** preach; — **tore** *m* preacher [beloved
prediletto preferred;
predilezione *f* preference
predire foretell
predominare prevail
prefazione *f* preface
preferire prefer
prefetto *m* prefect
prefiggere prefix
pregare pray; entreat
preghiera *f* prayer
pregiaro value; praise
pregio *m* value; repute
pregiudizio *m* prejudice
pregno pregnant
premere urge; press
premiare, premio reward; prize
preminente pre-eminent
premunire forewarn;
preoccupare preoccupy
preparare prepare [tion
preparazione *f* prepara-
preponderare preponder-
preporre prefer [ate
preposterò preposterous
prerogativa *f* prerogative
presa *f* taking; prize;
presciutto *m* ham
prescrivere prescribe
prescrizione *f* prescription
presentare offer; present
presentazione *f* presenta-
presente present [tion
presenza *f* presence
presentire foresee; presentimento *m* foresight; presentiment
preservare preserve
presidente *m* president
presidio *m* garrison
pressa *f* crowd; press;

200

- re urge; - nte urgent
pressione f pressure
prestidigitatore m juggler
prestito m loan
presto quick; sudden
presumere presume
presupporre presuppose
prete m priest
pretendere claim; pretend
pretendente pretender
pretensione f pretension
preterire omit; neglect
preterito past
pretesto m pretext
previo previous
previsione f foresight
prezioso precious
prezzare value; esteem
prezzo m price
prezzemolo m parsley
prezzolare pay; hire
pria before
priego m prayer
prigione f prison
prigioniero m prisoner
prima before
primario principal
primavera f spring
prim(ier)o first; former
primogenito m first-born
prince, principe m prince
priorità f priority
pristino old; former
privare deprive
privazione f privation
privato private; m water-closet
privilegio m privilege
pro m advantage; for
probabile probable
procedere proceed
procella f storm
processione f procession
processo m law-suit; progress [clamation
proclama(zione) f pro-
proclamare proclaim

procrastinare delay
procreare procreate
prode brave
prodigalità f prodigality
prodigo prodigal
prodigio m prodigy; - so prodigious
proditore m traitor
prodotto m product
produrre produce; create
produrre produce
produzione f production
profanare, profano pro-
proferire utter [fane
professare profess
professione f profession
profeta m prophet; - re prophesy
profezia f prophecy
profilo m profile [profit
profittare, profitto m
profondare dig; sink
profondità f depth
profondo deep [perfume
profumare, profumo m
profusione f profusion
progettare, progetto m project
programma m programme
progredire, progresso m progress
proibire prohibit
proibizione f prohibition
proiettile m projectile
prole f offspring
prominente prominent
promontorio m promontory
pronostico m prognostic
pronto quick; ready
pronunziare pronounce
pronunzia(zione) f pronunciation
propagare propagate
propensione f propensity
propinquo near
propizio favourable

proporre propose
proporzione f proportion
proposito m purpose
proposizione f proposition
proprietà f property;
– rio m proprietor; owner
proprio m proper
propulsare repel
propulsore m propeller
prora f prow; bow
prorogare prorogue
prorompere burst; rush
out
prosa f prose; – ico prosaic
prosperare prosper
prosperità f prosperity
prospettiva f perspective
prospetto m prospect
prossimità f proximity
prossimo nearest
prosternare prostrate
prostituta f prostitute
proteggere protect
protestante protestant
protesta(zione) f protestation [protest
protestare, protesto m
protettore m protector
protezione f protection
protrarre protract; draw
prova f proof; experi-
provare prove [ment
provenire proceed
provenienza f origin
proverbio m proverb
proverbiale proverbial
provincia f province;
le provincial
provocare provoke
provocazione f provoca-
provvedere provide [tion
provvisione f provision
provvisorio temporary
provvisto supplied; ready
pudico modest; chaste
pudino m pudding

puerilità f puerility
puerile puerile
puerizia f childhood
puerperio m lying in
pugna f fight; – re
fight; – le m dagger;
– lare stab [writing
pugno m fist; hand-
pulce f flea
pulcella f maid
Pulcinella m Punch
pulcino m chicken
puledro m colt; foal
puleggia f pulley
pulire polish; clean
pullulare swarm; spring
pulpito m pulpit
pulsazione f pulsation
pungere prick; sting
puntata f stab
punteggiare punctuate
puntualità f punctuality
puntuale punctual
pupilla f ward; pupil
purchè provided; if
pure also; however
purezza, rità f purity
purga f purge; – re purge;
– tivo purgative;
– torio m purgatory
purgatura f rubbish; dirt
purificare purify; – zione
f purification
puritano m puritan;
– nismo m puritanism
puro pure; clean;
– ramente purely
pusillità f smallness; vileness; – lo low
pustola f pustule
putativo supposed
putidezza f stink; – tire
stink; – tente, tido
stinking
putredine f rottenness;
– tredinoso, trido rotten

putrefare. tridire putrefy;
− **fazione. tridità. tri-**
putrefaction

puttella *f* young girl;
− **tello. tino.** to *m* young
boy

puzza zo *m* pus; stench;
− **zare** stink; − **zolente**
stinking

Q

quà here; hither; − **e là**
here and there; **di -**
this way

quaderno *m* sheet of
paper; writing book;

quadra *f* dial

quadragesima *f* Lent

quadrangolare quadran-
gular; − **lo** *m* quadrangle

quadrante *m* quadrant

quadrare quadrate; agree;
− **to** square

quaggiù giuso here below

quaglia *f* quail   [late

quagliarsi curdle; coagu-

qualche some; any;
whatever; whoever; −
duno somebody; − **cosa**
f something

quale who; whoever;
which; that

qualifica, zione *f* qualification; − **re** qualify

qualità *f* quality

qualmente how; like; as

qualora when; whenever

qualsisia. qualunque who-

quando when   [ever

quandochè when(ever)

quandunque whenever

quantità *f* quantity

quanto how much; how
many; − **a me** as for

me; − **prima** as soon
as possible

quantochè though
quantunque so much;
some; though

quaranta forty; − **tesimo**
fortieth; − **tinà** *f*
quarantine

quarantigia *f* guarantee

quare why   [days

quaresima *f* Lent; forty

quarta quart; quarter

quarterone *m* quarter
(moon)

quartiere *m* quarter;

quarto fourth [descent

quasi almost

quassù above

quattordici fourteen

quattro four

quetare appease; calm

qui here; − **dentro** herein

quietanza *f* acquittance

quinci herefrom; after

quindi therefore; hereby

quindici fifteen

quindicesimo fifteenth

quintale *m* hundred-
weight

quinta decima *f* full moon

quitare acquit

quinto fifth

quintuplo fivefold

quiproquo *m* blunder

quivi there; then

quota *f* quota; share

quotidiano daily

quoto *m* order

R

rabacchio, *m* baby;
child; boy

rabbia *f* rage; fury;
− **bioso** mad; furious

203

rabbonacciare lull; calm
rabbonire quiet; reconcile
rabbrenciare
rabbruscarsi darken; – **mento** *m* darkening
rabbuffare dishevel; disorder; fight; darken; – **fo** *m* rebuff; reprimand

raccapricciare frighten; terrify; – **ciamento** *m* fright; terror
raccartocciare twist
raccattare recover; redeem

raccenciare mend; patch
raccendere rekindle
raccennare beckon
raccertare assure
raccettare lodge; house – **tore** *m* lodger; – **to** *m* lodging; shelter
racchettare console
racchetta *f* racket
raccogliere gather
raccolta *f* drop; collection
raccomandare recommend
raccomandazione *f* recommendation [mend
raccomodare repair;
raccontare relate; tell
racconto *m* relation; tale

raccorciare shorten;
raccordare reconcile;

raddensare condense
raddirizzare redress
raddolcire soften; sweeten
raddoppiare redouble
raddormentarsi fall asleep
radere shave [again
radiotelegrafia *m* wireless telegraphy
radio *m* beam; ray
radioso beaming
radunanza *f* heap
radunare assemble

rafano *m* horse-radish
raffermare confirm; ratify
raffica *f* squall
raffilare sharpen; clip
raffinare refine
raffineria *f* refinery
rafforzare reinforce; fortify [cold
raffreddare cool; catch
raffreddore *m* cold
raffrenare refrain
ragazza *f* young girl
ragazzo *m* boy
raggelare congeal
raggiare beam; radiate
ragguardevole remarkable
ragia *f* resin; snare
ragionare reason; argue
ragione *f* reason; right; rate; firm; – **vole** reasonable
ragno(lo) *m* spider
rallegrare divert; rejoice
rallentare slacken; – **rama** *f* branch [lease
ramaccia *f* sled
ramancina *f* reprimand
rame *m* copper
ramaio *m* coppersmith
ramerino *m* rosemary
ramificare ramify
rammaricarsi grieve
rammarico *m* grief
rammassare heap up
rammendare mend
rammentare remind
ramo *m* branch; bough
raulaccio *m* radish
rampicare climb
rampollo *m* spring; shoot
rana, *f* **ranocchio** *m* frog
raucido rancid
rancore *m* grudge;
rapido rapid
rapina *f* rapine
rapire rob; ravish

204

rapparare learn again
rapparire reappear
rappellare recall
rappezzare mend
rapportare relate; refer
rapporto m relation
rappresentare represent
rappresentazione f representation
raschiare rasp; scrape
rasciugare dry up
rasentare graze; touch
raso m satin
rasoio m razor
raspa f; - re rasp; grater
rassegna f review; summons
rassegnare resign [marry
rassembrare resemble; gather [teach
rasserenare clear up;
rassettare mend; settle
rassicurare encourage
rassomiglianza f resemblance
rassomigliare resemble
rastione m brush
rastrello m rake
rata f portion; share
ratificare ratify
rattaccare reunite
rattaconare new-sole
rattenere detain; stop
ratto quick; ready; m rape; robbery; rat
rattoppare mend; patch
rattristare afflict; grieve
rauco hoarse
raucedine f hoarseness
ravanello m radish
ravvedimento m repentance
ravvedersi repent [tance
ravviare arrange; guide
ravvisare advise; inform
ravviure frighten
ravvivare revive
ravvolgere envelope; turn
razionale rational

razione f ration
razza f race; spoke
razzo m ray; spoke; fusee
razzolare scratch; file
re m king; - ale royal; - ame m realm
reale real; - mente really
realità f reality
realizzare realise
reato m crime; sin
reazione f reaction
rebbio m prong [liver
recapitare address; deliver
recapito m address
recere vomit
recesso m retreat; recess
recidiva f relapse
recinte m enclosure
recipiente m recipient
reciprocità f reciprocity
reciproco reciprocal
recita f representation; - re recite; perform
redazione f redaction
redentore m redeemer
redenzione f redemption
redimere redeem
redine f rein
regalare give; present
regale royal
regalo m present
regata f regatta [last
reggero rule; oppose;
reggia f royal palace
reggimento m regiment
regicida m regicide
regina f queen; regio
regione f region [royal
registrare registro m register
regnare reign
regno m kingdom; reign
regola f rule; law; order
regolare regulate; regular
regolarità f regularity
regolizia f liquorice
regola f rule; law

regolo *m* ruler
reietto waste; rejected
reintegrare reintegrate
reiterare reiterate
relativo relative
relazione *f* relation
remo *m* oar
remoto distant
rena *f* sand; gravel
rendere give back; render;
  yield; – si surrender
rendita *f* rent; revenue
rene *m* kidney; *pl* loins
renischio *m* sand
renitente obstinate
renna *f* rein-deer
renoso sandy
reo guilty; wicked
reparare repair
repellere repel; repulse
repente sudden
repertorio *m* repertory
replica *f.* – re reply;
  retort
reprimere repress; check
reputare esteem
reputazione *f* reputation
requiare rest; – quie
  requiem   [sary
requisito required; neces-
resa *f* surrender [cree
rescritto *m* rescript; de-
residenza *f* residence
residente resident
resina *f* resin
resistenza *f* resistence
resistere resist; last
respignere repulse
respirare breathe; exhale
respirazione *f* breathing
respiro *m* breath; pause
responsa *f* answer; –
  bile responsible; –
  bilità *f* responsibility
resta *f* repose; delay;
  fish-bone; – re remain;
  – nte residue; re-

mainder
restaurare repair; correct
resto *m* rest; del –
  besides   [train
restringere restrict; res-
restrizione *f* restriction
resultare, resultato *m*
  result
retaggio *m* inheritance
rete *f* net; snare
reticenza *f* reticence
reticolla *f* mantle
retina *f* retina
retribuire reward
retro behind; afterwards
retroattivo retroactive
retrogradare retrograde
retroguardia *f* rear-guard
retta *f* duration; resis-
  tance; dar – consent
rettangolo *m* rectangle
rettificare rectify
rettile *m* reptile
rettilineo rectilinear
retto right; straight
rettore *m* rector
rialzare raise
riamicare reconcile
riandare examine; search
riassumere sum up
riavere recover
ribalzare rebound
ribasso *m* abatement;
  discount
ribellione *f* rebellion
ribelle rebel   [berry
ribes *m* currant; goose-
riboccare overflow
ribrezzare tremble;
  shiver   [ing
ribrezzo *m* fright; shiver-
ributtare disgust; re-
ricacciare repulse [pulse
ricaggimente *m* relapse
ricalcitrare be reluctant
ricamare embroider

ricamo *m* embroidery
ricambiare reward; barter [reward
ricambio *m* exchange;
ricapito *m* remittance;
– lare recapitulate
ricattare redeem
ricavare gain; profit by
riccio *m* curl; curly;
hedgehog [richly
ricco rich; – camente
richiamare claim; call back [complaint
richiamo *m* reclamation;
richiedere ask; require
richiesta *f* demand;
petition
ricino castor-oil plant
ricogliere gather; reap
ricompense *f* – re reward;
compensate
riconciliare reconcile
rioncio seasoned
ricondire provide
riconoscenza *f* gratitude
ricondito hidden
riconfermare ratify
riconoscente grateful
riconoscere recognise
ricordare remind
ricordo *m* remembrance
ricorrente periodical
ricorrere have recourse
ricorso *m* refuge
ricoverarsi take refuge
ricreare divert; recreate
ricreazione *f* recreation
ricucire mend; sew again
ricuperare recover
ricusare refuse; challenge
ridda *f* country dance
ridere laugh; shine
ridicolo ridiculous
ridire repeat; blame
rividivere subdivide
ridondare overflow

ridotto *m* retreat; club
ridurre reduce
riduzione *f* reduction
riempiere fill; fill again
riescire succeed
rifare do again; repair
riferire refer; ascribe
rifinire cease; get tired
rifiutare refuse; renounce
riflessione *f* reflexion
rigattiere *m* broker
rigenerare regenerate
rigentilire beautify
rigetto *m* waste; refuse
rigido rigid [roam
rigirare turn round;
rignare neigh; grunt
rigoᵍlio *m* pride
riguardare look at; con-
riguardato prudent [cern
riguardo *m* look; regard
rilevante notable [up
rilevare lift up; – si get
rilievo *m* remnant; im-
portance; relief
rilucere shine; glitter
riluttante reluctant
rima *f* – re rhyme
rimandare restore; re-
rimanere remain [pudiate
rimanente remaining; re-
mainder
rimarcabile remarkable
rimbalzare rebound;
jump
rimbastire rebuild; baste
rimbellire beautify
rimborsare reimburse
rimbrottare reprimand
rimediare, rimedio *m*
remedy
rimembranza *f* memory
rimembrare remind; re-
member
rimessione confidence;
pardon
rimettere replace; remit

rimodernare modernize
rimounare whirl
rimondare cleanse
rimonta f remount
rimovere remove; dis-
rimpetto opposite [suade
rimpiagnere lament
rimpiazzare replace
rimproverare, rimprovero
m reproach; blame
rimunerare remunerate
rimuovere remove
rinascimento m revival;
renaissance [dearer
rincarare grow (make)
rincontra, alla go to meet
rincontrare meet
rincontro m meeting
rincrescere be sorry for
rinculare recoil; with-
draw [blame
rinfacciare reproach:
rinfrescare refresh; renew
rinfresco m refreshment
rinfuso confused; mixed
ringhiare growl; neigh;
snarl
ringhiera f pulpit; hust
ings [again
ringiovanire grow young
ringraziamento m thanks
ringraziare thank
rinomato celebrated
rintoppare meet; mend
rintoppo m meeting
rintrecciare interweave
rintracciare trace; search
rintuzzare resist; abate;
blunt
rinunciare renounce
rinvenire recover one's
self; meet; found
rinviare send back
riparare repair
riparabile reparable
ripartire share; divide
ripentirsi repent

ripercuotere repercuss
ripetere repeat
ripetio m dispute
riplego m expedient;
ripieno full [refuge
ripienezza f fullness
ripiguare retake
riportare report; win
riposare, riposo m rest;
riposto hidden [repose
riprendere recover; re-
primand
riprensibile reprehensible
riprensione f reprimand
ripresa f repetition;
reprimand
rirpresentare represent
riprodurre reproduce
riprova f proof; evidence
riprovare reprove
ripudiare repudiate
ripugnare repulse; resist
ripulsa f repulse
riputare repute; attribute
riputazione f reputation
risaia f rice-field
risaltare rebound; excel
risalto m projection
risarcire repair; com-
pensate
risata f derision; scorn
riscaldare warm
riscaldamento m heating;
riscattare redeem [anger
rischiarare explain
rischiare risk
rischio m risk; danger;
– so dangerous
risciacquare wash; rinse
riscontare discount;
abate [pare
riscontrare meet; com-
riscontro m meeting;
comparison; – d' aria
draught
riscorrimento m running

riscossa *f* recovery
riscuotere shake; redeem
risecare cut
riseccare dry up
risedere reside
risegnare resign [tion
risegna(zione) *f* resigna-
risicare, risicio *m* risk
risma *f* ream; faction
riso *m* laughing; rice
risolare resole
risolvere resolve; dissolve
risoluzione *f* resolution; distolution
risoluto resolute
risomiguare resemble
risonare resound [tion
risorgimento *m* resurrec-
risparmiare spare; save
risparmio *m* savings
rispettare respect; honour
rispettabile reapectable
rispetto *m* respect
rispettoso respectful
rispianato smooth; *m*
rispondere answer [plain
riposare remarry
risposta *m* answer
rissa *f*, - re fight; dispute
ritardo *m* delay
ritaglio *m* shred
ritegno *m* obstacle
ritenuto reserved
ritenere retain; keep
ritirata *f* retreat; W.C.
ritirarsi withdraw; retire
ritiro *m* retirement
ritmo *m* rhythm
rito *m* rite
ritocare revise; vex
ritornare, ritorno *m* return
ritrarre retire; paint a portrait
ritrattare retract [painter
ritrattista *m* portrait-
ritratta *f* retreat

ritrato *m* portrait
ritrosa *f* bird-net; snare
ritroso obstinate
ritto right; straight
rituale *m* ritual
riunire unite; reconcile
riuscire succeed; happen
riuscita *f* success
riva *f* shore; bank
rivale *m* rival
rivelare reveal
rivelazione *f* revelation
rivendere sell again
rivendicare revenge; [claim
rivenire return
riverenza *f* reverence
riverire revere; respect
riversare upset
rivertere return
rivertire convert
rivestire dress again; [clothe
riviera *f* river
rivista *f* review
rivoltella *f* revolver
rivoltoso rebel
rivoluzione *f* revolution
rizzare erect
roba *f* goods; gown
robaccia *f* trash; slut
robusto strong; sturdy
rocaggine *f* hoarseness
rocca *f* stronghold; rock
roccia *f* rock; dress
rogna *f* scab
rognone *m* kidney
rogo *m* wood pile
romaiuolo *m* ladle
romantico romantic
romanza *f* romance
romanzo *m* novel
romba *f* sling [turbot
rombo *m* hum; rhomb;
rombare resound; buzz
romitaggio *m* hermitage
romito solitary; *m* hermit
romore *m* noise; rumour
rompere break; interrupt

rompicollo *m* precipice; ruin
rompinoci *m* nut-craker
roncare weed
ronchio *m* block
ronda *f* round
ronzare buzz; ramble
rosa *f* rose
rosaio *m* rose-bush
roseto *m* rose-field
rosario *m* rosary

rotaia *f* rut; track
rotare rotate
rotella *f* knee-pan; wheel
rotolare roll
rotondo round [rupture
rotta *f* rout; defeat;
rotto broken; tired
rottura *f* rupture; gap
rovente red-hot
rovesciare overthrow; spill [reverse
rovescio *m* wrong side;
roveto *m* thorn-hedge
rovina *f*; – **re** ruin
rovo *m* briar; thorn
rozza *f* jade
rozzo rough; rude
rubare steal; rob
rubacello *m* topaz
rubicondo ruddy
rubino *m* ruby
rugginoso rusty
ruggine *f* rust; grudge
ruggire roar
rugiada *f* dew; comfort
rullo *m* roller
rullare roll
rum *m* rum
rumore *m* noise; rumour
ruolo *m* roll; list
ruota, rota *f* wheel; rota
ruoteggio *m* road
rupe *f* rock; – **pinoso** rocky
ruspare wind [snoring
russare snore; – **so** *m*
rusticaggine *f* rusticity

rutilare shine; glitter
ruttare belch; vomit
ruvido rough; rugged; – **damente** roughly

ruzzare jest
ruzzola *f* small; wheel; spinning-top
ruzzolone *m* large stone
ruzzoloni rolling

S

Sabato, sabbato *m* Sabbath; Saturday
sabbia *f* sand; gravel; – **bioso** sandy [hole
sabordo *m* (mar.) port-
sacca *f* sack; bag
saccardo *m* errand boy;
saccheggiare ransack; destroy; – **tore** *m* plunderer
sacco *m* sack; ransacking; – **coccia** *f* pocket;
sacerdote *m* priest; – **tale** priestly; – **tessa** *f* priestess; – **zio** *m* priesthood
sacramento *m* sacrament; oath; – **tale** sacramental; – **tare** consecrate; swear
sacrare consecrate; – **rio** *m* sanctuary
sacro, cra sacred; – **santo** holy
sadduceo sadducee
saetta *f* arrow; thunderbolt; lancet; – **tamento** *m* shooting; – **tore** *m* bowman
saggezza *f* wisdom; prudence; – **gio** *a* wise
saggiare try; taste; – **tore** *m* assayer
saggina *f* maize
saggitario *m* bowman

sagliente striking
sago *m* sago
sagola *f* sounding line
sagoma *f* counterpoise
sagra *f* dedication
sagrestano *m* sexton;
– **tia** *f* sacristy
sagro coronation; consecration
saio *m* robe; cassock
saime *m* pork; fat
sala *m* hall; dining-room
salace salacious; salty
salagione *f* salt provisions
salamandra *f* salamander
salame *m* salt meat;
salt-pork   [bow
salamelecche *m* profound
salamoia *f* brine; pickle
salamone *m* salmon
salare salt; – **to** *m* bacon
salariare pay; – **rio** *m*
salassare let blood [salary
salcigno twisted; uneven
sound; solid; *n* balance; – **damente** firmly
sale *m* salt; wit
salgemma *m* mineral salt
saliare splendid; sumptuous
saliera *f* salt-cellar [tuous
salificare salt; – **zione**
f salting; – **gno** no salt
salire go up; – **toio** *m*
ladder
saliscendi *m* latch-key
saliva *f* spittle; – **re**
salivate
salma *f* weight; ton
salmone *m* salmon
salnitro *m* nitre; saltpetre; – **trato** nitrous
salsedine *f* saltness; –
sugginoso salted
salsiccia *f* sausage; –
ciaio *m* sausage maker;
–**ciuolo** *m* slice of sausage

salso salted; sharp
salsume *m* salting; salt-meat   [bol
saltabeccare jump; gam-
saltamartino *m* fop
saltambarco *m* jacket
saltamindosso *m* short
jacket; scanty dress
saltare jump; dance;
– **tore** jumper;
saltuariamente from time
to time
salubre wholesome
salume salted meat or
fish; – **miere** *m* pork-
butcher   [salute
salutare wholesome;
saluto *m* salutation;
salute
salute *f* health; salute
salva *f* volley; proof
salvadanaio *m* money-box
salvaggina *f* game
salvaguardia *f* safeguard
salvare save; – **dore, tore**
m, saviour; – **mento** *m*
salvation; – **torio** *m*
asylum
salvietta *f* napkin; towel
salvigia *f* asylum; refuge
salvo save; excepted
salvocondotto *m* safe-
conduct
sanare cure; heal; be
cured; – **bile** curable
sancire decree
sandalo *m* sandalwood;
sandal
sangue *m* blood; race;
– **guifero** bloody;
– **nario** bloodthirsty; –
noso sanguine; con-
sanguineous; – **nità** *f*
consanguinity
sanguigno sanguine;
bloody
sanguinaccio *m* black

pudding
sanguinario sanguinary; cruel [sucker
sanguisuga f leech; blood
santificare sanctify; canonize; – **ceturo** m hypocrite; – **monia** f sanctity
santo holy; saint; m church; – **toccheria** f hypocrisy; – **tocchio** m hypocrite
santoccio m simpleton
santolo, la m & f godfather; mother [relic
santuario m sanctuary;
sanzionare sanction; – **zione** f sanction; confirmation
sapere know; understand; – **amente** know by heart; learning; knowledge; – **vole** learned; wise
sapienza f wisdom; school; – **temente** wisely
sapone m soap; – **naceo** soapy; – **naio** soapboiler
saporare relish; – **re** m savour; taste; – **roso** savoury; agreeable
sarchiare weed; – **mento** m weeding
sarcofago m sarcophagus
sarda f cornelian
sardella, dina f pilchard
sardonico sardonic
sargano m woollen-cloth
sargia f serge
sarpare weigh anchor
sarrocchino m pilgrim
sartiame m cordage;
sarto m tailor [shrouds
sassaiuola f stone; fight

Satan, tana m Satan; – **nico** satanical
satellite m satellite; policeman [satirical
satira f satire; – **tirico**
satiro m satyr; satirical poet [bail
satisdazione f security;
satisfare satisfy
saviezza f wisdom
savina f sabine
savore m savour; – **rare** savour; – **roso** savoury
savorra f ballast; cargo
saziare satiate; satisfy; – **zietà** f satiety
sbacoellare husk; shell
sbadataggine f inattention; – **to** inattentive
sbadigliare yawn ; – **mento** m yawning
sbagliare be mistaken; – **glio** m mistake; blunder
sbaldeggiare grow bold; – **dore** m courage
sballare unpack; brag
sbalordire astonish; confound; – **mento** m astonishment
sbalzare throw; leap
sbandare scatter; disband [exile
sbandire exile; – **to** m
sbaragliare rout; disperse; – **mento, glio** f rout; disorder
sbarazzare clear; rid
sbarbagliare scatter
sbarra f bar; barrier; – **re** bar; barricade; unbar; – **ro** m barrier obstacle
sbassare lower; abate
sbatsare unsaddle
sbattagliare ring (bells)
sbattere shake; torment; – **timento** m agitation
sbattezzare change reli-

gion [agitation
sbattito *m* confusion;
sbavagliare unmask
sbeffare laugh at; ridicule
sbellicarsi burst out
sbendare unveil; relax
sbevazzare sip; drink;
– **mento** *m* sipping
sbezzicare peck
sbiancare whiten; – **cato**
pale
sbiecare slope; – **co**, **sco**
aslant; crooked
sbietolare be moved
sbigottire frighten ;
terrify; – **mento** fright
sbilenco crooked; bandy-
legged
sbirbato cheated; deceived
sbirciare ogle
sbirro *m* policeman;
bailiff
sboccare overflow; break
off the neck(of a bottle);
– **co** mouth (of river)
sboccato improper; wild;
– **tamente** indecently
sbocciare open; expand
sbocconcellare nibble
sbombardare bombard
sbombettare tipple
sbordellare be lewd; –
mento *m* lewd life
sborsare disburse; –
mento, **so** *m* disburse-
ment [insult
sbottonare unbutton;
sbrattare cleanse; clear
sbrigare dispatch; hasten
sbrigliare unbridle; untie
sbrogliare unravel; clear
sbruffare besprinkle
sbruttare cleanse
sbucchiare skin; peel
scacchi *m pl* chess; – **era**
f chess-board
sacco *m* square; – **matto**

check-mate
scaglia *f* scale; – **re** throw
scagnardo ugly
scala *f* staircase; ladder
scalciare kick [pan
scaldaletto *m* warming-
scaldare warm; excite
scampagnata *f* excursion
into the country
scampanare chime
scampare save; deliver
scampol(ett)o *m* remnant
(of cloth)
scandalo *m* scandal
scandalezzare scandalize
scannare cut the throat
scanno *m* bench
scansare avoid; escape
scapigliare dishevel
scapolo *m* bachelor
scappare escape
scappellari salute
scarabocchiare scribble
scarabocchio *m* scribbling
scarafaggio *m* scarab
scaramuccia *f* skirmish
scarlattina *f* scarlet fever
scarlattino scarlet
scarmo *m* thole-pin
scarno emaciated
scarpa *f* shoe; slope
scarpino *m* light shoe
scarpione *m* scorpion
scarsella *f* purse
scarso scarce
scartabellare peruse
scartare discard; reject
scassare unpack
scastagnare flinch
scatola *f* box; case
scattare get loose; pass
(time)
scaturire spring; spout
out
scavare excavate; dig
scavo *m* excavation;
hollow

213

scegliere choose
scellerato wicked
scena f scene
scendere descend; invade
scenico scenic; theatrical
scesa f descent; declivity
scettico sceptic
scettro m sceptre
scettrato crowned
sceverare sever; divide
scheda f schedule; bill
schermire fence; defend
scherno m scorn; mockery
scherzare, scherzo m jest
schiacciare squash; crush
schiaffo m box on the ear
schiamazzare brawl; jest
schiantare split; rend
schiarire clear up; explain
schiatta f race; breed
schiavo m slave
schiccherare scribble

schiena f back; chine
schiera f troop; gang
schietto frank; candid
schifare shun; loathe
schiflà f modesty

schifo m disgust; boat
schifoso disgusting
schioppo m gun; musket
schiudere open; uncork
schiuma f. - re foam
scialacquare lavish;
sciallo m shawl [waste
scialuppa f shallop;
launch
sciamare, sciame m
swarm
sciampagna m cham-
pagne
sciarpa f scarf
sciatica f sciatica
sciattare botch
sciente learned; - mente
knowingly

scilinguare stammer;
to stammering
sciliva f spittle; saliva
scimunitaggine f stupi-
dity; blunder
scindere separate; loosen
scintilla spark; - lare
sparkle
sciocco stupid; fool
sciogliere untie; absolve;
- tore m deliverer
sciolezza f boasting
scioltezza f nimbleness
sciolto nimble; liquid
sciolvere breakfast
scionata, scione f squall;
whirlwind
sciorinare air; publish
sciorre untie; absolve
scipa m goose; blockhead
scipare waste; miscarry;
- tore m spendthrift
scipidezza f insipidity;
trifle
sciringa f syringe; - re
syringe; inject
scirocco m sirocco
sciroppo m syrup
scisma m schism; dis-
sension; - tico m schis-
matic
scissione f scission; cleft
sciugare wipe; dry;
- toio m towel [sume
sciupare squander; con-
sciupinio m squandering
scivolare rebound
sclamare exclaim; cry
out; - zione f exclama-
scoccolare pick off [tion
scodare crop; - to crop-
scodella f porringer [ped
scofacciare crush; flatten
scoffina f rasp; grater
scoglio m sand-bank;
reef; - gliera f shoal
scoiare flay; skin

scoiatto *m* squirrel
scolare *m* scholar
soolare drain; trickle
soolaresca *f* scholar
scolastico scholastic
scolatoio *m* sewer; strainer
scolatura *f* residue
scolazione *f* gonorrhœa
scommettere separate; embroil; bet
scommiatare dismiss; – **si** to take leave
scommuovere move; revolt
scomodare trouble
scompagnare separate; uncouple
scomparire disappear
scompartire distribute
scompigliare confound; disturb; – **mento** *m* confusion; disturbance
scomunica, zione *f* excommunication; – **re** excommunicate
scomuzzolo not at all
sconcare put; draw out
sconcertare disturb; disconcert
sconcezza *f* disorder; indecency
sconciare damage; –**cio** out of order; unbecoming; indecent
sconcorde discordant; – **dia** *f* discord
scondere conceal
sconfacevole indecorous
sconferma *f* confirmation; – **re** confirm   [own
sconfessare deny; disown
sconfidare mistrust; – **danza** *f* mistrust
sconfiggere rout; disturb
sconfondere confound
sconnettere separate; be

incoherent, – **ssione** *f* incoherence
scontraffatto deformed
scontramento *m* meeting; – **re** meet with; encounter;
scontro *m* meeting
sconturbare confound; – **bo** *m* confusion
scoperchiare uncover
sconoscere be ungrateful; – **scente** ungrateful; low; – **temente** inconsiderately; – **sciuto** unknown; low
sconquasso *m* destruction; – **sare** destroy
sconsacrare profane
sconsenso *m* approval
sconsentire refuse; dissent; – **mento** *m* refusal
sconsideratezza *f* inconsideration; – **to** inconsiderate
sconsigliare dissuade; – **tezza** *f* imprudence
sconsolare afflict; dishearten   •
scontare discount; expiate; – **to** *m* discount
scontentare discontent; – **mento, tezza** *m & f* discontent
scontinuare discontinue
scoppiare burst; come forth; – **mento, tura** *m & f* explosion; noise
scoppiettare crackle; explode   [cover
scoprire discover; uncover
scoraggiare, gire discourage; – **si** lose courage
scorare discourage
scorcare get up; to rise
scorciare shorten;

215

abridge; – **toia** f cross-road

scordare disagree; forget
scoreggiare whip; fart; – **ta** f whip
scorgere discover; guide; – **gimento** m discovery
scoria dross; scum
scornacchiare banter; laugh at; – **mento** m joke
scorno m insult; affront
scorta f escort
scortare shorten; escort
scortecciare peel
scortese discourteous; impolite; – **sia** f rudeness
scorticare peel; flay
scorto m bark
scorto prudent
scorza f rind; cuticle
scorzone m churl; serpent
scoscendere lop; split
scosciare disjoint; – **scio** m precipice [– re shake
scossa f toss; squall;
scostare remove; drive away; – **mento** m removal
scostumatezza m dissoluteness; indecency
scotennato m fat (pig)
scottare burn; scald;
scotto m share; Scot
scovare start; find out
scozzare shuffle (cards)
scozzonare break (horse); – **tore** m horsebreaker

scranna f folding stool; chair [tumacious
scredente infidel; con-
screditare discredit
scremento m excrement
scremenzia m quinsy
screpolare split; burst

screscere decrease
scriato slender; weak
scriba m writer; copyist
scrichiare clash; crackle
scriccio m wren
scrigno m jewel-box; – **gnuto** concave; concrima f fencing [vex
scrimaglia f defence
scrinare dishevel
scritta f writing; inscription
scritto written; erased; m writing; – **toio** m writing-desk; inkstand; – **tore** m writer; author; – **tura** f writing; scripture
scrivacchiare scribble
scrivere write; – **zione** f writing
scrollare shake; toss
scrosciare split; boil
scrupoleggiare have scruples; – **lo**, **sità** m & f scruple; – **so** scrupulous
scrutare tinare scrutinize; ballot; – **tinio** m ballot
scucire unstitch; undo
scudare shield; – **do** m shield; scutcheon
scuderia f stable; stud; – **diere** m equerry
scudisciare whip; – **scio** m switch; rod
scuffia f coif; head-dress; – **ra** f milliner
scuffiare swallow; devour
scultore m carver; engraver; – **tura** f sculpture
scumarola f skimmer
scuola f school
scusa f excuse; pretext; – **bile** excusable
scusare excuse; justify

216

scusso deprived; shaken

scutica f whip

sdegnare despise; decay; – si get angry; – gno m disdain; anger

sdicevole improper

sdilaciare untie; unlace

sdilinquire faint; – mento m fainting

sdormentare wake; – si

sdossare unload [awaken degree of doctor

sdottorare take away

sdraiarsi stretch one's self; lie down

sdurare quiet

se if; whether

sé one's self; himself; herself; itself; themselves

sebbene though

secante f secant

secca, gna f sand-bank; shallow [some person

seccafistole m trouble-

seccaggine f drought; importunity

seccare dry up; bother; waste; – ticcia f dry wood; – to dry; barren

secchia f pail; bucket; – ta f pailful

seccia f stubble [m drought

secco dry; flabby; thin;

secedere part; – cessione f defection; insurrection

secesso m retirement

seco with one's self

secolare profane; secular; – rizzare secularize

secolo m century; help

secondare help; second

secondario secondary; accessory

secreto m secret; confidant

secrezione f secretion; – torio secretary

sedizione f sedition; tumult; – so seditious

sedurre seduce; corrupt; – cimento m seduction; – duttore m seducer

sega f saw; – are saw; f reap; – tura f sawing; saw-dust

segale m rye

segaligno dry; lean

segavene m leech

seggetta f sedan-chair

segmento m segment

segnacolo m register; signet

segnalare signalize; – to illustrious; – tamente remarkably

segnale m description; token; signal

segnare note; sign; bless; bleed; – si cross one's self; be surprised; – to signed; marked; – tamente expressly; – tore m indicator; – gno m seal; signal; mark

sego m tallow; suet

segregare separate; – mento m separation

segreta f secret place; secret prayer; – rio, ro m secretary; – o m secret; confident; – tamente secretly

seguace, guitatore following; follower

seguitare follow; torment; – mento m following; pursuing; – to m suite; issue; – to part; reputed

sei six

selce, selice f paving-stone; f – ciare pave; – to, liciato m pave-

217

ment; – **cioso** stony
sella f saddle; chair;
– **laio** m saddler; – **re**
saddle

sembiante alike; resem-
bling; face; counten-
ance; – **brare** look;
appear

seme m seed; origin

sementa, za f seed;
origin; sowing; – **re**
sow; – **tore** m sower

semestre m space of six
months; – **trale** half
yearly

semi half; – **addottorato**
simple; – **cerchio, circ-
colo** m semi-circle; –
circolare semi-circular;
– **croma** f semi-quaver;
– **deo, dio** m demi-god;
everlasting; – **nare** perpetuate

semplice simple; pure;
– **mente** simply; – **cista**
m herbalist; botanical
garden; – **cità** f simpli-
city; candour

sempre ever; always;
– **che** so often as; **mai**
– for ever

sena f senna

senapa, pe f mustard-
seed; mustard; – **pismo**
m mustard-plaster

senario of six

senato m senate; – **tore**
m senator [senility

senile senile; – **lità** f

seniore senior; older

senno m sense; wisdom;
a mio – at my pleasure;
da – in earnest; **con**-
wisely

seno m bosom; intellect

se non if not; but

sensale m broker; agent;
– **seria** f brokerage

sensatezza f sense; prudence

sensazione f sensation

sensibile f sensible; per-
ceptible; – **lità, tività** f
sensibility; – **tivo** sensitive; scrupulous

senso m sense; feeling;
– **suale sensual**; – **lità**
f sensuality

sentarsi sit down

sentente feeling; hearing

sentenza f sentence;
maxim; – **zialmente**
sententiously; – **ziare**
judge; sentence; –
ziato m convict; – **zia-
tore** m judge [way

sentiere, o m path; bye-

sentimento m feeling;
judgment; – **tale** senti-
mental

senza without; **senz'-
altro** – without doubt;
– **che** besides; more-
over; – **più** without any
thing else

senziente sensible

sepa f snake

separare separate; remove; – **tamente** sep-
arately; – **mento, zione**
m & f separation

sera f evening; night;
– **le** evening [seraphic

serafino m seraph; – **fico**

serbanza f keeping; care

serbare keep; reserve;
delay; – **toio** m reservoir; – **tore** m deposi-
sere m sire; master [tary

serenare quieten; brighten; – **no** serene

serenata f serenade

sergente m sergeant;

bailiff

sergoncello _m_ sorrel

serico silk

serie _f_ series

serietà _f_ seriousness; – rio serious; – riamente, riosamente seriously

sermento _m_ vine-shoot

sermocinare, nare, neggiare preach; – natore _m_ preacher; – ne _m_ sermon; speech; salmon

serpe, pente _f_ & _m_ snake;

serpeggiare wind [serpent

serpentare plague; bore

serpere meander; creep

serpetta _f_ adder

serpillo _m_ wild thyme

serra _f_ mountain; dike; crowd [closure

serraglio _m_ seraglio; enserrare lock up; conceal; press; – to strained; close; – tamente tightly; briefly; – tura _f_ lock

serto _m_ garland

serva, vente _f_ maid servant [vitude

servaggio _m_ slavery ; serservare keep; hold; – tore _m_ keeper

servente _m_ servant; lover

servire serve; wait on; – dore, tore, vo servant; valet; foot-man; – gio, zio _m_ service; business; use; – vile servile

sesamo _m_ sesame

sessagono _m_ sexagonal

sessanta _m_ sixty; – tesimo sixtieth; – tina _f_ threescore

sessione _f_ session

sesso _m_ sex; – suale sexual

sessola _f_ scoop

sesta _f_ compass; sixth; – tante _m_ sextant

sesterzio _m_ sesterce

sestile _m_ sextile

sesto sixth; sixthly; _m_ order; compass

sestodecimo sixteenth

settanta seventy; – tesimo seventieth

sette seven

setteggiare revolt

settentrione _m_ north; – nale northern

settimana _f_ week; – le weekly; – nalmente weekly

settina _f_ seven

setto split; divided

settuplo septuple

severità _f_ severity; – ro severe; – ramente severely

sevizia _f_ ill usage [verely

sevo _m_ tallow; suet

sezione _f_ section

sezzaio, sezzo _m_ last; da sezzo late; too late

sfaccendato idle; unoccupied

sfanfanare waste; rum

sfardellare unfold

sfare undo; destroy

sfarinare grind; pulverize

sfarzo _m_ pomp; magnificence; – so pompous

sfasciare unswathe; pull down (walls)

sfastidiare pacify

sfatare scorn; disdain

sfatto undone; destroyed

sfavillare sparkle; glitter; – mento _m_ shine

sferza _f_ whip; discipline; – re scourge; imitate; – ta _f_ whipping

sfessatura _f_ slit

sfetteggiare cut in slices

sfiatare breathe; toil;

219

– to out of breath

sfibbiare unbutton

sfibrare enervate; – mento *m* enervation

sfidare challenge; mistrust; – da. damento *f* & *m* challenge; defiance; – tore *m* challenger

sfiduciato mistrust

sfigurare disfigure

sfilacciare unravel

sfilare file off; – ta *f* wiredrawing-iron; – to confused

sfingardaggine *f* idleness

sfinge *f* sphinx

sfinire finish; perfect; – mento *m* swoon

sfioccare unravel

sfiondare sling

sfocato cooled; cold

sfoderare unsheathe

sfogare evaporate; suppurate; – toio *m* airhole; tap; – mento *m* evaporation; relief

sfogliare strip of leaves; extenuate; – glia *f* metal sheet; spangle

sfogliazzo *m* diary

sfogo *m* evaporation; exhaling

sforacchiare drill

sformare disfigure; – to deformed; strange; – zione *f* deformity

sfortuna *f* misfortune; – to, tevole unfortunate

sfortunare make unhappy

sforzare constrain; ravish; – si endeavour; – to violent; unjust

sfracassare demolish

sfrattare dismiss; go away; – to *m* expulsion;

---

flight

sfregare rub; – mento *m* rubbing; – toio *m* duster; scrubbing brush

sfregiare undress; slap

sfregio *m* undressing; insult

sfrenare unbridle; – si live dissolutely; – mento, tezza *m* & *f* licentiousness; – to dissolute

sfriggolare fry

sfrontarsi make bold; – taggine. tezza *f* boldness; – to bold

sfuggevole perishable; – lezza *f* rapidity

sfuggire·fly from: avoid; – mento *m* flight; – to fugitive [colours

sfumatura *f* gradation of

sgabello, lino *m* stool

sgagliardare weaken

sgallinare fuddle; banquet [get tired

sgangherare disorder; dislocate

sgannare undeceive

sgaraffare deceive

sgarare rire surpass; vanquish

sgargarizzare gargle; – zo *m* gargling

sgarrare be mistaken

sgavazzare guttle; riot

sgelare thaw

sghembo oblique; tortuous; *m* obliquity

sghermire get loose; let go [throat

sgherro *m* bully; cut-

sghiacciare thaw

sghignare laugh at; deride; – gnazzare burst out laughing; – mento. ta *m* & *f* burst of laughter

sgocciolare distill; drop; – **toio** *m* gutter; – **tura, lo** *f & m* dripping

sgombinare, gominare jumble

sgomentare frighten; – **si** be frightened; – **mento** *m* fright; – **tevole** frightful

sgorgare overflow; chat

sgovernare govern; treat badly [swallow (insult)]

sgozzare cut throat of;

sgradire disagree; disgust; – **devole** disagreeable

sgraffiare scratch; etch

sgraffignare steal

sgranare shell out

sgravare unburden; relieve; – **mento, vio** *m* relief

sgravidare be delivered; lie in; – **danza** *f* lying-in

sgraziato clumsy; unfortunate

sgretolare break; hash

sgretolio *m* fermentation

sgricchiolare crackle

sgridare scold; – **tore** *m* grumbler

sguardare look at; consider; – **ta** *f* glance; – **tore** *m* looker-on

sguarnire guernire strip

sgufare jeer

sguinzagliare set (dogs) on; provoke

sguisciare swim; shell

siamese *m* Siamese

sibarita sybaritic; sybarite

sibilare, billare whistle; incite; – **tore** *m* whistler; – **lio, lo** *m* whistle

sicario *m* hired assassin

sicchè so; also; thus; therefore

siocità *f* dryness; drought

siccome as; so; as soon as; owing

siclo *m* cycle

sicomoro *m* sycamore

sicumera *f* pomp; ceremony

sicuranza *f* security; boldness; – **rare** assure; secure; – **rezza, rità, curtà** security; – **ro** assured; firm

sido *m* great cold

sidro *m* cider

siepaglia *f* thicket

siepare enclose with a hedge; – **pe** *f* hedge;

sigillare seal; confirm; – **latamente** exactly; – **lo** *m* seal

signifero *m* ensign; standard-bearer

significamento *f* signification; notice; – **cantemente, cativamente** significantly; – **care** signify; give notice; – **cativo significative**

signora *f* lady; mistress; madam; – **rina** *f* miss

signore *m* Lord; God; sir; mister [govern

signoreggiare domineer;

signoria government; lordship; – **rilità** *f* lordship; – **rilmente** lordly

sillaba *f* syllable; – **re** pronounce

sillogismo *m* syllogism;

simpatia sympathy; – **tico** sympathetic; – **tizzare** sympathize

simplificare simplify; – **zione** *f* simplification

simposio *m* symposium

simulacro *m* image; likeness

simulare simulate; dissemble; – **mento, zione** *m & f* feint; dissimulation

simultaneità *f* simultaneity; – **neo** simultaneous; – **neamente** simultaneously

sinagoga *f* synagogue

sincerare justify; – **zione** *f* justification

sincerità *f* sincerity; candour; – **ro** sincere; – **ramente** sincerely – **gizzare** argue

silvano sylvan

silvestro, tre wood

simboleggiare symbolize; – **leità, lità** *f* analogy; – **lo** *m* symbol; creed

simigliante alike; same; – **temente** in the same way; – **za, litudine** *f* comparison; – **gliare** resemble; imitate

similare similar; – **le** alike; same; – **milmente** similarly

simmetria *f* symmetry; – **trico** symmetric

singolare, gulare singular; only; – **rità** *f* singularity; – **lo** each

singulto *m* sob; sigh

sinistra *f* left; left hand; **da** – on the left hand; – **tro** left; sinister

sino till; until; as far as; **sin adesso** till now; hitherto; – **a che** till; until; **sin dove** ? how far? – **sin qui** hither

sinonimia *f* synonymy; – **mico, mo** synonymous; – **mo** *m* synonym

sintassi syntax

sintesi *f* synthesis; – **tico** synthetical

sintomatico symptomatic; – **mo** *m* symptom

siroccbia *f* sister

sirte *f* quicksands

sisimbrio *m* watercress

sistema *m* system; – **re** regulate; classify; – **tico** systematical

sistro *m* timbrel

sitare stink

sitibondo thirsty; covetous; – **re** be thirsty

sito situated; *m* site; stink

situamento *m* situation; – **zione** *f* situation

slacciare untie; unfold

slanciamento, cio *m* spring; – **re** throw; dart

slargamento *m* widening; – **re** widen

slegamento *m* loosening; – **re** loosen

slitta *f* sledge

slogamento, tura *m & f* dislocation; – **re** dislocate

slungare lengthen; remove [depreciate

smaccare crush; vilify;

smacchiare break cover

smagamento *m* astonishment; – **re** be astonished; mislead; – **smago** *m* fright; error

smagramento, grimento *f* growing thin; – **grare, grire** grow thin

smaliziato sharp; cunning

smallare peel

smaltare enamel; pave; – **mento, tura** *m & f* enamelling

smanceria *f* affection;
– **cinato. roso** affected

smania *f* & *m* fury;
frenzy; – **re** get furious;
rave; – **niante, nioso**
furious; frantic

smaniglia *f* & *m* bracelet

smantellare dismantle

smanziere *m* beau; dandy

smargiassare bully

smarrire mislay; – **si**
lose one's way

smascherare unmask

smembrare dismember

smenomare diminish

smentire belie

smeraldo *m* emerald

smerare clean; polish

smerciare sell; deliver;
– **cio** *m* sale; delivery

smerdare soil

smerigliare polish with
emery; – **glio** *m* emery

smeriglione *m* swivel

smerlo *m* merlin

smettere leave

smezzamento *m* parting

smillanta *m* bully; – **re**
bully

smilzo delicate; feeble

sminchionare jeer

sminuire lessen; – **mento**
m diminution

sminuzzare hash; detail

sminuzzolare hash; explain

smodamento *m* disorder;
– **dato** immoderate

smoderamento, ezza *m*
& *f* excess; immodera-
tion

smogliato bachelor

smovitura *f* movement;
commotion

smozzicare maim

smozzicatura maiming

smugghiare bellow; roar

smugnere dry up; wither

smunire restore

smuovere move; excite

smurare demolish

smussare blunt

snaturare alter; – **tezza**
f cruelty; – **to** cruel

snebbiare clear up

snellezza *f* agility

soave sweet; gentle;
– **mente** *ad* sweetly;
gently; – **vità** *f* sweet-
ness

sobbalzare tremble

sobbarcare conquer; – **si**
submit

sobbollire boil gently

sobborgo *m* suburb

sobbornare suborn

sobillare seduce; – **mento**
m seduction

soccorrere help; agree;
– **vole** helpful; – **ri-
mento, so** *m* help;
– **ritore** *m* helper

sociabile sociable; – **ciale**
a social; sociable;
– **lismo** *m* socialism;
– **lista** *m* socialist; – **lità**
f sociability

società *f* society

socio *m* comrade; partner

soda *f* soda

sodale *m* comrade; companion; – **lizio** *m* company; fraternity

sodare consolidate; bail

soddisfacente, cevole
satisfactory; – **mente**
satisfactorily; – **cimento, zione** *m* & *f* satisfaction; – **fare** satisfy

sodezza *f* solidity; constancy; – **do** constant;
intrepid; *f* guarantee

sodomia *f* sodomy

sofà *m* sofa

sofferenza *f* suffering;

223

patience; – **revole** bearable; – **rire** suffer
soffermare stop
soffermata f pause; stop
soffiare blow; excite; move; m breath; – **il naso** blow one's nose
soffocare conceal; hide
soffice soft
soffornato vaulted
soffraganeo suffragan
soffratta f want; penury
soffreddo coldish
soffriggere fry; – **fritto** m fricassee
soffrire suffer
soggettare subject; subdue; – **bile** subject; – **gezione** f subjection; – **getto** m subject; object
sogghignare smile; – **gno** m smile
soggiacere surrender; – **cimento** m subjection; submission
soggiogare subdue; surpass; – **mento, zione** m & f subjection
sorgolo m gorget; double chin
soglia f threshold; sole (fish) [hold]
soglio m throne; thressogliola f sole (fish)
sognare dream; imagine; – **tore** m dreamer; – **gno** m dream; revery
soia f flattery; – **re** wheedle
solaio m floor; wainscot
solamente only
solare solar; – **zio** sunny; southern; m sunny place
solata f sun-stroke; sunshine

soldare recruit
soldato m soldier; – **tesca** f soldiery; – **tesco** soldierly
soldo m sou; pay; war
sole m sun; year
solecchio m parasol; canopy
solecismo m solecism
solenne solemn; – **neggiare, nizzare** solemnize; – **mente** solemnly – **nità** f solennity; – **zione** f solemnization
solere be accustomed to
solerte careful; vigilant; – **zia** f care; vigilance
soletta f sole (stocking)
soletto alone
solfa f gamut; music
solfatara sulphur mine
solfato m sulphate
solfo f sulphur; brimstone; – **nello** m match; – **rico** sulphuric
solimato m sublimate
solingo alone; solitary
solio m throne
solitario, ria solitary
solito; usual; accustomed; m habit; **al** – usually
solitudine f solitude
solivago alone; only
sollazzare amuse; entertain: – **lazzo** m amusement; sport
sollecitare solicit; urge; incite; – **tore** m suitor;
sollievo m ease; comfort
sollo soft; flabby
solo alone; only
solstizio m solstice
soltanto only; but; solely; – **che** provided
solubile soluble; separable; – **lità** f solubility

solvere dissolve; free‡ – **vibile** solvent; – **lità** *f* solvency

soma *f* load; burden; – **ro. miere** *m* pack-horse; beast of burden

somiglianza *f* likeness; resemblance; – **gliare** compare; resemble

somma *f* sum; summit; result; **in –** in short

sommaco *m* morocco leather [amount to

sommare sum up;

sommario summary

sommergere submerge; sink; – **gibile** submersible; – **gimento, sione** *m* & *f* submersion

sommessione. missione *f* submission; obedience; – **sivo** submissive

somministrare supply; administer; – **tore** *m* purveyor; – **zione** *f* supply; provision

sommità *f* summit

sommo; ma supreme; *m* summit; – **mamente**

sonare, suonare ring; play (instrument); **suono** *m* sound

sonettare make sonnets; – **netto** *m* sonnet

sonnacchiare. necchiare doze; slumber

sonnambulismo *m* somnambulism; – **lo, la** *n* somnambulist

sonno *m* slumber; rest; – **lente, lo to** sleepy

sonorità *f* sonorousness; – **ro** sonorous

sontuosità *f* sumptuousness; – **so** sumptuous

soperchiamento *m* superabundance [ceed

soperchiare surpass; ex-

sopercheria *f* cheat; insult; – **chio** superfluity; superabundantly

sopire quiet; quench; – **pore** *m* lethargy; – **rifero, fico roso** soporific

soppalco *m* ceiling

soppanare line; trim;

soppressa *f* press; – **re** mangle; press; – **pressione** *f* oppression; suppression; – **primere** oppress; abolish

soppressata *f* sausage

sopra on; above; beyond; about; towards **soprabbondante, devole** superabundant; – **danza** *f* superabundance; – **dantemente, devolmente** superabundantly

soprabbuono very good

sopraccapo *m* superintendent; director

sopraccaricare overload; – **co** *m* overload

sopraccarta *f* envelope

sopracchiedere ask too much for

sopracchiusa *f* cover

sopracciglio *m* eye-brow

sopracinghia *f* surcingle

sopracciò *m* superintendent; director

sopraccomperare overpay

sopraccoperta *f* counterpane; envelope

sopraccorrere rush upon

sopraggirare turn round

sopraggiugnere supervene; surprise; – **giunto** caught; surprised; *m* addition

sopraggravare overload

soppraintendenza *f* superintendance

soprallodare praise ex-

225

sopralzare lift [cessively
sopramabile most amiable
soprammattone m brick-wall [excessively
soprammisura extremely;
soprammodo inordinately
soprammontare grow; surpass
sopranimo passionately; with animosity
soprannaturale supernatural; – **lmente** supernaturally
sopransegna f regimentals
soprantendente, ditore m superintendent
soprappeso m overload
soprappigliare seize upon; take too much
soprappiù m surplus; addition; **di** – into the bargain; besides
soprapporre add; load; – **ponimento, sizione** m & f superposition
soprapprendere surprise; – **dimento** m surprise
soprapprofondo very deep
soprarrivare supervene
soprascritta, scrizione f inscription; epitaph
soprascrivere superscribe
soprasoldo m extra-pay
soprassegnale m description; – – **gno** make a mark; – **gno** m mark; sign
soprassello m surplus
soprasseminare sow again
soprassalare salt too much [much
soprassapere know too
soprassedenza f suspension; delay; – **dere** suspend
sopravvedere supervise
sopravvenire supervene

sopravvento m windward
sopravvesta, te f sleeve-less coat; pretext
sopravvincere surpass
sopravvivenza f reversion; – **vere** out-live; survive
soprecedente superabundant; – **za** f super-abundance [lent
sopreccellente most excel-
sopreminente most high; sublime [tend
soprintendere superin-
soprosso m splint; trouble
soprumano supernatural
soprusare misuse; abuse; – **so** m misuse; injury
soqquadrare overthrow; – **dro** m ruin; confusion
sorare cast (hawks)
sorbetto m sherbet; ice-cream; – **tiera** f ice-mould
sordaggine, dezza f deafnes ; – **do** deaf; – **domuto** m deaf and dumb; – **dità** f deafness
sordido sordid
sorella f sister; nun
sorgente m spring; origin;
sornacchiare cough and spit; – **chio** m fit of coughing
sornuotare float
soro low; dark; m booby
sorpassare surpass; excel
sorprendere astonish; deceive; – **dente** surprising; – **presa** f surprise;
sorradere graze [deceit
sorreggere prop; bear up; – **si** stop
sorridere smile; – **dentemente** smilingly; – **riso** m smile
sorsaltare start up

sorsara, sorseggiare sip
sorta *f* sort; manner
sorte *f* fate; hazard; luck
sortiere, tilego *m* sorcery;
   – legio *m* witch-craft
sortire go out; draw lots
sorvenire supervene
sorvivere survive
sorvolare excel; float;
   – lante surpassing;
floating
soscrittore *m* subscribe; –
   vere subscribe; –
   scrizione *f* subscription
sospendere hang; defer;
   – dimento, sione *f* suspense; suspension; –
   sorio *m* truss; – peso
suspended; irresolute
sospettare, picare mistrust; suspect; – petto,
toso suspicious; *m* suspicion; mistrust; – tamente, tosamente suspiciously
sospirare sigh; long for;
   – tore *m* lover; – spiro
m sigh; minim rest
sossopra upside down
sostegno *m* prop; protection
sostenenza *f* toleration;
aliment; – nere sustain;
tolerate; last; – tore *m*
protector
sostentare prop; nourish;
   – mento, zione, *m* & *f*
sustenance, support
sostentatore *m* protector
sostenutezza *f* gravity;
   – to sustained; detained
sostituire subatitute; –
tuto *m* substitute
sostituzione *f* substitution
sottacqua under water
sottacqueo subaqueous
sottana *f* cassock; petti-

coat   [stealth
sottocchi secretly; by
sotterfugio *m* subterfuge
sotterra under ground
sotterraneo subterraneous
sottomettere submit; –
   messione, missione *f*
submission; subjection
sottomurata *f* foundation
sottordinare subordinate;
   – ordinato subordinate;
subaltern
sottoscritta, scrizione *f*
subscription; – tore *m*
subscriber; – vere subscribe
sottosopra upside down
sottosquadro *m* cavity
sottoterra under ground
soitovoce low voiced
sottraimento, zione *m* &
f subtraction; – trarre
substract; deceive
sovente frequently
soverchiare exceed; fall;
sovero *m* cork   [sink
sovra on; upon
sovrabbondanza *f* superabundance
sovradescritto aforesaid
sovraggrande very great
sovrapossente almighty
sovrapiù *m* excess
sovrasaltare throb
sovrastamento *m* superiority; – stante *m* superintendent
sovreccellente most excellent
sovrempiere fill up
sovresso over; on; upon
sovroffesa *f* offence
sovrumano supernatural
sovvenenza, nimento *f* &
m help; – nevole helpful; – nire aid; relieve;
   – nitore, ventore *m* benefactor; – venzione *f*

help; subsidy
sovversione *f* subversion
sozio *m* comrade
sozzare soil; corrupt;
– zo profligate; dirty
spaccare divide; cleave
spaccamonti *m* bully
spacciare sell; abbreviate; kill; – bile sale-
able
spada *f* sword; sword-
fish; a – tratta entirely
spaderno *m* fishing - line
spadina *f* hunting-knife
spadone *m* back-sword
spadulare drain
spagnolata *f* bragging

spalla *m* shoulder; top
spalletta *f* epaulet
spalliera *f* back (seat);
espalier
spampanare thin out
(vines) [*f* ostentation
spampanare brag; – ta
spandere shed; pour
spanditoio *m* drying-room
spanna *f* span; hand
spannare baffle; sweep
spantanare drain a march
spantare be frightened
sparagnare save; pardon;
– gno *m* frugality
sparalembo *m* apron
sparare forget; disfigure

sparecchiare take away;
swallow; clear
spareggio *m* disparity
spargere spill; shed;
spartamente separately
spartatamente apart
spartire divide; assess;
– bile divisible; – mento,
to *m & f* division
sparutello, to, weak;
meagre [hawk
sparviere, ro *m* sparrow-

spasima, mo, spasmo *f &*
m convulsion; spasm;
– smodico spasmodic
spassarsi enjoy one's self
spasseggiare walk; take
a walk; – gio *m* walk
spassevole diverting
spasso *m* pastime
spatola *f* spatula
spatriare exile
spauracchio *m* scarecrow; terror
spavalderia *f* impudence;
sauciness; – do bold;
impudent
spavenio *m* spavin
spaventacchio *m* bugbear
spaventare frighten; fear;
– tevole, toso fearful
spavento *m* fright; alarm
spaziare extend; stretch
spazieggiare distance; –
zievole spacious
spaziosità *f* width; – so
wide; spacious
spazzacamino *m* chimney-
sweeper [ade *m* idler
spazzacampagne, contr-
spazzamento *m* sweeping;
– zare sweep; dust
spazzino *m* sweeper;
floor-scrubber
spazzo *m* pavement
spazzola *f* brush; – re
brush
specchiare look in a glass;
look at; examine; –
chio *m* looking-glass
speculare observe; speculate; meditate; trans-
parent [cavern
speculo *m* looking-glass;
spedale *m* hospital
spedarsi get tired; – da-
tura *f* fatigue; weari-
ness [venient

spediente opportune; con-
spedire send; hasten;
  - **tezza** *f* quickness;
  - **tivo** expeditious

spegnere extinguish; destroy

spelda, spelta *f* spelt

spellare skin; - **mento** *m*
flaying

spelonca *f* cave; den

speme *f* hope; expectation

spendente lavish; - **dere**
spend; employ; *m*
spendthrift [*m* plume

spennachiare pick; - **chio**

speranza *f* hope; confidence; - **rare** hope

sperdere lavish; dissipate; - **si** die; faint

sperimentale experimental; - **tare** try; experiment; - **to** experienced;
skilful; - **to** *m* experiment

sperma *m* sperm; seed

spermaceti *m* spermaceti

spernere despise; scorn

sperone *m* spur

sperso scattered

sperticato long-legged;
exaggerated

sperto expert; skilful

spesa *f* expense; cost

spessamente frequently;
often [frequent

spesso thick; hard;

spesseggiare, sicare reiterate; repeat

spetrare soften; calm;
free

spettacolo *m* spectacle

spettatore *m* spectator

speziale special; - **lità** *f*
speciality; - **lmente** especially

spezie *f* species

spiacenza, cevolezza *f*
dislike   [region

spiaggia *f* beach; coast;

spianare level; explain

spiantare level; eradicate; raze; - **to** ruined;
miserable [- **tore** *m* spy

spiare spy; seek out;

spiattellare speak freely

spiccare detach; unhook;
distinguish one's self

spiccatamente brilliantly

spicchio *m* clove

spicciare spring; spout;
pronounce clearly; urge

spiedo *m* boar spear; spit

spiegare unfold; explain;
  - **bile** explicable

spiegazzare fumble

spietatezza *f* cruelty;
inhumanity; - **to** *a*
inhuman; cruel

spietrare soften

spigolare glean; - **tore** *m*
gleaner; - **tura** *f* gleaning

spigolo *m* lavender

spigoso full of ears

spilla *f* pin   [wool

spillaccherare cleanse

spillare tap; pour; distil; sponge   [gimlet

spillo *m* pin; sting;

spilorceria *f* avarice;
greediness   [awl

spina *f* thorn; fish-bone

spinace *m* spinach

spinetta *f* trimming

spinosità *f* prickliness;
difficulty; - **so** thorny;
difficult

spinta *f* shock; thrust;

spiritale vital; spiritual

spiritare possessed by the
devil; be frightened

spirito, spirto *m* spirit;
breath; wit

spiritosità *f* spirituality;

– so spirituous; – tuale
spiritual
spiro m breath; spirit
spiumacciare shake; – ta
/ slap
splebeire ennoble
splendente splendid; –
mente, didamente splen-
didly; – dere shine;
sparkle
spoglia / spoil; pod;
cast off; – re spoil;
strip naked; – toio m
place for undressing;
– tore m plunderer
spogliazza / flagging;
furniture; spoil; – to
half naked
spoglio m spoil; furniture
spollonare sweep; cleanse;
– tura / cleansing
spolverare dust; search;
– tura / dusting; – riz-
zare pulverize
sponda / bank; shore
spongiosso fungous
sponimento m exposi-
tion; explanation
sponsale nuptual; – zio
m wedding
spontaneità / spontaneity;
– neo spontaneous
spontone m pontoon
spopolare depopulate;
– zione / depopulation
spoppare wean
sporre expose; explain
spossare debilitate
spossedere, sessare, spo-
destare dispossess
spostare change; remove
sprecare squander; waste
spregiare despise; dis-
dain   [juiced
spregiudicare be unpre-
spregnare bring forth
spremere squeeze out

sprezzare despise; disdain;
– sprezzo m contempt;
acorn
sprillare squeeze out
sprimacciare make a bed
sprimere express; state
sprizzare spring; irrigate
sprocco m shoot; sprig
sprofondare sink; dig;
ruin   [differ
sprolungare prolong;
sproporzionale dispropor-
tioned; – lità, ne /
disproportion
spropositaggine, to / &
m blunder; – tare act
or speak foolishly
sprotetto unprotected
sprunare prune
spruneggio, neggiolo m
dwarf holly   [rain
spruzzaglia / drizzling
spugna / sponge
spurare, purgare purge;
cleanse
spurgo m purge; spit
spurio, ria spurious;
bastard
sputacchiare sputter; –
chiera / spittoon; – tare
spit
spuzzare stink
squaccherare, querare
squirt; bungle; – chera
/ squirt   [manifest
squadernare peruse;
squadra / square; squad-
ron: – re quarter
squadronare marshal;
– ne m squadron; troop
squalidezza / paleness;
– lido squalid; wan
squalo m shark
squama, squamma /
scale (fish); mail; –
moso scaly
squarciare lacerate; rend

230

squarcione m boaster
sjuarquoio disgusting
squartare quater; brave;
- toio m butcher's knife
squassare shake; agitate;
- mento, so m shaking;
shock
squilla f splinter; bell;
- re ring; resound
squinanza f quincy
squisitezza f excellence;
- to exquisite; excellent
squittinare ballot
squittire bark; yelp
sradicare eradicate
sragionevole unreason-
able   [orderly
sregolato irregular; dis-
sreverente irreverent; -
temente irreverently;
stabile firm; durable;
- lire establish; ap-
point; - mento m es-
tablishment; - lità f
stability; - bilmente
firmly; constantly
stadera f steelyard
stadico m hostage; sheriff
stadio m stadium
staffilare whip
staggire seize; arrest
staggio m stick; sojourn;
hostage   [mitigate
stagionare ripen; season;
stagione f season
stagliare hack; compute;
- to distinctly; quickly
stagnare stanch; tin;
stagnate; - ta f tin-ware
stagno m pond; marsh;
staio m bushel   [tin
stalattite f stalactite
stalla f stable; stall;
rest; - tico m dung;
- liere m ostler   [tion
stallo m house; habita-
stamane, mattina this

morning   [bow
stambecchino m archer;
stambecco m wild goat
stamberga f garret
stamburare beat the
drum   [thread
stame m carded wool;
stampa f printing; press;
print; kind; stamp;
- re print; bore; - to
printed; engraved; -
tore m printer; coiner;
- tura f printing
stampanare tear
stampella f crutch
stanare break cover
stancare tire; - si be
tired; grow faint; -
chezza f weariness; -
chevole tiresome; - co
fatigued
stanga f bar; row of
pegs; - re bar [night
stanotte to-night; this
stante being; m moment;
since; afterwards; dur-
ing
stanziale permanent
stare be situated; live;
stop; stand; cost;
last; go; work; bail;
produce; become; sig-
nify; come sta? how
are you?
starnazzare shake; beat
starnutare, tire sneeze;
- mento, to m sneezing
statista m politician;
minister; - tico political
statistica f statistics
stato m rank; quality
statua f statue; - ria
statuary
statuire ordain; enact
statura f stature; posture
statuto m statute
staza f gauge; - re
gauge; - tore m gauger

231

stazione *f* dwelling; railway station; **- nale, rio** stationary

stazzo *m* rag; **- nare** fumble [knife; cue

stecca *f* splinter; paper-

steccadente *m* tooth-pick

steccheggiare switch

stecco *m* thorn; straw; tooth-pick

stecconato *m* palisade; **- ne** *m* paling

stefano *m* paunch

stella *f* star; fate; **- lante, lato, lifera** scintallating

steniare decamp

stendere spread; display; **- dimento, sione** *m* & *f* extension; extent

stenebrare illuminate

stenografia *f* stenography; **- nografo** *m* stenographer

stentare want; labour; vex; **- stento** *m* toil; suffering; **a -** with difficulty

stentoreo stentorian

stenuare extenuate; emaciate; **- tivo** extenuating; **- ione** *f* extenuation

steppi, steppe *f* steppe

sterco *m* dung; excrement

stereoscopia *f* stereoscopy; **- po** *m* stereoscope

stereotipare stereotype

sterile sterile; **- lità** *f* sterility; **- lire** sterilize

sterlino *m* sterling

sterminare exterminate; desolate; **- nio, ione** *m* & *f* extermination; desolation

sternuto *m* sneezing; **- nutare** sneeze

sterpare, extirpate; **- mento** *m* extirpation

stidione *m* spit

stigare excite; instigate

stige *f* styx

stigma *m* mark; seal

stile *m* style; way

stilettare stab; **- ta** *f* stab; **- to** *m* stiletto

stilla *f* drop; tear; **- re** distil; drizzle; **- tore** *m* distiller; **- ione, leria** *f* distillation; distillery [brocation

stillicidio *m* (med.) em-

stima *f* esteem; regard; **- bile** estimable; **-**

stimolare stimulate; provoke; **- lante, lativo** stimulating

stinco *m* shin-bone

stinguere extinguish; kill

stipendiare hire; **- dio** *m* stipend [maker

stipettaio *m* cabinet-

stipite *m* stalk; stake

stipito *m* pier

stipula *f* thatch; stubble

stipulare stipulate; **- zione** *f* stipulation

stirare stretch; strain

stirpare extirpate

stirpe *f* stock [peevish

stitico costive; stingy;

stivalarsi put on one's boots; **- to** booted; **- le** *m* boot; fool

stivare heap up; stow

stizza *f* anger; wrath; **- zarsi** be angry; **- zire** provoke

stoccata *f* thrust; pass; **- cheggiare** thrust

stoccofisso *m* salt codfish

stoffa *f* stuff

stoffo *m* stock; quantity

stoggio *m* flattery

stogliere dissuade

stoico *f* stoic; stoical

stola *f* stole

stolidezza, dità *f* stupidity; foolishness

stoppia *f* stubble; stubblefield

stoppinare light with a candle; - **no** *m* wick; rush-light   [dislocate

storcere twist; untwist

stordire stun; astound

storia *f* history; story; - **rico** historical; historian; - **re** illustrate

storione *m* sturgeon

stormo *m* troop; storm

stornare turn aside; dissuade

stornello *m* starling

storpiare, stroppiare maim; cripple

stracaro very dear

stracca *f* weariness

straccaggine *f* disgust; languour   [harness

straccale *m* breeching;

straccare tire; vex; - **chezza** *f* weariness; anger

stracciafoglio *m* scraper

stracciare scrape; tear

straccicalare chat

straccuocere overdo; - **cotto** overdone   [fied

stracontento very satisfied

strada *f* road; street;

strafalciare run; neglect

strafficare sell; make; dispatch

strafigurare disfigure

straforare bore; - **ro** *m* boring

strage *f* slaughter

stragrande gigantic

stralciare prune; finish

strale *m* arrow; disgrace

straignare degenerate

stralunare look every way

stralunato squinting

s'amazzare knock down faint

strambellare break; tear to pieces

strambo crooked; bandy

strame *m* bay or straw; litter; lair

strampalato extravagant; - **teria** *f* extravagance

stranare alienate; sell

strangolare strangle; suffocate; - **mento** *m* strangulation

strangosciare grieve

stranio strange; foreign

strano strange; rare

straordinarietà *f* strangeness; - **rio** extraordinary

straparlare slander   [ary

strapazzare despise; disdain

strapuntino *m* counterpoint; - **to** *m* bolster

straricchire become wealthy; - **ricco** wealthy

strarpare overflow; - **mento** *m* overflowing

strasciare nare draw along; - **strascico** *m* drawing along; train of a gown

strascioni dragging

stratagemma *m* stratagem

strategia *f* strategy; - **gico** strategic

stravalicare pass beyond

stravasare extravasate

stravero most true

stravestire disguise; - **mento** *m* disguise

straviziare feast; banquet

stravolgere twist violently

straziare provoke; tear; squander; — **io** *m* injury; slaughter

stregua *f* share

stremare cut; diminish

stremo extreme

stremenzire debilitate; extenuate   [need

stremità *f* extremity;

strenna *f* new year's gift

strenuità *f* courage; strenuousness; — **nuo** courageous; gallant

strepere, pitare re·ound

strepito *m* noise

stretta *f* squeezing; distress; defile; — **tezza** *f* straightnes ; — **to** narrow; squeezed; *m* strait

strettoia *f* bandage

stridere cry; ecream; crackle; — **dente, dulo** noisy; sharp

strigare rid; disentangle

striglia *f* curry comb; — **re** curry

strignere confine; bind

strillare shriek; — **lo** *m* shrieking

strimpellare play badly (instrument); — **mento, tura** *m* & *f* discordance

stringa *f* tag; lace

strippare eat too much

striscia *f* scarf; serpent; — **re** crawl; elide

strofinaccio *m* duster; dish-cloth; — **nare** rub; — **mento, nio** *m* rubbing; friction

strologo *m* astrologer

strombazzare bettare proclaim; trumpet

stromento *m* instrument; deed

stroncare cut off

stronzare maim; retrench

stropicciare rub; scour

strozza *f* throat; windstrozsare throttle [pipe

strozziere *m* falconer

strozzule *m* throat; gullet

strumentare compose music; — **tale** instrumental; — **to** *m* instrument   [— **pro** *m* rape

strupare force; violate;

struttura *f* structure; disposition

struzione *f* destruction

struzzo, zolo *m* ostrich

stuccare plaster with stucco; sicken

stucchevolare annoy; disgust; — **chevole** tedious

studente student; — **diare** study; — **dio** *m* study; school-room; diligence;

stuolo *m* troop; crowd

stuonare be out of tune

stupefare stupefy; astonish; **stupefarsi** be astonished; — **zione** *f* stupefaction

stupendo admirable; splendid; — **diamente** splendidly

stupire be astonished; — **mento** *m* astonishment; — **pore** *m* stupor; amazemen·

stuprare rape; violate

sturare uncork

sturbare disturb; — **bo** *m* disturbance

su concerning; on; over; near; **su e giù** up and down; **su! su!** cheer up!

subalternare subalternate; — **no** subaltern

subastare auction; — **zione** *f* auction

subbia *f* chisel

234

subbietto, subbietto *m* subject

subbissare overthrow; destroy; **- so** *m* ruin; wonder

subcutaneo subcutaneous

subdividere subdivide

subillare suborn

subiugare subjugate

subiuntivo *m* subjunctive

sublimare exalt

sublime sublime; **- mità** *f* sublimity

subodorare smell; foresee

subordinare subordinate;

- zione *f* subordination; **- to** subordinate

subornare bribe

succedere succeed; happen; **- dimento** *m* event; success; **- tore, cessore** *m* successor

successibile successible; **- sione** *f* succession; success; **- vo** successive; **- so** *m* success; event

succhiare suck

succhiellare drill; bore

succhio *m* juice; sap

succiare suck

succissangue *f* leech

succinto succinct; tucked up; **- tamente** succinctly

sudacchiare perspire

sudare sweat; perspire

sudario *m* winding-sheet

suddetto *m* aforesaid; above mentioned

suddiacono *m* sub-deacon

suddito *m* subject

suddividere subdivide; **- sione** *f* subdivision

sudiceria *f* dirtiness; **- cio** nasty; dirty

sudore *m* sweat; toil

sufficente, ciente sufficient; **- mente** sufficiently; **- ficienza** *f* sufficiency

suffragio *m* vote; suffrage

sufolare whistle; hiss

sufclo *m* whistle

sugare suck; blot; **- gente** blotting

suggellare seal; print

suggere suck

suggerire suggest; **- mento, gestione** *m* & *f* suggestion; **- tore** *m* prompter

suggestivo deceitful

suggettare subject; constrain [tree

sughero *m* cork; cork-

sugna *f* grease; hog's lard; **- gnoso** greasy; fat

sugo *m* juice; sap

suo his; her; its; **suoi** their

suocera *f* mother-in-law; **- ro** *m* father-in-law

suola *f* sole; hoof

suolo *m* ground; hoof

suono *m* sound; song

suora *f* sister; nun

superare surpass; surmount; **- bile** conquerable

superbia *f* pride; haughtiness; **- bo** proud; haughty

supercilio *m* eye-brow

superficiale superficial

superfluità *f* superfluity; **- fluo** superfluous

supericrità *f* superiority; **- riore** *a* & *n* superior; **- rmente** masterly

superlativo superlative; **- vamente** superlatively

supernale supernal; di-

vine; – **nalmente** supernaturally
suppedaneo *m* floor
suppellettile *f* *pl* furniture; chattels [d :ive
supplantare supplant;
supplementario supplementary; – **plente** substitute; – **plire** supply;
substitute; – **plemento**,
plimento *m* supplement
supporre suppose; substitute; – **sizione** *f* supposition; – **posto** supposed; supposition
suppregare supplicate
supprimere suppress;
conceal; – **pressione** suppression
supremazia *f* supremacy;
– **mo** supreme; – **ma-
mente** supremely
sur on; upon; over
surgere come out; begin
surretizio surreptitious
surto elevated; ready
suscettibile, tivo susceptible; – **lità** *f* susceptibility
suscitare revive; excite
susina *f* plum; – **no** *m*
plum-tree [interruption
suspensione *f* suspension;
suspicace suspicious; –
care suspect; doubt;
– **pizione** *f* suspicion
sussecutivo, **guente**,
quente subsequent; –
guentemente subse-
quently
sussiego *m* seriousness;
gravity
sussistenza *f* subsistence;
– **tere** subsist
sussulto *m* surprise;
start
susta *f* pack-cord; spring

sustantivo *m* substantive
sustanza *f* substance;
– **ziale** substantial
sustentazione *f* sustenance
sustituire substitute; –
zione *f* substitution
svagolare wander
svaligiare strip; rob
svampare evaporate
svanire evaporate; disappear
svantaggio *m* disadvantage; detriment; –
gioso disadvantage
svaporare vent; evapor-
svariare vary [ate
svecchiare renew; reform
sveglia *f* alarm clock;
– **re** wake; – **si awake**;
– **toio, glierino** *m* alarm
clock
svelare discover; reveal
sveltezza *f* nimbleness;
– **to** nimble; slim
svenare kill [unfortunate
svenevole disagreeable;
svenire faint; – **mento**
m swoon; eclipse
sventare fan; air; winnow; fail
sventura *f* misfortune;
– **to** unfortunate; miserable
svergogna *f* dishonour;
insult; – **to** impudent
svernare winter
svignare scamper
svigorire dibilitate
svilire abase; undervalue
svillaneggiare insult; out-
rage [plain
sviluppare discover; ex-
svincolare untie
svisare scratch
svista *f* error; oversight
svitare unscrew

sviticchiare take away; snatch

sivivagnato stupid

sviziare amend

svociechiare discredit

svogliare disgust

svolare fly

svo¹azzare flutter; vault

svolere alter one's mind

svolgere unfold

svoltare tolare turn aside; dissuade; **– ta** f .turn; bending; **–tura** f fold; plait

svolvere unfold; dissuade

T

tabacco m tobacco; **caio. caro, chino** m tobacconist; **– care** take snuff: **– chiera** f snuff-box; **presa di –** pinch of snuff

taballo m kettle-drum

tabano slanderous

tabarro m overcoat

tabe rottenness; **– fatto, bido** putrefied

tabella f rattle

taccia f notch; gap;

taccagneria f stinginess

taccato spotted; speckled

tacchino. m peacock

taccia f defect; stain; **–re** accuse; blame

tacco m clog

taccola f magpie; sport

taccolaia f prattle

taccolino m babbler

tacconare mend

taccuino m pocket-book; almanack

tacere hold one's tongue

tacito tacit; **–tamente** tacitly

taciturnità f taciturnity;

– no silent; taciturn

tafanario m bottom

tafano m horse-fly

tafferia f wooden board

tafferugia, tafferuglio m riot; tumult

taffettà f taffetas

taglia f killing; tax

tagliaborse m cut-purse

tagliamento m cut; slaughter

tagliando m paring

tagliapietra m stone-cutter [cheat

tagliare cut; tax; carve;

talché so that

talco m talc

tale such; like; **un –** such a one; **– lmente** so; so much [agreeable

talentare please; be

talento m talent; ability; **mal – grudge**

talismano m talisman

tallero m thaler (coin)

tallire seed

tallone m heel

talora, volta sometimes

talpa f mole

taluno some; any somebody

tamanto so great

tamburello. retto rino m tambourine; **–** kettle-drum; **–rino** m kettle-drummer; **– ro** m trunk; drum; **– rone** m big drum

tambussare beat; bang

Tamigi m (geog.) Thames

tampooco not even; neither

tana f hole; den; socket

tanaglia f pincers; **–re** torture

tantino very small; a little

tanto so; so much; so many; as many; non – notwithstanding; per – however; a – per – at this rate; – per uno so much apiece; so long

tantosto immediately

tappete m carpet; cover

tappezzare hang with tapestry; deck; – zeria f hangings; tapestry; – ziere m upholsterer

tara n defect; waste

tarabuso m bittern

tarantella f tarantella; tarantula

tarantello f & m overplus

tarantola f tarantula

tarare abate

tarchiato strong-limbed

tarlare rot; get worm-eaten; – to rotten

tarma f worm; wood-louse

taroccare grow angry

tarsia f marquetry; miser

tartagliare stammer; – mento m stammering; – glione m stammerer

tasca f purse; pocket; –chino m purse

tassa f tax; duty; –re rate; assess; – tivo taxable; –tore m assessor

tassellare restore; repair

tassello m cape (cloak)

tassetto m hand-anvil

tasso m yew; badger

tastare, teggiare touch; try; sound

tastiera f key-board

tattamella f chat; tittle-tattle; –re chat

tattica f tactics; – co m tactician

tatto m touch; feeling;

taverna f tavern; pot-house; –naio, niere m tavern-keeper; drunkard

tavola f table; index

tavolare board; floor

tavolata f tableful

tavolato m wood-partition; floor; shed

tavoletta m small table

tavoliere m chess-board; card-table

tavolozza f pallet

tazza f cup; cupful

te thee

te m tea

teatro m theatre

technico technical; –nologia f technology; – gico technological

teco with thee

teda f wild fir; larch-tree

tedio m tediousness; disgust; – diare annoy; disgust; – so tedious; disgusting

tegame m earthen saucepan

tegghia pie-dish; linendrier

tegnente tenacious; sticky; – za f tenacity; stickiness [tile-maker

tegola f tile; –iaio m

teismo m theism

tela f linen; picture; snare; – io m loom; painter's frame; – laiuolo m weaver; – leria f linen drapery

telegrafia f telegraphy; – fo m telegraph; – gramma m telegram

telescopio m telescope

teletta f fine linen

tema n theme; subject;

/ fear; alarm

tempera *f* hardening; (paint) distemper; disposition; a – in water-colours

temperamento *m* temperament

temperante temperate; – **ranza** *f* temperance

temperare harden; agree; moderate; – **tivo** *a* sedative; – to temperate

temperatoio, rino *m* penknife [ture; hardening

temperatura *f* temperature

temperie *f* temper

tempesta *f* tempest; – **tare** be stormy; storm; trouble; – **toso** stormy; tempestuous

tempestivo seasonable

tempia *f* temple (of the head)

tempio *m* temple; church

tempissimo (per) very early

tendenza *f* tendency; – **dere** stretch; set (snares); tend; aim at

tendetta, dina *f* small tent; awning

tendine, done *m* tendon

tenebrare be dark; darken; – **bre** *f pl* darkness; – **broso** dark; gloomy

tenente lieutenant

tenere *m* handle; power

tenere hold; keep

tenerezza *f* tenderness

tenero tender

tenta *f* probe; try; – **tivo** *m* attempt; trial experiment

tentare try; urge; probe; – **zione** *f* temptation

tentellare resound

tentennare vacillate

tenue tenuous; thin; – **amente** thinly; – **ità** *f* tenuity

tenuta *f* possession

tenuto kept; reputed

tenzonare fight; contest; – **ne, zione** *f* contest

teologale divine

teologia *f* theology; – **gico** theological; – **ologo** *m* theologian

teorema *m* theorem

teoria *f* theory

tepefare, pificare warm

tepido lukewarm; tepid

terapeutico therapeutic

terchio rough; coarse

tergemino triple

tergere cleanse; purge

teriaca *f* treacle

termale thermal

terme *f pl* hot baths

terminare terminate; – **zione** *m & f* termination; – **ne** *m* end; limit; term

termometro thermometer

terno *m* terne

terra *f* earth; land; ground; – **racqueo** ter-raqueous; – **ferma** firm land; continent

terreno worldly; *m* ground; land; **pian** – ground floor

terretta *f* borough; village

terribile terrible

terriccio *m* mould

terriere *m* citizen

terrigno of the earth

territorio *m* territory; terse; – **riale** territorial

terrore *m* terror; – **rismo** *m* terrorism; – **rista** *m* terrorist

tersezza *f* neatness

terzo third; – **zo, zeria**

m & f third part
terzuolo sparrow-hawk
tesa f brim of a hat
teschio m skull
tesi f thesis
teso bent
tesoro m treasure; —
  reria f treasury; — **riere**
  m treasurer
tessera f sign; token
tessere weave
testa f head; chief; —
  tardo, tereccio head-
  strong
testare make one's will;
  — **mento** will; testament; — **tore** m testator
teste m witness; — **tificare**
  bear witness
testè lately; just now
testicolo m testicle
testuggine m tortoise;
  turtle; vaul   [dark
tetricità f darkness; — **tro**
tetta f teat; — **te** suck
tetto f roof; house;
  — **toia** f pent-house
ti thee
tiara f tiara; mitre
tibia m shin-bone
ticchio m whim
tiepidare grow lukewarm;
  — **do** tepid; timid
tifo m typhus
tifolo m cry; squeak
tifone m typhoon
tiglio m filament; lime-
  tree
tigna f scurf; scab;
  — **gnoso** scurvy
tignamica f avarice
tignere dye
tignone m back-hair
timone m pole; helm;
  — **niere** m helmsman
timore m fear; alarm;

— **rato, soro** timorous;
  fearful
timpanista m kettle-
  drummer
timpano m tympanum
tino m tub; tun; vat;
  — **nozza** f basin
tinta f dying; tint
tintillo, tinnio m jingling
tintinnare ring; tinkle
tinto m tint; shade
tintore m dyer
tipo m type; model;
  — **pico** typical
tipografia f typography;
  — **fico** typographical;
  — **fo** m printer
tira f debate; dispute
tiralinea m ruler
tiranno m tyrant
tiranneggiare tyrannize
  over; — **nesco, nico** a
  tyrannical; — **nia, nide**
  f tyranny
tirante m boot-strap
tirare draw; attract;
  extend; shoot; — **si**
  escape
tirone m apprentice;
  novice   [consumptive
tisichezza f phthis; — **co**
titano m titan; — **nico**
titillare titillate [titanic
titolo m title; pretext;
  — **lare** titular; entitle;
  — **to** entitled
titubare waver; stagger
tizzo, tizzone m brand;
  firebrand
to' oh!   [brocade
tocca f gold or silver
toccare touch; move;
  — **ta** m feeling; prelude
tocca a me it is my turn
toeletta f toilet; dressing
toga f toga   [table
togliere take; take away

tolda f deck   [table
toletta f toilet; dressing
tollerare tolerate; – **bile** tolerable; – **ranza** f toleration
tolletta f theft
tolta f theft
tolto taken
tonare thunder; roar
tondare round; make round; – **tura** f pruning; shavings
tondeggiare be round
tondere shear (sheep etc.); – **duto** shorn; – **ditura** f shearing; parings
tondezza f roundness; rotundity; – **do** round; simple; – **do, dino** m sphere; plate; saucer
tonello m cask
tonfo m fall; noise of a fall; – **lare** fall; make a noise in falling
tonica f tunic; refuge
tonico tonic
tonnara tunny-net
tonneggiare tow; – **gio** m tow; towing
topografia f topography; – **fico** topographical; – **fo** m topographer
toppa f lock; door-lock
toppè m toupee
toppo m stump; stock
torace m thorax
torba f turf
torba, torbida f muddy water; – **bidare** trouble; make muddy; – **bido** thick; troubled
torcere twist; turn
torchio m press
torcia f torch; taper
torcigliare wrap up
torcimanno m interpreter

torcolare press; – **liere** m pressman
tordo m thrush
tormentare torment; inrest; – **to** m torment; grief; – **tore** m tormenter
tornaletto m basement
tornare come back; remember; mend
tornasole m sunflower
torneo m tournament; compass; – **nitore** m turner; – **nio** m turningwheel   [big; strong
toro m bull; bed; – **so**
torpedine f torpedo; laziness
torpere grow torpid; – **pido** torpid
torpiglia f torpedo
torta f tart; twisting; – **telleta, lina** f small tart; – **tello** m pancake
tortola, ra f dove
tortore m tormenter
tortuosità f tortuosity; – **so** tortuous
torvità f haughtiness; – **vo** haughty
torzione f extortion
torzone m lay friar
tosa f young girl; lass
tosare shear; shave; **tosco** m poison   [prune
tosone m golden fleece (order of); fleece
tossa, tosse f cough; – **simento** m coughing; – **sire** cough
tossicare poison; – **co** m poison; venom
tosto quick; saucy; – **tamente** quickly; soon
totale total; whole; – **lizzare** sum up
tovaglia f table-cloth

tovaglietta, gliuola, gliolo *f & m* napkin; towel

tozzetto *m* small bit

tozzo short; big; heavy; bit; piece

tozzolare beg

tra between; with

trabacca *f* hut; stall; tent

trabaccolo *m* ship

trabalderia *f* theft

traballare stagger; vacillate; **– lio** *m* swing

trabocchello, chetto *m* snare; deceit

tracannare sip; drink hard; **– tore** *m* drunkard

tracheggiare defer

traccia *f* track; treaty; **– mento** *m* plotting; **– ciare** trace; track

trachea *f* wind-pipe

trachiare most clear

tracocente very hot

tracollare be sleepy; tumble; nod

traconfortare console

tracotaggine, tanza *f* arrogance; **-te** arrogant

tradigione, mento *f & m* treason; **– re** betray; **– tore, trice** *m & f* traitor; traitress

tradimenticato forgotten

tradizione *f* tradition

tradurre translate; extend; **– dotto** translated; **– ducibile** translatable; **– citore, duttore** *m* translator; **– zione** *f* translation

trafitta, tura *f* wound; puncture

trafoglio *m* trefoil

traforare pierce

traforeria *f* deceit; trick

traforo *m* point-lace; hole [with

trafugare rob; run away

tragrande huge

traguardare level; foresee; **– do** *m* level

trainare pull; haul; **– no** *m* cart-load; train; sledge

tralasciare cease; omit

tralazione *f* translation; transport

tralignare degenerate; decay; **– mento** *m* adulteration; degeneration

tralineare get out of line

tralucere be transparent; shine; **– cente** transparent; shiny

trama *m* plot; woof; weft; **– re** conspire

tramaglio *m* drag-net

tramandare transmit

tramazzare overthrow; **– zo** *m* riot

trambasciare grieve

tramessa, messione *f* interposition; mediation

tramesso *m* side-dish

tramestare revolve; mingle [transmit

tramettere interpose;

tramezza *f* partition; lane

tramezzare interpose; insert; **– mento** *m* interposition; mediation; **– tore** *m* mediator

tramischianza *f* shuffle

tramite *m* path; way

tramoggia *f* hopper; feeder (machine)

tramontana *f* north-wind

tramontare set (sun, etc); go down; **– to** *m* set

tramortire faint; swoon

trampoli *m pl* stilts

tramutare transmute; transplant; **– zione** *f*

transmutation; change
trana cheer up! all right
tranare draw; struggle
tranellare deceive; cheat;
– leria, lo f & m deceit;
snare

transatare transact; –
satto, sazione m & f
transaction; comprom-
ise [lantic
transatlantico transat-
transfiguramento, zione
m & f transfiguration
transfondere decant;
carry [expire
transire pass; fade;
transitivo, torio transi-
ive; transitory; **–to**
m transit; death
transizione f transition
translucido pellucid
transuntare extract; –
zione f extract
transustanziare transub-
stantiate; **– rione** f
transubstantiation
trapanare trepan; **– toio,
no** m trepan; **– zione** f
trasalire, saltare jump
trasamare love fondly
trasandare pass beyond;
slight
trasattarsi apply; fit
trascegliere choose; –
glimento m choice
trascendentale, dente
transcendent; **–dere** surpass; excel
trascinare draw
trepaning
trapassare pass beyond;
cross over; transgress
trapelare distil; filter
trapensare mediate
trapprendere undertake;
trapuntare stitch; quilt;
– to stitched; stitch

traricchire grow wealthy
trarre draw; pull; reap
trarupare precipitate
trascolare distil
trascolorare change colour
trascorrere pass quickly;
escape; omit; repeat;
– rente, revole transitory
trascorsivo cursory
trascorso m error; oversight [copy
trascrivere transcribe;
trascurare neglect; abandon; **– raggine, ranza,
ratezza** f negligence
trasecolare be astonished;
astonish
trasferire transfer; convey; **– si** go; repair;
–ribile transferable
trasfigurare transfigure;
be transfigured; **– zione**
f transfiguration
trasfondere transfuse;
communicate; **– fusione**
f transfusion
trasformare transform;
– zione f transformation
trasgredire· transgress;
trespass; **– dimento,
gressione** m & f trans-
gression; **– ditore** m
transgressor
trasmettere transmit; –
missione f transmission
trasmigrare transmigrate
– zione f transmigration
trasmutare transmute;
transform; **– mento,
zione** m & f transmuta-
tion

trasordinario extraordinary; **–riamente** extra-
ordinarily [excess
trasordine m disorder;
traspallarsi rush upon;
trasparenza f transpar-

243

ency; – **rire** get transparent   [transfer
traspiantare transplant;
traspirare perspire; – **zione** *f* perspiration
trasporre transfer
trasportare transport; – **to** *m* transport; carriage   [treat
trassinare touch; ill-
trasvolare fly swiftly; rise
trasvolgere overturn
tratta *f* pull; space; throw; draft
trattatore *m* negotiator; interpreter
trattenere entertain; amuse; – **nimento** *m* amusement
tratto shot; pull; stroke; space; trot; **ad un** at once; **ad ogni** – every moment; **di primo** – at first; **tratto tratto** from time to time
trattoso kind; tractable
trattura *f* pulling
travagliare work; afflict; – **glio** trouble; labour
travalente most skilful
travasare decant; transfuse
trave *f* beam; high tree
travecchiezza *f* ancient
traversino *m* bolster
traverso oblique; **a** – across; through
travestire disguise; – **mento** *m* disguise
traviare mislead
travisare deceive; disguise; –**so** *m* mask;

travolare fly beyond
travolgere, volvere overturn

trazione *f* attraction
tre three
trebbia *f* flail; – **re** thrash (corn); – **mento, tura** *m & f* thrashing of (corn)
trecca, treccola *f* hawker; – **cheria** *f* greengrocer
treccia *f* tress; curl
trecciera *f* knot of ribands
treccolare chat
treccone *m* retailer; fruiterer; huckster
trecento three hundred; – **tesimo** three hundredth
tredici thirteen; –**cesimo** thirteenth

tremare shiver; tremble; – **mante, mebondo** timorous; – **rella** *m* panic
trementina *f* turpentine
tremola *f* torpedo (fish)
tremolare shiver; tremble; – **lio** *m* shivering; – **lante lo** tremulous; shivering
tremula *f* aspen
tremuoto *m* earthquake
treno *m* train; sledge; – **diretto** fast train
trenta thirty; – **tesimo** thirtieth
trepidare tremble; fear; – **dazione** *f* trepidation
treppiede *m* trivet
tresca *f* brawl; scrape
trespolo *m* trestle; prop
triaca *f* treacle
triangolo *m* triangle; – **lare** triangular
tribbiare smash; grind

tricolore tricoloured
tricorno with three horns
tricuspide *m* with three points
tridente *m* trident [points
trifoglio *m* trefoil
triforcato, cuto with

triforme with three forms

trigesimo thirteenth

trigono *m* triangle; - metria *f* trigonometry

trilatero trilateral

trillare hum; trill

trillione *m* trillion

trilogia *f* trilogy

trilustre fifteen years old

trimestre *m* quarter; -trale quarterly

trina *f* fringe; lace

trincare tipple

trincea, ciera *f* trench; entrenchment

trincerare entrench; -mento *m* entrenchment

trinciare carve; cut up

trincone *m* drunkard

triplicare triplicate; - ce plo triple; treble

tripode *m* tripod

tripudiare dance; - tore *m* dancer; reveller

triregno *m* tiara

trisavolo *m* great great grand-father

tristanzuolo thin

tristarsi be sad; grieve

tristezza, tristizia *f* sadness; melancholy

tristo sad; wicked

tritare, tolare, turare grind; examine

tritatoio, tritapalgie chaff-cutter

tritello *m* coarse flour

tritico *m* corn

tritone *m* triton

triumviro *m* triumvir; - rato *m* triumvirate

trivella *f* probe; borer - re bore; bruise

trombone *m* trombone; trombone-player

troncare cut off, mutilate; - co *m* trunk;

bust; - cone *m* stump; large trunk [tedly

troncatamente interrup-

trono *m* throne; thunder

tropico *m* tropic; - cale tropical

troppo too much excess; much

trota *f* trout

trottare trot; go quick; -tore *m* trotter; -to *m* trot

trottola *f* top

trovare find; observe; - tore *m* inventor; minstrel; -trovato found; invention; discovery

trovatello *m* foundling

truce ferocious

trucidare massacre; - tore *m* murderer

truffa, feria *f* lie; deceit

truffare cheat; dupe; - tore *m* deceiver; cheat

trullare fart; - lo *m* fart

truogo, truogolo *m* trough

truppa *f* troop

tu thou

tuba *f* trumpet; horn

tubare coo; - bante cooing

tubercolo *m* tubercle; - loso tuberculous

tubero *m* truffle; medlar-tree

tubo *m* tube; pipe; socket; -bulare tubular

tuffare dip; plunge; - tore *m* diver; - fo, folo *m* immersion

tuffete suddenly

tugurio *m* hut; cottage

tulipano *m* tulip

tumefare tumefy; - more *m* tumour

tumulo *m* tumulus; tomb

tumulto *m* tumult; uproar; – **tuante, tuoso** tumultuous

tunica f tunic

tuo, tua thy; il – thine own; i **tuoi** thy family

turba f crowd; mob

turbante m turban

turbare trouble; disturb; –si get angry; darken; – **mento** m trouble; disturbance

turbina f turbine [order **turbinarsi** whirl round

turbine, turbino, bo m whirlwind; storm; – **noso** stormy

turbo thick; disturbed

turchino blue; dark blue; – **niccio** bluish

turcimanno m interpreter

turco m Turk

turfa f crowd

turgenza, gidezza f swelling; – **gere** swell; – **gido** swollen; bombastic

turibolo m censer

turma f troop; crowd

turno m turning-wheel; turn

turpe base; indecent; – **mente** shamefully; – **pezza, pitudine** f vileness: shame

tutore, trice m & f guartor

tuttafiata, via, volta however; as often as; nevertheless; always

tutto, ta all; every; whole; tutto tutto entirely

tuttochè almost; though

tuttodì always

tuttora still; always

U

ubbia f bad omen; – **bioso** superstitious

ubbidire obey; – **diente** obedient; – **dienza** f obedience; submission

ubbriacare, ubbriacare fuddle; – **co** drunk; tipsy; – **chezza** f intoxication [fertile

uberifero full-breasted;

ubero m breast; teat

ubertà f plenty; – **toso** plentiful

ubicazione f situation

ucchiello m button-hole

uccidere kill; cut off; – **sione** f murder; – **cisore** m murderer

udire hear; listen to; – **bile** audible; –**dienza** f audience; – **zione** f hearing; – **tore** m auditor

ufficiale m official; officer

ufo (a) at other people's expense

uggia f shade; omen; avere in – to hate; essere in – be hated

uggiolare howl

ugnere anoint; – **gnimento** m anointing

ugnome m claw

ugola f uvula

uguagliare equal; match; – **glianza, lità** f equality; – **le** equal; – **lmente** ad equality

ulcera m ulcer; – **re** ulcerate; – **mento, zione**

ultimare finish; – **mato**

finished; ultimatum; – zione f conclusion; – mo last; –mente at last

ululare howl; – lato, lulo m howling

umanarsi take human flesh; – nità f humanity; – no human

umbè therefore

umbelico, bilico m navel

umettare wet; moisten

umidezza, dità f moisture; – dire moisten

umido, detto moist; damp

umile humble; – liare humble; quiet; – zione humiliation; – milmente humbly; – miltà f humility

umore m humour; moisture; – rista m humorist

unicità f particularity; – co only; sole

unicorno m unicorn; – nuto one-horned

unificare unify

uniformare conform; – me uniform; – mità f uniformity

unigenito m only son

unire unite; – nione f union

unisonanza f concordance

unisono m unison; connissimo only [cord

unità f unity; – to united; –tamente jointly

universale universal; –lizzare generalize; – sità f university; generality; – so m universal; universe

uno, na one

unqua, quanco, quema¹ never

uomo m man; husband (pl uomini)

uopo m usefulness; need

uracano, gano m hurricane

urano m Uranus

urbanità f urbanity; – no polite

urente burning

uretra f urethra

urgente urgent; – za f urgency; – gere urge

urlare howl; –mento, liolo m howling

urna f urn

urta (aver in) f hate

urtare knock; hit

usare use; frequent; – sanza f use; habit; – to, sitato usual; habitual; – uso usual; use

usciere m porter; usher; – scio m door

uscire go out

uscita f way out

usuale usual; – lità f habit; – lmente usually

usura f usury; – raio, riere m usurer; – reggiare practise usury

usurpare usurp; –mento, zione m usurpation; – tore m usurper

utensile m utensil

utero m uterus; womb

utile useful; profitable; m advantage; – lità f utility; profit; –littare, lizzare utilize

utre m leather-bottle

uva f grapes; – spina gooseberry; – secca raisin

V

vacante vacant [tion

vacanza f vacancy; vacavacca f cow; – ro m cowherd;

vaccina f cow-pox; – re

vaccinate; – **tore** *m*
vaccinator; – **zione** *f*
vaccination

vacillare vacillate; –
mento, **zione** *m & f*
vacillation

vacuare evacuate; –
zione *f* evacuation;

vacuità *f* vacuity; – **cuo**

vado *m* ford. [vacuous

vagabondare wander; –**do**
vagabond; vagrant

vagamente gracefully

vagare ramble

vagheggiare court; – **tore**
m sweet-heart

vaglia *f* merit; courage

vagliare sift; despise;
– **tore** *m* sifter; lover

vago vague

vagolare wander

valere *m* value; courage;
be worth; –**za**, **zia** *f*
courage; virtue

valeriana *f* valerian

valetudine *f* health

valicare ford

validare ratify; confirm;
– **dità** *f* validity; – **do**
valid; strong

valigia *f* portmanteau;
valise

vallare surround; fortify

vallata, **le**, **lea** *f* valley;
trench; dale; – **letto** *m*
dale; – **lo** *m* valley;
– **ligiano** *m* inhabitant
of a valley

valorare confirm; fortify;
– **re** *m* courage; price;
– **roso** valorous

valuta *f* value; price;
– **re** appraise

valva *f* shell [waltzer

valzare waltz; – **zer** *m*

vampa *f* flame; ardour

vampiro *m* vampire

vanagloria *f* vainglory;
– **riarsi** boast; – **so**
vainglorious

vanare dream; rave

vandalismo vandalism

vaneggiare rave; – **mento**,
gio *m* raving; furor;

vanezza *f* vanity; inanity

vanga *f* spade; mattock;
– **re** dig; – **ta** *f* spade-
ful; – **tore** *m* digger;

vaniglia *f* vanilla

vanire vanish; disappear

vanità *f* vanity; – **toso**
vainglorious; – **no** vain

vanni *m pl* wings

vantaggiare favour; – **gio**
m advantage; fortune;
– **gioso** advantageous;
– **samente** advantage-
ously

vantare praise; extol;
– **si** boast; – **to** celebrated; – **tore** *m* braggart

vaporarsi steam; – **zione**
f evaporation

vapore *m* vapour; steam;
– **vole** volatile; – **riera**
f steam-boat; steamer;
– **rosità** *f* vapour

varare launch (ship);
board

variabile variable; – **lità**
f variableness

variare, **rieggare** vary;
differ; – **mento**, **rietà**
m & f variety; change;
– **riante** variable;
– **riazione** *f* variation

vascolare loso vascular

vascolo *m* small vase

vaso *m* vase; – **sellame** *m*

dishes and plates; plates
vasello *m* vase; ship
vaso *m* vase; vein; vessel; – **da fiori** flower-pot
vasto vast; immense
vate *m* poet
Vaticano *m* Vatican
ve you; there
vecchia *f* old woman; – **chiaia, chiezza** *f* old age; – **chiardo, da** *m & f* old man, woman
vece *f* time; place; **in – instead** [derstand
vedere see; know; un-
vedetta *f* sentry
vedova *f* widow; – **vanza** *f* widowhood; – **vo** lonely; *m* widower
veemente vehement; –**za** *f* vehemence
vegetare vegetate; – **zione** *f* vegetation
vegghia vigil; evening-party; – **ghiare** wake; watch
veggia *f* cask; vessel
veglia *f* sentry; evening-party; –**re** watch
vegliardo *m* old man
vegnente future; next
veicolo *m* vehicle
vela *f* sail; boat
velare veil; – **si** take the veil; –**me, mento** *m* veil; –**tamente** secretly
veleggiare set sail; sail; – **mento; leggio** *m* sailing; –**tore** *m* sailor
velenare poison; – **noso** poisonous; – **no poison**
veleno *m* poison; venom
veleria *f* sails
veletta *f* sentry; top-man; –**tare** stand sentry
veliere pull out; separate

vellicare prick; stimulate
vello *m* fleece; wool; – **so** hairy; woolly
velluto *m* velvet; – **tato** like velvet
velo *m* veil; crape; skin
veloce swift; quick; – **mente** swiftly; – **cità** *f* velocity; swiftness;
vendere sell
vendita *f* sale; – **tore** *m* seller; vender; – **all'asta** sale by action; **acontanti** ready money sale
vendetta *f* revenge
vendicare avenge; vindicate; –**tivo** vindictive; – **tore** *m* avenger
venerare venerate; – **bile** venerable; –**ranza, zione** *f* veneration
Venere *r* Venus; – **reo venereal** [– **le** venial
venia *f* pardon; mercy;
venire come; arrive;
venti twenty; – **tesimo, – simo** twentieth
ventiera *f* ventilator
ventilare ventilate; examine; – **zione** *f* ventilation [– **ticello** *m* breeze
vento *m* wind; vanity
ventola *f* fan; eyeshade
ventolare fan; winnow
ventosa *f* cupping-glass; – **re** cup
ventoso windy
ventraia *f* belly; tripe
ventrata *f* litter
ventre *m* stomach; bosom
ventuno twenty-one
ventura *f* luck; chance; – **riere** *m* adventurer
venturo future; – **to** lucky
venustà *f* beauty
venuta *f* arrival; **ben –**

vepre *f* briar [welcome
ver towards; against
verbo *m* word; verb;
– a – word for word;
– so verbose

verdastro, dognolo greenish; – **de** green; young
verdeggiare be verdant;
– **detto** greenish; verdict
verdetto greenish; sourish; verdict
verdume, ra *m & f*
verdure; greenness
verecondia *f* bashfulness;
decency; – **do** modest
verga *f* rod; want;
stripe; – **to** striped
vergella *f* rod; switch
vergheggiare flog; switch
vergine, netta *f* virgin;
maid; Virgin Mary;
– **nale, neo** virginal;
– **nità** *f* virginity
vergolare put commas
veridicità *f* veracity
verificare verify; prove;
– **zione** *f* verification;
– **tore** *m* examiner
veriloquio *m* report;
relation
verisimiglianza *f* likelihood; – **milmente** likely
vermigliare paint vermilion; – **glio** scarlet
vernaccio *m* hard winter
vernacolo vernacular
vernale vernal
vernare winter; be very
cold; winter; – **nereccio**
wintery; – **no** *m* winter
vernicare, ciare varnish;
– **ce** varnish
vero true; certain
versare pour; pay; overthrow [f versatility
versatile versatile; – **lità**

versato poured out;
skilled
versatore *m* versifier;
– **setto** *m* small verse
versione *f* version
versipelle astute; crafty
verso *m* verse; air;
way; towards; concerning
versorio *m* compass
versuto astute; cunning
vertebra *f* vertebra
vertente (anno) the present year
vertenza *f* controversy
verticale vertical
vertice *m* top; zenith
vertigine *f* vertigo; – **noso** giddy
veruno none; no; nobody
verzicola *f* flux
versiere *m* orchard;
kitchen-garden
verzotto *m* cabbage
vescia *f* puff-ball; chatter
vesciaia *f* chatter-box
vescica *f* bladder; blister
vesta, te *f* coat; robe;
– **tiario** *m* vestry
vestale *f* vestal
vestibolo, bulo *m* vestibule; porch
vestigio *m* step; trace
vestimento *m* garment;
– **re** clothe; dress
veterano *m* veteran
veterinaria *f* veterinary
art; – **rio** veterinary
vetero old
veto *m* veto
vetraia, trata *f* glasshouse; glass-window;
– **traio** *m* glazier
vetrice *f* osier; – **ciaio**
m osier-bed
vetrina *f* show-window

vetriolo, triuolo *m* vitriol

vetro *m* glass; – **so** glassy; vitreous

vetta *f* top; ridge

vette *f* lever

vettina *f* pipe; duct; canal

vettone *m* shoot; sprig

vettovaglia *f* & *m* victuals; – re victual

vettura *f* car, carriage; freight; – le *m* carrier; – reggiare carry; – rino *m* carrier; cabman

vetustà *f* age; –to old; ancient

vezzeggiare flatter; caress

vezzo *m* amusement; sport; caress; – **so** charming

vi there; you

via *f* way; road; street; away

viadotto *m* viaduct

viaggiare travel; journey; – giatore viandante *n*. traveller; –gio *m* travel; journey

viale *m* avenue

vicenda *f* return; event; vicissitude; a – reciprocally; – devole reciprocal; mutual; – lezza *f* vicissitude

vicenome *m* pronoun

viceprefetto *m* vice-prefect

vicinanza, nità *f* neighbourhood

vicinato *m* vicinity

vicino neighbouring; neighbour; near

vicissitudine *f* vicissitude

vico, lo *m* lane

vidente *m* seer; prophet

vidimare authenticate

vie much; by far

viera *f* ferrule

vietare forbid; – tivo *a* vieto old [prohibitive

vievia directly

vigere subsist; last

vigesimo twentieth

vigilante, le vigilant; – lanza *f* vigilance; – lare watch

vigilia *f* vigil; eye

vigliacco cowardly; vile

vigliare choose; elect

viglietto *m* note; billet

vigna *f* vine; vineyard; – gnazzo, gneto *m* vineyard

vignetta *f* headpiece

vigore ria *m* & *f* vigour; strength; – rare strengthen; –so vigorous

villania *f* injury; filth; roughness; –no peasant; rough [try

villareccio lereccio country

villata *f* borough

villeggiare enjoy one's self in the country; – tura *f* country life

villese, lico *m* farmer; peasant

villoso hairy; woolly

viltà *f* vileness; – lume *m* trifles

vincastro *m* rod; switch

vincere conquer; – cente victorious; – ta *f* victory; conquest; – citore *m* conqueror

vincido soft; flabby

vinciglio *m* band; tie

vincolare chain; bind by contract; –lo *m* band; tie

vinello *m* small wine

vino *m* wine; – lento intoxicated; – lenza *f* intoxication

vinto vanquished

251

viola f violet; viol

violare violate; **– zione** f violation

violentare force: constrain; **-tore** m transgressor

violente, to violent; impetuous; **–mente** violently; **–za** f violence

violetta f violet

violino m fiddle; violin;

virgineo virginal; **-nità** f virginity; maidenhead

virgola f comma; **– re** put commas   [shoot

virile virile; **– lità** f virility; **–lmente** manly **– ro** m adult; man

virtù, de, te f virtue; power   [virtually

virtuale virtual; **–lmente**

virtuoso virtuous; able; m virtuoso [f virulence

virulento virulent; **– za**

visaggio m visage; face

viscera f viscera; bowels

visciola f morello (black cherry)

visconte m viscount; **– tessa** f viscountess

visibile visible; **– lità** f visibility; **– lmente** visibly

visiera f vizor; mask

vivace lively; sprightly; **– cità** f liveliness

vivagno m shore

vivaio m fishpond; nursery

vivanda f food; victuals

vivandiera, re f & m sutler; caterer

vivere live; **– vente** living

vivezza f vivacity; **– vido** vivacious

viviparo viviparous

vivo living; lively

vivuolo m clove-tree

vivuto lived

viziare vitiate; **– mento** m adulteration

vizzo flabby; withered

vocabolario m vocabulary **– lo** m word; term

vocale vocal; oral; m vowel

vocalizzare vocalize

vocalmente vocally

vocare call; name; **– zione** f vocation

voce f voice; word; vote; **a viva –** by word of mouth; **sotto – in** a low voice

vogare row; **– tore** m rower

voglia f will; desire; **– glievole, so** desirous

voi you

volare fly; **– bile, lante** flying; **-ta** f flight

volatile volatile

volcano m volcano

voleggiare flutter

volere will; consent; **– lente** willing; **– lentieri** willingly

volgare vulgar; common; **– rizzare** vulgarize; **– rità** f vulgarity; **–**

volontà f will; wish; **– rio** voluntary; **–riamente terosamente** voluntarily; **–tieri** willingly

volpe f fox; **– paia** f fox's hole; **–peggiare** be astute; **–picino** m fox's cub; **–pone** m cunning (old) fox

volta f vault; turning; time; **alla – towards:** **alcune volte, alle volte**

voltaica (pila) voltaic pile

voltare turn; change

volteggiare flutter; fly about; **-tore** *m* tumbler; sharp-shooter

volto, ta turned; *m* vault; face

voltoio *m* cup

voltolare turn; rove; roll

volubile voluble; **-lità** *f* volubility

volume *m* volume; book; mass; **-noso** voluminous

voluttà *f* delight; voluptuousness; **-tuoso** voluptuous; sensual

vomere mire vomit

vorare devour

vortice *m* whirlpool; vortex; **- coso** giddy

vosco with you

vostro yo r; yours

votaborse expensive

votacesso *m* night-man

votare empty; cleanse; vote; dedicate; **-tezza** *f* vacuum; emptiness

votivo *m* votive

voto empty; inane; *m* vow; suffrage

vulcano *m* volcano; **- nico** volcanic

vulnerare wound; hurt; **- rio** vulnerary; **-to** wounded

vulturno *m* north-east

vulva *f* womb; uterus

vuotare empty; · to empty; vacancy

W X Y

The **W**, **X** and **Y** letters do not exist in the Italian language

The letter **S** is used for **X**, and the letter **I** for **Y**.

Z

zambracca *f* prostitute; **- re** prostitute one's self

zampa paw; talon; **-re** claw; **-ta** *f* scratch

zampettare begin to walk

zampetto *m* sausage

zampillare spout out

zampilletto *m* drunkard; feeding-bottle

zampillo *m* purveyor; water-spout

zampogna *f* blow-p:pe

zana *f* basket; cradle; cheat; **-iuolo** *m* basket-maker; **-ta** *f* basketful

zanca *f* leg; claw; **-to**

zanco left-handed [coiled

zanna *f* tusk; fang; **- re** smooth

zappa *f* sap; mattock; spade; **-re** sap; dig; hoe; **-tore** *m* sapper; **- ne** *m* mattock; pick-axe

zara *f* risk; danger;

zecca *f* mint; **-re** stamp coin

zecchino *m* sequin

zeffiro, zefiro *m* zephyr

zelo *m* zeal; ardour; **- lante, loso** zealous; **- tore** *m* zealot

zenit *m* zenith

zenzero *m* ginger

zeppa *f* cradle; wedge

zeppare fill up

zerbineria *f* conceit; **- no, notto** *m* fop; dandy

zero *m* zero; cypher;

zibibbo m raisin

zigrino m shagreen

zis zag m zigzag

zimbellare call birds;
– mento, tura m & f
bird-call; – tore m bird-
caller; – lo m decoy-
bird; lure

zimino m fish; sauce

zinale m apron

zineo m zinc

zingano, ro m gipsy

zinna f nipple; breast

zinnale m apron

zinnare sip; – tore m
tippler; – zino m
zio m uncle [draught
zitella f young girl; – lo
m young boy

zittire make a noise
– to n & int silence

zizzania f dissension;
discord

zocco, lo m sandal;
slippers; wooden-shoe;
– laio m sandal-maker;
– lare wear sandals

sodiaco m zodiac

solfa f gamut

solfo m sulphur; brim-

stone; – tanaria, tara
fiera f sulphur-pit;
– naio m match-seller;
– nello, ferino m match

zoologia f zoology; – co
zoological; – gista, go
m zoologist

**zoppaggine,   picatura,
mento** f & m lameness;
– peggiare, picare go
lame; – picante lame;
– picone, ni lame; –
po lame; defective

zoticaggine,   chezza f
roughness; – co harsh

zuccaro. chero m sugar;
– cherare sugar; swee-
ten; – riera f sugar-
basin; – rino m sweet-
meat

zuccotto   m   helmet

zuffa f riot; strife

zufolare play the flute;
whistle; – mento, lio m
whistling; – lo. lone m
flute; whistle

zuppo full; saturated

zurlare   play;   sport;
– lo. ro m merriment;
play

254